AF361353

Market Affect and the Rhetoric
of Political Economic Debates

Studies in Rhetoric/Communication
Thomas W. Benson, Series Editor

Market Affect and the Rhetoric of Political Economic Debates

Catherine Chaput

Published by the University of South Carolina Press
Columbia, South Carolina 29208

uscpress.com

Printed in the United States of America

Library of Congress Cataloging-in-Publication Data
can be found at http://catalog.loc.gov/.

ISBN 978-1-61117-994-1 (hardback)
ISBN 978-1-61117-995-8 (ebook)

Contents

Series Editor's Preface

In *Market Affect and the Rhetoric of Political Economic Debates,* Catherine Chaput asks how capitalism as an idea and a system has resisted criticism in the rhetorical public sphere. Her investigation traces the debate by pairing a series of advocates of capitalist theory and "free markets" with a major critic of each—Adam Smith and Karl Marx, John Maynard Keynes and Thorstein Veblen, Friedrich Hayek and Theodor Adorno, Milton Friedman and John Kenneth Galbraith. In each case, argues Chaput, the critics of capitalism fall short in the rhetorical encounter because they allow their own arguments to be staged in and limited to the realm of ideology, material power, and rational choice. Chaput reasons that the much-needed critique of capitalism has been handicapped by its failure to understand the affective biopolitics of capitalism, a realm of analysis most fully explored by Michel Foucault. Affect theory, states Chaput, offers the possibility for a reinvigorated rhetoric of affective democratic critique and governance.

Thomas W. Benson

Acknowledgments

I would like to thank the editorial staff at the University of South Carolina Press. They have been incredibly responsive, helpful, and professional throughout this process. There are some exceptional colleagues in rhetoric who deserve my thanks. Robert Asen, M. Lane Bruner, Ronald Greene, Mark Longaker, and Brian Ott all volunteered to read this manuscript even among so many other pressing obligations. Each of you represents the kind of scholar—one with equal doses of curiosity and generosity—that I hope to become. Additionally, I wish to thank the anonymous reviewers of the manuscript. Their nuanced reading and insightful comments demonstrated a careful engagement with my ideas, for which I am grateful. I am fortunate to have a local community of such commentators in my colleagues in the Department of English at the University of Nevada, Reno, and especially in the rhetoric and composition faculty. I have learned much from them as well as the graduate students with whom I have worked. I am particularly indebted to the informal reading group of graduate students and faculty who have studied Marx and Foucault with me. These discussions have sometimes been fast-paced and dynamic while at other times they have been thoughtful and lighthearted, but they have always been intellectually and personally fulfilling to me. A final thanks goes to my family and, in particular, to Madeline Chaput, who has become my touchstone in the world, reminding me that is it easier to theorize change than to practice it.

Introduction

A Genealogy of Affect in Market Thinking

On a Sunday, a little more than a week before the August 2011 deadline for Congress to raise the United States debt ceiling or risk defaulting on our national obligations, the news media highlighted neither the Democrats nor the Republicans as rhetorical actors in this historical scene. Instead, the agent was the ephemeral entity we have placed our faith in for over two hundred years: the market. CNN's correspondent contended that the market, in fact, was the only adult at the discussion. The Democratic and Republican leadership were cast as children who placed their interests and agendas above economic laws. It was, therefore, up to the market to ensure a debt-ceiling increase and free finance capital from arbitrary constraints. That same Sunday's *New York Times* featured an article on the American diet that staged its argument similarly: healthier eating habits and healthcare cost savings would be accomplished by the market on its own accord. Here too the human agents of change were absent. In short, the news media that day declared that the market would negotiate our federal budget and implement a better national diet. This is far from anomalous. The economic imaginary present in these examples pervades contemporary political economic and cultural landscapes, distancing human agents from their social and individual choices.

These two examples and others like them simultaneously exemplify Adam Smith's invisible-hand metaphor and Marx's notion of alienation. Smith, the adopted father of free-market capitalism, is perhaps most remembered for his theory that conscious decisions to plan the economy often backfire. Deliberate interventions interfere with natural market processes that operate as though they were guided by an overarching invisible hand. His theory characterizes economic agency as an invisible force that silently instructs. For Marx, these extrahuman qualities derive from the market's origins in the human mind; the market, he says, is the alienated power of human beings. Human beings abdicate their world-making responsibilities by externalizing them within the fantasy of market forces. As we place our faith in this all-knowing construct, we displace our own agentive powers. The market shapes our political life—making decisions about the national debt, for instance—just as much as it contours our everyday lives—determining whether we make healthy lifestyle choices, to use the other example. The market comes to the table, acts appropriately, and determines future courses of action. A tried and true political economic agent, the market not only exists but thrives and proliferates. The question that needs to be answered, the question that underscores this book, is not whether the market exists but what the market is and how it cajoles so invisibly, effortlessly, and yet authoritatively.

At least part of the answer, the part on which I focus, suggests that the market is an affective force that influences rhetorical action by linking bodily receptivities to economic persuasion. The market *feels* real because it is the nominalization we give to the very real affective energies circulating throughout our lived experiences. An often-slippery concept, "affect" signifies a set of theories tracking diverse relationships among emotion, sensation, and everyday practices. Affect studies, across a range of approaches, has reinvigorated explorations of people's conscious and unconscious behaviors that had more or less come to an explanatory impasse in theories of ideology. In the Marxist tradition, ideological criticism presupposes an economic base that supports a multiplicity of cultural and political practices in the superstructure. Ideological inclinations, that is, derive from the specifics of our daily economic relations. Unmasking these causal relationships produces a different consciousness and thus different life patterns. Affect theory complicates this connection between materiality and consciousness by exploring the unconscious bodily mediations that influence how we understand and interact with the material world prior to conscious thought.

In the cultural studies tradition, for instance, Raymond Williams uses the term "structure of feeling" and Richard Hoggart refers to a "felt quality of life" to account for the perceived milieu constructed by the many factors underwriting individual and group sensibilities. They challenge the idea of an economic base and offer a more complex formula for understanding ideology. This initial rethinking has been expanded by a second generation of cultural theorists who benefit from the post-structural philosophies of such scholars as Gilles Deleuze and Félix Guattari. Deleuze and Guattari add desire to the social relations between materiality and consciousness, changing understandings of both ontological and epistemological ways of inhabiting the world. Thinkers such as Lawrence Grossberg, Lauren Berlant, and Melissa Gregg make use of affect through a nonlinear lens that seriously engages both the many facets of our consciousness and the radical open-endedness of identity and power relations. They replace "rational" and "irrational" as the terms for identifying nonideological from ideological thinking with a spectrum of affective and emotional assemblages, each of which offers a way of understanding and engaging in public debate. For them, it is just as important to study how communities habituate embodied ways of knowing as it is to analyze the cultivation of particular kinds of thinking.

A parallel, though sometimes overlapping, trajectory of affect studies focuses not on representation (the articulation of desires and ideologies to material objects) but on valuation (the process of producing material possibilities). Rather than locating the nodal point in Williams's structure of feeling, this thread is inspired by Louis Althusser's work. Among Althusser's chief contributions is the claim that Marx's base/superstructure model is ultimately overdetermined by a range of sociohistorical factors. Ideological state apparatuses such as schools, churches, and social organizations all hail individuals into complex subject positions serving, in the last instance, the economic base. Taking a cue from his teacher, Michel Foucault theorizes "biopower"—the indirect regulation of civil society that "focused on the species body" or the statistical averages of "the population" (*History of Sexuality* 137). This reorientation from the sphere of production to the sphere of reproduction (what the autonomist Marxists call the social factory) forms the foundations for Michael Hardt and Antonio Negri's analyses in their books *Empire, Multitude,* and *Commonwealth,* which collectively rearticulate value from the bottom up and privilege biopower as it fuels ordinary people in their daily lives.[1] They emphasize how people in and out of work produce value through their consumptive and reproductive behaviors, coining the term "affective labor" to represent this value production.

Each of these affective traditions offers a path beyond the ideological cul-de-sac of conscious rhetorical agency, and so I am indebted to their modes of thinking. Although different in their critical orientation, both traditions tend toward a definition of affect as a psychological or emotional state, and in that sense each rationalizes the affective as a mode of cognition. I diverge from them because I am interested not only in theorizing these affective moments but also in engaging the productive powers of affect that recuperate and redirect market agency. If affect is indeed operating invisibly within the material terrain, then it must be bundled into political economic analysis and production at a foundational level. As I explain in more detail later, my understanding of affect is inspired by such thinkers as Brian Massumi, Teresa Brennan, and Patricia Clough, among others. What holds this group together is a common belief in affect as a concrete physiological, as opposed to psychological or metaphorical, component of lived experience. In this theory, affect moves like an energy between two bodies—one affecting and the other being affected. Adhering to this tradition, I reserve the term "affect" to reference the physiological energies inhabiting the world; I use "sensation" to mark the bodily recognition of this energy; and I rely on "emotion" to denote the rationalizing of that sensation.[2] Affect, as a physical entity, moves through all matter—human or nonhuman as well as living or nonliving—and, through its circulating charge, connects the dots between people and the world they inhabit. The connections are not equal as the affective charge shifts according to both the environment of its movement and the bodies involved. Two people could be confronted simultaneously with the same affective charge emanating from the same body and each sense it differently. Although there exists no linear causation written into the movements of affect, its repetitive circuits do produce orientations—what Louis Althusser's dialectic characterizes as the kernel of capitalism fused from the accumulation of encounters. Consequently, all affectively charged experience is at once open to an indeterminate range of potential responses, and yet, in a given political economic context, those responses remain narrowly predictable.

The pervasive intertwining of matter by means of circulating connectivity is not a theoretical proposition but a material fact capable of being tracked through entanglement, pheromone secretion, and neurological activity (Barad; Brennan; Lakoff). Even though I rely on this literature to ground my proposition that affect is a physiological, semiautonomous entity traveling through objects and enabling different responses, I am not trying to develop or apply the scientific data as are many neuroscholars and cognitive psychologists.[3] As a theoretical project, I am interested in the process by which affective encounters create rhetorical dispositions toward the market. I want to know what a theory of affect adds to rhetorical investigation generally and how such a theory might shift our thinking about the rhetoric of economics specifically. My speculation is that it challenges and expands the traditional rhetorical repertoire, making biopolitical production part of its invention strategies and repositioning the *ethos-pathos-logos* triangulation from the symbolic onto the bodily.

With these provocations in mind, this project explores how different approaches to capitalism conceive of the market as a process that circulates an affect-like *dunamis* or *energeia* as part and parcel of capitalist ontology. As a synecdoche for rhetorical being, the market lives and propagates in arguments that favor capitalism, founded in many ways by Adam Smith's *The Wealth of Nations*, as well as in arguments against capitalism, initiated in similar ways by Karl Marx's *Capital*. These two texts represent rational expressions of differing positions on the material soul of the capitalist political economic system. By reading them and the traditions they foster through the lens of affect, I seek to emphasize that each author conceptualizes capitalist power as a being that moves through the production and consumption of capitalist goods and that these differing theories bolster their primary texts as well as the traditions that follow. While Smith identifies this primal political economic source to help us understand and participate more deeply in our capitalist processes, Marx uses it to promote a critical distance from our commonsense participation with Smith's market.

A rereading of Marx's early work through the lens of affect serves as a model for how I read economic theorists throughout this project. As human beings, economic thinkers are situated in particular historical contexts and explore the economic problems of their times via bodily hunches, philosophical theories, and logical claims. This interdisciplinary and extradisciplinary complex becomes the means by which ideas are tested and defended. Rather than the chronological maturation of ideas, economic thinking reflects significant recursivity within and among economic theorists who regularly return to the curious agentive power that lies beyond conscious human authority. Like a beacon, this affect-like core draws thinkers to the calming shores that synchronize with their embodied dispositions, belying the myth of economics as a pure science.

To understand the vast network of human relationships embedding into Marx's argument in *Capital*—his most important contribution to political economy—one must understand the problems that led him to seek exile in England, live in relative impoverishment, and make daily trips back and forth to the British Museum's library, where he constructed his critique.[4] Like many of us, Marx spent his life pursuing questions that arose from a coincidence of early events. The decisive event for Marx was almost certainly the confluence of revolutionary perspectives he encountered during his short Paris sojourn. Engaging in lively political debates, he brought his Hegelian philosophical training into dialogue with French and English political economic theory. In the process of measuring each against the other, Marx developed a radically new critique of bourgeois political economy.[5] This was more than a cognitive process; it was an embodied, experiential, and social process as well. This youthful period is too often quarantined from the later Marx.

Althusser's Marx and the Challenge of Affect Theory

Too much has been made of Louis Althusser's claim that Marx's early "ideological" work is separated from his later "scientific" work by an epistemological break. For Althusser, young Marx believed that capitalism impoverished workers while it enriched owners, whereas mature Marx used a scientific method (dialectical materialism) to show how capitalism accomplished this feat. The early work is ideological because it engaged political economy through the lens of speculative philosophy, relying on such concepts as alienation, species-being, and essence.[6] This approach, he claims, differs from the later scientific work, which developed a theory of value to explain the social phenomena of capitalism. Certainly Althusser offers a useful distinction between the different approaches exemplified in Marx's work; yet, its division has demonstrated so much staying power that it often goes unchallenged. Consequently, cultural critics tend to make use of the early ideological Marx, while economic and political critics reference the later scientific Marx, leaving the role of Marx's early thinking in his more developed critique of capitalism underexplored.

In some ways, this rigidity conflicts with what Althusser argues. He never suggests that the epistemological shift was a fundamental rupture in which Marx was born anew. On the contrary, he argues that in addition to the theoretical method found in his later work, one can also find "Marx's philosophical theory" ("From *Capital*" 32). As Althusser makes clear, this philosophy is neither Hegelian nor the simple reversal of Hegel.[7] Marx, he says, "shows us in a thousand ways the presence of a concept essential to his thought, but absent from his discourse" (30). The crucial concept alluded to here and in other places lies in the notion of a materialist, as opposed to Hegelian, dialectic, which Althusser locates in his mature work. Following this symptomatic practice of reading a text as an answer to a question not directly posited, I too explore how Marx's *Capital* answers questions posed by his early work. Contra Althusser, I maintain that the founding principle of his early work is not ideological as much as the development of an ontological theory of social energy. Althusser says that Marx's early work is ideological in that it performs its investigation "from a whole *conception of Man*" ("The '1844 Manuscripts'" 159). I disagree. Marx does not start from a fully developed conception of man but invents his notion of species-being through the process of abstracting the energetic forces that animate worldly objects. If we rethink this early work as a theoretical exploration of intuited knowledge about what holds people together, the focus on something like affect, rather than an ideologically impassioned plea, comes into relief.[8]

Althusser, for instance, cites the theoretical leap that separates mature Marx from young Marx as his ability to locate and analyze embodied, social processes; although he characterizes this as a leap toward scientism, it equally reflects the essence of worldly being. Marx's scientific investigation of capital, defined as a set of dynamic relations and not a concrete or static thing, focused less on accumulated wealth or the means of production and more on the process by which those things enlist people and institutions toward the production and distribution of social wealth. As Althusser says, this "object is an abstract one: which means that it is terribly real and that it never *exists* in the pure state" ("Preface to *Capital*" 77). The capitalist production of value, as an abstraction, "is 'invisible' (to the naked eye)" (77). The abstraction under investigation, though invisible, contorts bodies in the workplace, directs them into the marketplace, and shapes their consumption habits. Strikingly, those bodies do not readily perceive this ever-present force. One way to approach this value theory is through a mathematical lens that quantifies and discloses with numerical precision. Another way to think about it is that all this invisible corralling takes place on an unconscious level. It operates in what Brian Massumi calls the "missing half second" (the gap between when our brains make a decision and when we are conscious of that decision) or what Slavoj Žižek calls the "fantasy structure" (the fact that we ideologically disassemble the material arrangements that nevertheless maintain our life activities). No doubt, Marx's later work approaches capitalist relationships through a complex explanatory schema that includes the manipulation of algebraic equations, but his ability to abstract and theorize capital in this way derives from engagement with bodily experiences as his centrally located chapter on the working day illustrates.

Through his simultaneous theorization of experiential, textual, and institutional practices, Marx explains how the entire assemblage of the capitalist mode of production creates what Althusser calls a "society effect." He accounts for capitalism's influence on how "men consciously or unconsciously live their lives, their projects, their actions, their attitudes and their functions" as social beings (Althusser, "From *Capital*" 66). To investigate this network of relationships requires, says Althusser, the "cognitive appropriation of the real object by the object of knowledge" (66). It involves understanding the "mechanism that produces it, not the reduplication of one word by the magic of another" (66). What makes something scientific knowledge is the empirical exploration of how it works rather than an impassioned defense or analysis based on untested beliefs. Althusser thus divides Marx's knowledge production into two parts, maintaining that one is a philosophical exploration of capitalist thinking and the other is an explanation of the mechanisms by which that system is produced. Using this taxonomy, he characterizes Marx's early work as ideological because it lays bare the relationship between a set of ideas and their material consequences.[9] Yet these early critiques rely on an innovative conception of individual and social life that is shot through his theory of value. Marx's early work abstracts not capitalism proper but the affordances of being under capitalism.

This early sensibility toward life energy—what Althusser dismisses as intuition—is part of the historical, intellectual, and lived experience that cannot help but dwell in his later work. Early Marx was driven by a profound interest in the full potentiality of human beings, leading him to explore how that development was stymied. In the "Preface" to his *A Contribution to the Critique of Political Economy,* written in 1859 in the time between his two supposedly different periods of inquiry, Marx explains that this text was "written not for publication but for self-clarification" (19). The collection of work was developed during respites between exiles from Germany, Paris, and Brussels as well as in his adopted home of London, where he would stay for the rest of his life. After a university education dedicated to studying philosophy, history, and law, Marx entered the sphere of public discourse and, in his own words, "found [himself] in the embarrassing position of having to discuss what is known as material interests" (19). Ongoing policy discussions about public land, wage labor, taxes, and international trade existed at a concrete level with which Marx had not previously engaged. In this adjustment to materiality as conditioned by the hard realities of life, Marx recognized (both intellectually and viscerally) that the political state and its legal apparatuses do not represent the unfolding of Hegel's World Spirit but that "they originate in the material conditions of life" (20). He asserted what Foucault reverses in his biopolitical lectures: "the anatomy of this civil society," according to Marx, "has to be sought in political economy" (20). Understanding and intervening in capitalism requires interdisciplinary study, deliberation, invention, and communication. In practice, Marx was an ethnographer, an economist, a politician, and a philosopher; and in all these modes, he attended to society's animating powers, whether called species-being or value.

I want to call attention to the rhetorical nature of this dynamic thinking. Marx entered a public sphere in which particular problems were being debated. This discussion changed his thinking, orienting it to the needs of civil society or everyday life and the world in which it plays out. In this way, he discovered that political economic knowledge needs to be theorized in relationship to lived experience. Although Marx insists that this work was intended for "self-clarification," he did not explain what it was that he was trying to clarify (19). Althusser takes it for granted that his object of study was capital, but the fragments of Marx's early work suggest a reoccurring interest in human relations—practices at the heart of rhetorical inquiry. Capital and its institutions are only symptomatic of his larger interest: the process in which lived experience conflicts with species-being or full human potential. To reify an epistemological break between an ideological Marx (who argued against a free-market belief with another belief) and a scientific Marx (who exposed the process by which capitalism produces profit) ignores his struggle to engage this affect-like component of life as well as the rhetorical importance of such engagement. Refusing to ignore these aspects produces a different conclusion than the one that James Aune forwards when he characterizes Marx as arhetorical.[10]

Marx's abstraction of species-being authorizes a critical practice whereby one can track the theorization of affect in his early work and use that theory as a lens through which to view his later work, but it also begs the question of whether there might be a parallel trajectory with Adam Smith and other economic thinkers. Indeed, just as Marx's economic analyses take on different significance if his earlier theories—ones focused on an inchoate concept of affect—are taken into account, so too do Smith's market ideas acquire a slightly differentiated meaning if viewed from the perspective of his earlier work. Indeed, Smith's nascent theory of affect is developed at length in *The Theory of Moral Sentiments,* a text that, as Roger Franz, Jerry Muller, and others argue, very much informs *The Wealth of Nations. The Theory of Moral Sentiments* explores how we connect to or repel from others and form ideas based on the presence or absence of what Smith called sympathy and what I interpret as affect. Before outlining the full book project, which places incongruent economic thinkers in dialogue so as to illuminate the importance of capitalist affect, I offer a short explanation of what I mean by the fact that affect plays a role in how Adam Smith and Karl Marx differently assess the marketplace.

Adam Smith and Karl Marx: Invitations toward the Affective Powers of Capitalism

Smith limits his discussion of production to the opening pages of *The Wealth of Nations* and even there focuses narrowly on how developed societies make use of the division of labor to increase productivity. He famously suggests that while a single worker can make, at most, twenty pins per day, a group of ten workers who divide the pin-making tasks among themselves can make 48,000 pins per day, increasing productivity by an extraordinary 24,000 percent (10–11). This remarkable anecdote aside, the majority of his nearly six-hundred-page tome details how the market system circulates goods, motivates people, secures profits, and distributes wealth through proper cultural, political, and economic organization. Take, for example, his discussion of the way free trade benefits nation-states. Smith offers an analogy between individuals and states, proposing that

> Private people who want to make a fortune, never think of retiring to the remote and poor provinces of the country, but resort either to the capital, or to some of the great commercial towns. They know, that, where little wealth circulates, there is little to be got, but that where a great deal is in motion, some shares of it may fall to them. The same maxims which would in this manner direct the common sense of one, or ten, or twenty individuals, should regulate the judgment of one, or ten, or twenty millions, and should make a whole nation regard the riches of its neighbors, as a probable cause and occasion for itself to acquire riches. (384)

People are drawn to places by the circulation of capital or the hustle and bustle of the marketplace. The more items that are in motion, the more wealth it signals, and the more likely are one's chances of sharing in that wealth. By the same argument, nation-states can reasonably expect to benefit from the profits of their wealthy neighbors; therefore, there is no need to impose regulations that impede the circulation of commodities across borders.

Although economists make much of the free-market tone of such passages as the one above, they often leave unasked the question of how circulating wealth pulls individuals toward commercial centers. This force, encapsulated in the invisible-hand metaphor, features significantly not only in this text but also in Smith's *The Theory of Moral Sentiments.* Rather than allowing the legislature to manipulate people like pieces in a chess contest, Smith prefers to leave social control to the natural sentiments that regulate individual conduct for the collective good. "In the great chess-board of human society," he says, "every single piece has a principle of motion of its own" (*Theory of Moral Sentiments* 275). Individual moral sentiments, whether innate or habituated, suffice as social motivation. Given the careful attention he gives to such forces in his early work, *The Wealth of Nations* takes for granted (as do many of its interlocutors) the sentiments animating the marketplace.

Adam Smith's defense of free markets is deeply indebted to how sentiments regulate production and exchange activities. Ranging from self-interest to benevolence and from fear to confidence, individual sentiments in all their apparent caprice conspire to construct the market as a public space that negotiates and ultimately persuades through fair and open exchanges. As long as there are no constraints, the forces that naturally regulate individual choices maintain a functioning political economy. But capitalism, Marx states, includes more than just the sphere of commercial exchange. It includes the semiprivate spaces of work, whose operations seem unfair, opaque, and secret even to Adam Smith. Opposed to the frenzy of visible activity in the marketplace, the workplace remains closed to outside observers. This difference is key to Marx's contribution to the political economic conversation, suggesting that the secret to profitmaking lies in the private relations of production rather than, as Smith indicates, in the public sphere of exchange.

Marx's *Capital* dramatizes this departure from the public marketplace, calling its audience into the unexplored space of production: "let us therefore, in company with the owner of money and the owner of labour-power, leave this noisy sphere, where everything takes place on the surface and in full view of everyone, and follow them into the hidden abode of production, on whose threshold there hangs the notice 'No admittance except on business'" (279–80). This invitation is interrupted by a reflection on the Smithian marketplace, a space shaped by the Enlightenment values of freedom, equality, property, and self-interest. The sphere of exchange, Marx admits, is an "Eden of the innate rights of man," wherein individuals are perfectly free and fully equal.

Parodying Smith, he states that the entire range of disparate activities comes together because of an external power. As he explains, "the only force bringing them together, and putting them into relation with each other, is the selfishness, the gain and the private interest of each. Each pays heed to himself only, and no one worries about the others. And precisely for that reason, either in accordance with the pre-established harmony of things, or under the auspices of an omniscient providence, they all work together to their mutual advantage, for the common weal, and in the common interest" (280).

For Smith and other classical political economic thinkers, the proper functioning of the individualized system requires an externalized force beyond human comprehension. Marx enters instead into the workplace, searching for the source of this chaotic system within concrete and observable practices. In this space, people become characters of capital: one transforms into a smirking and self-important owner of production and the other into a timid and fearful worker. This transformation suggests an affective shift: the people remain the same, and yet their affectivities have been recalibrated. The comportment, demeanor, and identity of this dramatis personae modify according to the new spatial and environmental location. Marx does not combat the marketplace's image as fair and full of good cheer but notes that the workplace recapacitates those inside its borders. Affect, for him, alters according to the relations, modalities, and spaces of capitalist circulation.

Both Marx and Smith agree that capitalism operates according to rational laws as well as bodily investments. Thus, investigation into this complex system requires embodied as well as intellectual engagement. Marx emphasizes this by ending both his "Preface" to *A Contribution to the Critique of Political Economy* and the "Preface" to the first edition of *Capital* with Dante quotes. In the former he says, *"Qui si convien lasciare ogni sospetto / Ogni viltà convien che qui sia morta,"* which translates as "Here must all distrust be left; / All cowardice must here be dead" (23). The objects of these statements are the bodily dispositions—distrust and cowardice—that prevent individuals from engaging his critique. If such sentiments are removed, then presumably Marx's argument will be given the same deliberative space as the arguments of bourgeois economists. The "Preface" to *Capital* extends this gesture by inviting dialogue. Marx paraphrases Dante, saying, *"Segui il tuo corso, e lascia dir le genti,"* which translates as "Go on your way and let the people speak" (93). Marx not only demands openness but also directs his readers to engage in discussion.

Marx invests himself—politically, emotionally, and intellectually—with the arguments put forth in *Capital* just as Smith invests himself in the arguments outlined in *The Wealth of Nations.* These are not isolated scholarly endeavors but engagements with an ongoing conversation about the role of human relations within the political economy of capitalism. This conversation has continued, more and less vociferously, over the last several hundred years, with economists and theorists tending toward one or the other of these affective investments. The question yet to be addressed is this: How do these parallel but differing accounts of the relationship between affect and capital influence the ongoing debates about capitalism that tend to engage these foundational thinkers?

Affective Investment as Rhetorical Being under Capitalism

Affect is a possible bridge among multiple materialisms—traditional agent-centered materialism, post-structural discourse-centered materialism, and the posthumanist focus of new materialism. Theorized as a physical force acting in the world and on those agentive subjects, affect complicates the traditional materialist position at the same time that it grounds post-structuralist and posthumanist arguments that often lack an operationalizing mechanism by locating immanence in the deep tissues of our fleshly existence. To construct this bridge, I comb the rhetorical tradition for an implicit understanding of affect conceived as circulating passions. This nascent conception of affect, although not well theorized, is nonetheless significant to our rhetorical tradition. Combining this marginalized focus with a particular thread of contemporary affect theory, I propose a fluid lens for exploring the materialist power of rhetorical being in Smith and Marx as well as those who follow in their footsteps.

This affective sensibility leads into a comparative analysis of the marketplace in Adam Smith and Karl Marx. As I have already indicated, I argue that the early work of each author contains a different implicit account of affect that helps one understand the rhetorical effect of his later work. Whereas for Smith commerce is an ongoing process of persuasion that circulates affect along three related pathways invisibly mobilizing people into the proper activities that produce and distribute the requisite products, for Marx capital is a process of coercive labor that traps naturally dynamic life energies within the commodity form, wherein they remain stuck. Proponents of capitalism have left many of Smith's arguments behind but have held tightly to his theory of affect—concretized in his invisible-hand metaphor—while anticapitalist proponents, following Althusser's famous account of the fissure between the young and mature Marx, ground themselves in Marx's "scientific" arguments without taking account of his earlier work on alienation, which, since the Frankfurt School's recuperation of this material, has been redirected into the study of culture. These divergent paths lay the foundations for how future audiences receive arguments supporting and opposing capitalism.

The first such moment is the global political economic crisis that engendered the World Wars. Multiple economic crises leading up to and including the Great Depression marked capitalism as an unstable system in need of rethinking. Both John Maynard Keynes and Thorstein Veblen theorized the major shifts of capitalism during the beginning of the twentieth century so as to understand this increasing instability. In doing so, Keynes and Veblen reimagined the affective structures of Smith and Marx. Each thinker determined that the economic trouble of their day resulted from the improper transmission of affect among human beings who occupied a dramatically changing environment. Keynes viewed individual economic choices as driven by animal spirits rather than rational needs, whereas Veblen claimed that the instinctual drives of species-being were redeployed by modern institutional traditions. Both sought a rational intervention into what were, in Smith and Marx respectively, unencumbered human bonds that enabled or questioned the evolution of the capitalist marketplace. Taming the ontological within the rational (government regulations for Keynes and matter-of-fact thinking for Veblen), these theorists compromised the affective integrity of the foundational arguments for and against capitalism. Thus, this moment weakened the persuasive force of both Smith's invisible hand and Marx's species-being.

Such thinking precipitated the post–World War II phase of capitalist theorization wherein a new variant of classical economics gradually overtakes the state capitalism constructed through Keynesianism. It is worth exploring this process by analyzing the affective shifts—ones undergirded by a psychological rewriting of the founding principles—that take place within capitalism. Paradigmatic of the divergent psychological interventions into theories of capitalism are Friedrich Hayek and Theodor Adorno. Hayek introduces cognitive psychology to explain why the market does not operate rationally and should not be rationally managed. He bolsters Smith's invisible hand with neurological evidence of how individuals and communities thrive through unconscious mimicry, requiring only minimal rules to enable a strong world market. Adorno, on the other hand, reads the crisis of capitalism through Freudian depth psychology, suggesting that people have forfeited their ability to rationally negotiate unconscious individual and social desires. According to him, the individual ego has been replaced by the external ego of group psychology, and thus there is no one to resist capitalism's more pernicious aspects. Although both Hayek and Adorno address the economics of monopoly capitalism, their theories circle around questions of affect and its agentive mobilization. In answering these questions, Hayek tends to strengthen Smith, while Adorno ironically moves away from Marx in an effort to retrieve Marxism from its problematic implementation in state communism.

John Kenneth Galbraith and Milton Friedman both engage the nascent neoliberal moment barely hinted at by Hayek and Adorno. I argue that Friedman surpasses Galbraith in the court of popular opinion, the stage on which they play out their alternative theories of capitalism, because of his superior treatment of affect. Friedman translates Adam Smith's invisible hand—the shorthand for a broader theory of affective regulation—into the persuasive scientific lexicon of his "*as if* by rational choice" doctrine, whereas Galbraith abandons positive affective production in his description of a postindustrial world in which corporations manipulate individual desire and governments rescue society with greater aesthetic and cultural attention. I demonstrate that the tidal wave of support for Friedman's monetary economics owes a significant debt to the fact that his rational-choice theory buries the affective circuitry of capitalism under the ground of a scientific landscape, whereas Galbraith builds the conspicuous wires of corporate power across a fairly barren world of individual relationships. Friedman continues to work from the affective traditions of Smith, Keynes, and Hayek but does so under the guise of scientific rationality, while Galbraith dismisses all traces of affect in the political economic traditions (both classical and Marxist) as little more than magical incantations. In short, I contend that the reception of their economic positions largely reflects their substitutes for affect—rational choice or corporate power—and that the liquidation of positive affective possibilities from Galbraith's critical position leaves it severely handicapped.

Insights from these various authors indicate that it is possible to reinvigorate a critique of capitalism by insisting on the importance of affective value to the rhetorical constitution of agentive subjects. This approach relies heavily on the collaboration between Marx and Foucault, a pairing that, as Jamie Merchant suggests, helps enrich our understanding of the rhetorical situation. In particular, Foucault's biopolitical work in conversation with his discussion of *parrhesia* complements the Marxist critique of capital with a positive proposal for developing a critical subjectivity capable of discerning, speaking, and acting according to affectively determined truths even in the face of opposition. Rhetorical practice must rethink its standard handbook to include the biological production of agency within its notion of invention and in doing so give serious attention to ethos as not only the evolving constitution of subjectivity but also as the foundation for what is emotionally and logically persuasive.

1 Affect as Capitalist Being

Bridging the Materialist Traditions

The critic is not the one who debunks, but the one who assembles. The critic is not
the one who lifts the rugs from under the feet of the naive believers, but the one who
offers the participants arenas in which to gather.

Bruno Latour, "Why Has Critique Run Out of Steam?"

Since the eighteenth century, capitalist materiality has signaled a set of
political economic processes that produce and distribute surplus wealth
according to spontaneous market operations. Spontaneity, however, does
not exist outside the procedures that funnel motion along particular trajectories. Involuntarily jumping to one's feet at the site of a spectacular sport-
ing accomplishment or the inability to prevent oneself from tearing up at a
sentimental scene represents the cultural habituation of spontaneity and not
raw biological instinct. From this perspective, capitalism requires the market's
invisible orchestrating force to circulate throughout the world's many dynamic unfoldings and imprint itself onto this vast complex so that its desired
responses spring forth as if by nature. Reinforcing such a conjecture, theorists
like Stephen McKenna and Mark Longaker assert that the production of capitalist nature emerged as a consequence of rhetorical practices that trained
Enlightenment subjects in the *belles lettres* tradition. Enculturation into bourgeois style saddled the individual with a stable identity that predicated other
practices, including economic decision making. One could argue that the process of repetitive instruction transformed raw affect into a semiautonomous
capitalist judgment. Indeed, capitalist theorists consistently stage arguments
at this level—the market's ability to organize a frenetic world through the
unwitting cooperation of instinct-riddled human beings. Alternatively, critics
of capitalism tend to censor market ideology as a fiction that contributes to
the uneven distribution of material resources. In short, market thinkers accept

agency as the unconscious alignment between economic responses and market signals while antimarket thinkers call on agentive subjects to consciously manipulate the political economic field.

These debates reflect a rhetorical asymmetry wherein critics use reason to fight advocates who rely on passion. Even those post-structuralist thinkers who locate the possibilities for change in the discursive process of performative practices subjugate bodily spontaneity to carefully reasoned cause-and-effect dynamics. Much of the materialist scholarship that came out of the 1990s, for instance, highlighted the signifying practices of material texts from memorials and museums to bodies and the genetic code. Overwhelmingly, such objects were studied as a visual display that produced rhetorical effects or as the material effect produced from the rhetoric of popular representations, public policy, or disciplinary knowledge. These artifacts, according to the scholarship, participate in a relationship between discourse and materiality that, although it may be reciprocal, remains confined to a linear diagram of power: discourse produces reality and reality determines discourse. So conceived, rhetoric subscribes to what Barbara Biesecker has famously called the "logic of influence." Informed by a range of new materialist thinking that views the human as hybrid (Haraway), bodies as entangled (Barad), and environments as unconsciously priming our dispositions (Rickert), this project locates materialism not at a structural level nor at a local level, but at the level of circulating affect. This shift in perspective places the capitalist debate on a single materialist plane—the invisible force that informs our ostensibly instinctual economic behaviors.

This standpoint does not object to anthropomorphizing the market (acknowledging a living undercurrent to economic choices) but does object to locating market forces beyond human intervention. Such positioning transforms humans into biological conduits who synchronize themselves to the currents of their environments by following the imperceptible tug of affect. Anticapitalist theories often highlight this unthinking subject and call for critical agency tied to rational, if not scientific, economic policies and practices. In doing so, they commit themselves to the founding principles of Aristotelean rhetoric (rational deliberation in organized arenas among fully agentive subjects) and abandon those practices that lie on the outskirts of this tradition (the circulating passions of becoming and the philosophical practice of world making). Because, as market discourse never tires of expounding, humans are animals whose efforts at rational behavior often fail, we need to recraft rather than quarantine, quell, or outreason our instinctual bodies. So, while I locate world-making prospects within the affective realm, I neither abdicate reason nor ground myself in it; instead, I reimagine reason as that which must be practiced, negotiated, and transformed as a living, embodied training. Such production falls within a broadened terrain of rhetorical arts that includes bodily instincts and the discernment of truth.

The possibilities for alternative political economic paradigms exist in the energetic becoming of our rhetorical being. As Jane Bennett describes it, "an active becoming, a creative not-quite-human force capable of producing the new, buzzes within the history of the term nature. This vital materiality congeals onto bodies, bodies that seek to preserve or prolong their run" (*Vibrant Matter* 118). If this is so, capitalism's recalcitrant nature—its adaptability within an evolving historical terrain and its capacity to absorb difference into niche commodity markets—cannot be pinpointed in political structures, cultural representations, nor even in human beings themselves. Its endurance stems from the rhetorical work of the vibrant materiality moving through each of these layers to constitute an invisibly entangled infrastructure that merges myriad moments into a single, though dynamic and differentiated, force. This rhetorical constitution of being predisposes individuals to capitalism even though the circulating being, at its core, remains "ontologically multiple" and thus open to different becomings (Bennett, *Vibrant Matter* 8). Raw affect contains innumerable potentialities unactualized by the rhetorical training of habituated being. Although not obviously present, these forms of being are neither destroyed nor lost to history, but they lie untapped in the materiality of affect. Capitalist instinct will only give way to a new instinct, one that must be symbolically crafted but biochemically and energetically circulated.

What I am proposing is perhaps an additional materialism but only in the sense of locating and engaging the rhetorical energy moving throughout the nesting dolls of other materialisms.[1] Traditional materialism positions its critique of capitalism at the largest scale—those political economic structures that ensure the production and consumption of commodities as well as the social relations they engender. Discursive approaches narrow the scope by focusing on particular sites of materialization. Another materialism studies the biopolitics of capitalism or the communicative labor that produces human beings with particular capacities to affect and be affected. New materialism goes to the flesh of the matter, exploring the physical relations among bodies, things, and spaces. This project maintains each of these materialisms by adding another: a circulating affective materiality whose accumulating traces ossify into particular rhetorical dispositions. As the energetic substance that creates order out of the world's chaotic materiality, affect attests to the rhetorical being that both maintains life as it is and reminds us of the freedom to become other than we are. The soil in which rhetorical responses take root, affect inscribes rhetoric's discursive template of *ethos, pathos,* and *logos* onto bodies that emote and calculate according to deep-seated, though evolving, modes of being-in-the-world. This rhetorical being pervades the political economic world, and although it cannot be directly altered through structural changes or positively asserted by the demand for recognition, it can be nudged, modulated, and motivated by ancillary practices that break its rhythmic waves and build up different patterns. If the critic's task, as Bruno Latour says, is to assemble arenas in which to gather, then this proposition could be understood as a new assembly of old formations. What were separate materialist passages that led us in different directions become fused through affective circuits that illuminate an entirely uncharted cartography.

Although different from ideological rhetorical analysis, affective analysis seeks to answer the same question: why do people experience and understand things in such vastly different ways? Louis Althusser's "Preface to *Capital* Volume One" answers this query when he asserts that the working class endorse Marx more easily than the intellectual class because of their differing life experiences.[2] He goes on to describe ideology as an active agent that sabotages knowledge by causing people to be "literally blinded" to certain ideas (74). With this explanation, Althusser, the godfather of ideological critique, offers an implicit theory of affect—the material entity that circulates among people and everyday objects to enhance or impede their capacity to engage. It is no wonder that Althusser has reemerged in new materialism as well as the many posthumanist theories indebted to Foucauldian biopolitics: ideological analysis differs from, but is not incompatible with, affect studies.[3]

As I have said elsewhere, the resilience of capitalism against ideological critique requires rhetorical theory and criticism to enhance such analyses with attention to affect.[4] However different in their approaches and regardless of the depths of their insights, critical rhetoricians espousing ideological analysis—Michael McGee, Raymie McKerrow, James Arnt Aune, and Dana Cloud, among others—work from the warrant that more and better information will energize audiences, who will then act in accordance with that knowledge.[5] Assuming that increased consciousness prompts political economic change, critics work diligently to debunk and disarticulate deeply held ideologies. There is, however, a futility in this consciousness raising: one belief system gives way to another ad infinitum, preventing the actuality of a nonideological worldview. Even as we learn to see things differently, our practices resist adjusting to that knowledge, doing so inconsistently and at a snail's pace. Recalibrating the critical lens from ideology to affect, a perspective that may be dormant in traditional theories of ideology, replaces the Sisyphean task of outpacing worldviews with the study of how the open-ended rhetoricity of instinctual capacities has sealed itself within capitalist being.

The goal here is to locate this agentive capacity in our traditional rhetorical theories, enhance it with contemporary materialist perspectives, and develop a practice through which to glimpse, and later engage, the affective sensibilities of political economic theories. I begin by skimming the rhetorical tradition, from the classical to the contemporary, for its implicit understanding of affect, arguing that the idea of an independent motivating force moving through bodies functions as a latent part of that history. Although barely puncturing the surface, this cursory review demonstrates how the question of an unnamed bodily force persists unanswered within the canon of rhetorical theory. This concern plays an important role, one I survey in more detail, in the work of rhetoricians who study the materiality of language and its relationship to political economy. Although diffuse, there exists a constant desire among such scholars to theorize rhetoric's motivational energy and connect it to the political economic power relations of its production. Combining the key propositions of this rhetorical scholarship with insights from affect theory, the chapter ends by offering a flexible methodology for tracking how theorists of capitalism conceive this vibrant force—one that directs my investigations in subsequent chapters.

The Materiality of Affect: Reassessing the Rhetorical Tradition

Although only recently part of our critical vocabulary, affect speaks to crucial questions that have haunted rhetoricians since the classical era, during which both sophistic rhetoric and Platonic critique of such rhetoric offered materialist alternatives to the Aristotelian characterization of rationalized emotional appeals. Indeed, before Aristotle neatly codified pathos as one of his three rhetorical proofs, others described passion—what I call affect—as a powerful force moving among and working on embodied participants.[6] Visceral and seemingly uncontrollable desires are, for Aristotle, beyond the purview of rhetoric as they reflect inartistic components of human motivation; nonetheless, rhetoric's suasive powers cannot free themselves from the existence of seemingly compulsory responses. Persuasion gathers its strength from a force, an energy, or a charge within speech and so, across a range of explanations, the possibility prevails that rhetoric may require an uncodified and possibly uncontainable material power.

According to Thomas Cole's history of ancient rhetoric, for instance, Gorgias, perhaps the most studied sophistic practitioner, understood rhetorical persuasion as tapping into an innate capacity for bodies to manipulate one another. For Gorgias, the "state of being persuaded does not have to be externally, or even self-, induced. It is more like the natural state of humankind" (Cole 148). Rhetoric, part and parcel of the human condition, exists separate from but works through speech to inspire individuals. Speech, in Gorgias's view, is "a powerful lord, which by means of the finest and most invisible body effects the divinest works: it can stop fear and banish grief and create joy and nurture pity" (41). Two aspects of this description stand out: first, rhetoric works through an invisible agent within the speech itself that evokes and modulates the hearer's emotions and, second, that invisible agent has a body. An invisible, though material, entity contained within words, passes from speaker to auditor in order to effect its energetic charge. Further, according to Gorgias, "the effect of speech upon the condition of the soul is comparable to the power of drugs over the nature of bodies. For just as different drugs dispel different secretions from the body, and some bring an end to disease and others to life, so also is the case of speeches, some distress, others delight, some cause fear, others make the hearers bold, and some drug and bewitch the soul with a kind of evil persuasion" (41). The agent of change within speech is not only a material thing but one that alters the bodies of its recipients. Like a drug, it triggers corporeal processes that ignite emotional valences. By affecting the embodied state of its audience, a rhetorical agent unleashes psychological states that motivate rhetorical effects. The varied responses of an audience derive from rhetoric's ability to change bodily disposition.

There is no need to privilege the sophists for this definition of rhetoric, however. More detailed and less evaluative, this sensibility parallels Plato's well-known comparison of rhetoric to a spice. According to Plato's "Gorgias," rhetoric is a "habitude" intended to produce "gratification or pleasure" (70). Even as this dialogue positions Socrates in opposition to Gorgias and his rhetorical instruction, it proposes a definition of rhetoric quite similar to the one posed earlier by Gorgias: rhetoric has an ontological existence that adjusts and infuses the setting so that an audience is more disposed to accept a given proposition. The practice of orienting an audience contains multiple branches, including such things as rhetoric and cookery. The unifying characteristic of these branches is the fact that they change the essence of a thing through shortcut alterations that change bodily reception. Like a drug, a spice changes our instinctual response to something else—we detest even our favorite foods if they have been oversalted but accept our least favorite ones if they have been creatively seasoned. Similarly, rhetorical persuasion materially alters one's body so as to convince quickly, replacing arduous and time-consuming logical propositions with familiar commonplaces. If Plato's "Gorgias" outlines his suspicions about rhetoric's ability to redesign the material capacities of its listener, his "Phaedrus" concedes a role for these passions if properly tethered to philosophy—a practice of accommodation mimicked by medieval theorists of rhetoric who sought to redirect bodily desire toward Christian doctrine.

In the Christian era, both rhetoric and the philosophical tradition so antagonistic to it suffered—one for its attention to the earthly world and one for reliance on a panoply of pagan gods. Although their reputations waned, these pursuits and their engagement with the passions did not disappear. Instead, they were appropriated for the pedagogical and ascetic practices of the Church. In the process, rhetoric and philosophy were transformed into pursuits that, like other bodily desires, should be replaced with religious zeal. The idea that passions are to be corralled and guided can be found as early as the second century's "On the Sublime." This treatise, generally attributed to Cassius Longinus, explains that "the great passions, when left to their own blind and rash impulses without the control of reason, are in the same danger as a ship let drive at random without ballast. Often they need the spur, but sometimes also the curb" (13). The problem, of course, is that true passion "bursts out with a kind of 'fine madness' and divine inspiration, and falls on our ears like the voice of a god" (17). Whether writing, preaching, or practicing a monastic lifestyle, one must be careful to align one's passions with an emergent Christian faith. This shift takes its quintessential form in the fourth and fifth centuries with the work of St. Augustine and St. Jerome. After their respective conversions, each man replaced ancient rhetorical and philosophical texts with biblical study and kept a vigilant eye on bodily yearnings. Although one could never shed these nagging impulses, constant self-assessment could reorient earthly desire toward heavenly contemplation. As St. Jerome explains, "desire is quenched by desire": the only way to curb embodied passion is to funnel it through an individual, inward, and frequently secluded relationship with God (4). Not surprisingly, these men and their followers isolated themselves from the secular public, protecting their passions against alternative circulating energies.

In their recuperation of classical thinking, Renaissance rhetoricians returned to the passions to ground their sense of rhetoric as the material power and driving force of external persuasion.[7] As in the classical period, this led some to embrace the passionate function of rhetoric and others to critique such an elusive thing. Both positions envisioned rhetoric as a circulating force over which individuals—speakers as well as audience members—have only partial control. Revelatory of this viewpoint, the Italian Francesco Patrizi, in his "Ten Dialogues on Rhetoric," represents rhetorical force as beyond one's control: "But when I'm in the process of speaking, I'm like an unbridled horse that doesn't slow down at all no matter how much the rider pulls on the reins until it goes headfirst into a wall or something and breaks its neck. I'm filled with grief that Nature has given me such ardent spirits that transport me against my will" (193). Rhetorical power derives from its ability to mobilize nature's passions, altering the body and forcing it to act apart from one's conscious will. This uncontrollable pull occurs, Petrarch says, when words "caress my ears and gradually flow into me, stimulating me through the force of their sweetness . . . and with their hidden barbs transfiguring me deep within" (17).[8] By directly working on the body, passions set the stage for speech to rouse or settle its audience. For these authors, passions move through speech, dispose the embodied listener, and allow speech to work regardless of its reasonableness. Passions represent the uncontrollable and sometimes unpredictable sea within which rational debate treads water; to stay afloat, argument must buoy itself on these invisible beings.

Describing rhetorical power as an invisible agent over which individuals have limited control fell out of fashion during the modern period dominated by reasonable speech and empirical data. The Scottish Enlightenment thinkers, for instance, privileged unambiguous language, purity of style, and psychological explication. Their goal was to categorize and classify the passions as a means to both legitimate historical action and calibrate contemporary judgment according to a unified moral standard. As George Campbell contends, rhetoric's ability to influence the will of an audience requires "an artful mixture of that which proposes to convince the judgment, and that which interests the passions, its distinguished excellency results from these two, the argumentative and the pathetic incorporated together" (147). Housed within individual bodies, where it can be cajoled for rational purposes, passion—conceived variously as sentiment (Adam Smith), taste (Hugh Blair), and vivacity (George Campbell)—matched words, images, and actions in an Enlightenment matrix of propriety. For these theorists, the alignment of rhetorical being makes organized society, including a burgeoning economic sphere, possible.

Amid this rational worldview one passion—self-interest—dominated all others to establish a consistent political economic and cultural context. The success of self-interest arose in part from the tripartite relationship among democracy, capitalism, and rhetoric. Capitalism emerged in the same Italian city-states that witnessed the rebirth of rhetoric and spread along similar pathways through northern Europe and into the British Isles.[9] Grappling with the rising democratic state and the economic shift into capitalism, early modern thinking accounted for the predictable worker-citizen through recourse to passions that opposed other passions in order to stabilize individuals within predictable patterns of behavior. Because the passions could not be tamed by reason, countervailing passions emerged as controlling entities. According to Albert Hirschman, self-interest rose above the fray to become the single countervailing passion capable of training all others and ultimately maintaining social order. Individual avarice disciplined wage workers and free citizens, whose enterprising efforts held out the possibility of participating in a limitless marketplace. So intertwined with rational choice, self-interest gradually became defined more as reason than as passion. Measured by the moral standards of Enlightenment judgment, it was not unreasonable to want more earthly goods or to desire a governing voice as such self-interestedness serendipitously regulated society. Consequently, the sophistic and Platonic traditions, which gestured toward an embodied definition of rhetorical being as including non-rational modes of persuasion, slowly disappeared from the modern period, during which reason dominated.[10]

The lacuna of rhetorical passions prevailed until postmodernism resuscitated this dubious alternative tradition and gave it pride of place. In response, rhetoric exploded into its ubiquitous form—the so-called big rhetoric.[11] This notion of rhetoric, as John Bender and David Wellbery state, redirected attention such that the "sea of invisible communicative transactions that the tradition of classical rhetoric did not and could not take into account becomes . . . a privileged object of study" (34). This new focus, they say, "displaces the rhetorical operations to an unconscious sphere" and "finds its theme in the impersonal domain of what occurs among us, unnoticed and without deliberation" (34). Rhetorical investigation, following this logic, must attune itself to nonagentive impersonal operations that function so inconspicuously as to bleed into the natural background of life activities. What holds this new perspective together, according to David Fleming, is a sensitivity to the way that rhetoric frequently operates "independent of and prior to human agency" and thus, at times, is "insusceptible to reason" and "*outside* of our control" (175, 176). Even though Bender and Wellbery frame this definition of rhetoric against the classical tradition, it seems more accurate to acknowledge it as a particular insight that has existed alongside and underdeveloped within that tradition.

In the *longue durée* of rhetorical theory, this alternative tradition has taken a back seat to Aristotle's seemingly more legitimate description of rhetoric as the practical art of persuading specific audiences about probable truths (28). His taxonomy locates, names, and organizes the entire apparatus of rhetoric, leaving nothing invisible and rationalizing appeals according to social and psychological norms. Aristotle's rhetoric provides a pragmatic structure for lodging arguments in publics populated by relatively homogenous groups that listen carefully and make decisions based on thoughtful assessment of a proposition's credibility, reasonability, and moral applicability.

The alternative perspective I put forward seeks to expand and augment, rather than displace, this tradition by making the passions coextensive with the rational and understanding both as simultaneously embodied and trans-bodied. To investigate persuasion from its affective core, the critic must begin with the effects and work backwards to find their embodied rhetorical provocations. Further back than appeals, lines of argument, and rhetorical frames, such work takes us to the question of what enables these signifying structures to work their magic in the first place. This form of inquiry has already inspired a range of materialist rhetorics. Kenneth Burke's attempt to merge materialism with psychoanalysis, Michael Calvin McGee's materialist rhetoric, and James Aune's ideological approach all, in different ways, demonstrate both a sensibility to the persuasive capacity of embodied experience and a commitment to studying rhetorical power within the political economic terrain.

Affect as the Circulation of Rhetorical Being

Although fundamentally drawn to psychological explanations of rhetoric, Kenneth Burke constantly flirts with a materialist definition of persuasion. Indeed, his rhetorical contributions rely so heavily on embodiment that overemphasizing the psychic pull of identification misses a more complex understanding of his work. Take, for instance, *Counter-Statement,* which defines literary form as the construction and appeasement of desires in an audience. The satisfaction of one's expectation can be read as the fitting of form to consciousness; however, it can also be read as a materialist conformity. Burke uses the embodied metaphor of nourishment to explain that we become conscious of our appetite for these forms through bodily sensations, which serve as "the material on which eloquence may feed" (40–41). Rhetoric moves audiences through some kind of "charge," and the intensity of this charge moves from author to audience through form as well as word choice (163–65). The charge converts one person's sensibilities into textual form, and these sensibilities reemerge in the audience. Manipulating style to match the purported expectations of an audience serves the rhetorical function of identification, a process that is just as much the work of an invisible material agent as it is a function of an identifiable ideological association.

The traditional approach to Burke's notion of identification organizes itself around stylistics while ignoring the materiality of identity. Scholars frequently cite Burke's conjecture that "you persuade a man only insofar as you can talk his language by speech, gesture, tonality, order, image, attitude, idea, *identifying* your ways with his" and leave unacknowledged the preceding sentence, which characterizes this as "the simplest case of persuasion" (*Rhetoric of Motives* 55). To discover the more complicated cases that function through rhetorical charges, we must turn to Burke's other descriptions of identification. The identification and division underscoring rhetorical action takes place through consubstantiality—the sharing of a physical substance that unites separate individuals with and against each other. Identification requires the sharing of material substances: "in being identified with B, A is 'substantially one' with a person other than himself. Yet at the same time he remains unique, an individual locus of motives. Thus, he is both joined and separate, at once a distinct substance and consubstantial with another" (*Rhetoric of Motives* 21). People act together, he asserts, because a common substance moves between individuals and orients their embodied actions such that physical experiences articulate with psychological ones.[12] In addition to adopting a particular style, identification requires the material transformation of one's rhetorical being.

Several recent studies have revisited Burke in relationship to the body and its capacity to influence rhetorical knowledge, underscoring the prescience of his multidimensional theories. Engaging Burke through Freud and contemporary philosophy, Diane Davis, for instance, argues in her *Inessential Solidarity* that Burkean rhetoric's condition of possibility is identification—being drawn into communion with others—and resistance—taking a critical stance to that identification process (20).[13] According to Davis, this work presumes a differentiated body with flesh, bones, and organs contained by its own skin and an identification process that works through a psychological rather than embodied connection. As Burke's later work explains it, the body is individuated and separate, while the person—the ideological construct—is dispersed through the process of identification ("Methodological Repression" 413).

Davis challenges this account of ideology through a brief excursion into neuroscience, which asserts that bodies, in addition to being psychically connected, are often physiologically identified. By way of example, she notes that mirror neurons fire regardless of whether one's body executes a particular action or one observes another body executing the same action. In the case of these neurons, bodies and their thinking minds fail to distinguish between themselves and others; this is an essential part of Adam Smith's theory of sympathy. Along with a host of other research on the body, such phenomena suggest that one's rational decision processes can hardly be exclusive, given that one's mind "doesn't manage to consistently distinguish between self and other" (Davis 24). Thus, Davis cautions against a reliance on individual reason as either the origin or *telos* of rhetorical inquiry. She maintains instead that we need "to think the limits of reason by tracking the implications—for society, for politics, for ethics—of a radically generalized rhetoricity that precedes and exceeds symbolic intervention" (36). Davis makes a convincing case that Burke relies on the notion of a self-contained individual whose body differs from his or her mind (and this is certainly the preferred reading of his work). But perhaps, as Debra Hawhee suggests, his concept of identification entails something of this radically generalized rhetoricity—a power Davis associates with its affectability—as evidenced by Burke's exploration of the intersection between intellectual work and practices such as mysticism and drug use (19).

In *Moving Bodies* Hawhee explores Burke's reoccurring interest in the body as a source of invention, suggestion, and communication. Through an excavation of both his early work and his own biography, she pieces together a Burkean philosophy in which unintentional bodily motions play a role in the intentional manipulation of language: bodies, for Burke, "enable critical reflection on meaning-making . . . from a perspective that does not begin by privileging reason or conscious thought" (2). Rather than offering a definitive reading of Burke's understanding of that role, Hawhee walks the reader through his many-layered discussions of the body's rhetorical function, while ultimately holding Burke open to an even richer interpretation of how the material world persuades. Hawhee ends her book with a quote from the afterword to Burke's third edition of *Permanence and Change,* where, she notes, he declares "the body of the human individual is the point at which the realms of physiological (nonsymbolic) motion and symbolic action meet" (167). According to Hawhee's reading of Burke, the nonsymbolic material world serves as "something like 'pre-performative,' or the force (motion) on which a successful performative depends" (165). Material bodies and the world in which they move condition our rhetorical abilities. From this perspective, the Burkean tradition offers a materialist rhetoric that recognizes the power of the body to influence through and beyond speech. The ambiguous and sometimes contradictory passages of Burke's extensive rhetorical theories lend themselves to multiple divergent readings; they all, however, signal the importance of the refracting relationships among materiality and language, a project taken in other directions through materialist rhetoric.[14]

As is well documented, Michael McGee provided the first positive assertion of materialist rhetoric in his "A Materialist Conception of Rhetoric," but even before that watershed publication, he advocated that rhetoricians ground themselves within political and material debates. McGee's "In Search of the 'People'" establishes an early agenda for exploring "the reciprocal relationship between rhetoric and social theory" and, specifically, one willing to "participate in the serious Hegelian and Marxist dialogues" that, he says, "have greatly affected life in our own time" (350). Such a call simultaneously invokes a materialist tradition and zeros in on a conversation between two different forms of dialectic—one oriented toward consciousness and the other toward historical materialism. The differences between these two dialectics is among the crucial conversations of the Marxist tradition (purportedly separating the young, ideological Marx from the scientism of his mature work), but it also evokes the conundrum at the heart of Burkean rhetoric: how do the body and its material existence shape consciousness or the ability to act reasonably? To investigate such a question, critical theory often focuses on the way that groups are formed, motivated, and pacified through institutional apparatuses, language, and other cultural forces.

Following this pathway, James Aune takes McGee up on his suggestion that rhetoricians simultaneously explore the dialectics of consciousness and materiality. Using Burke's process of identification as his point of departure, Aune locates a foundational link between rhetoric and dialectic. Rhetoric discursively unites human beings who are materially divided from each other. He says that "insofar as division or alienation has been a constant feature of human societies, the rhetorical impulse appears to be a natural development of other coping mechanisms such as magic or ritual" ("Historical Materialist Theory" 10). Rhetoric emerges at the intersection between material dialectics (lived experiences of division and unification) and the dialectics of consciousness (psychological divisions and connections). Through this insight, Aune develops a multilevel model of ideological investigation that moves from the abstract to the concrete and shuffles between imposed and organic social constructs. This historical materialist form of rhetorical criticism adds sophistication and clarifies the ideological picture. It does not, however, get at the undergirding process that makes rhetoric like magic and ritual.

To understand rhetoric's spellbinding potentiality requires attention to affect in addition to ideological analysis, a proposal Aune makes in his later work. In "Democratic Style and Ideological Containment," he returns to Burke as he contemplates the role of affect within political discourse, noting in his discussion of form another possible opening for a Hegelian-Marxist dialectic. He interprets Burke's definition of form as a kind of material force that creates "an appetite in the mind of an audience" so that "when one hears the first clause of an antithesis, one feels compelled to complete the figure with the second clause" (482). Form creates a visceral desire and, in Pavlovian fashion, audiences are moved toward its fulfillment: form literally induces bodily responses. For Aune, discourse exploits biological inclinations by symbolically mimicking their innate rhythms and desires. Democratic discourses, in particular, tap into "the universal human experience of tension and release, generalize them into mechanisms for the expression and resolution of anxieties, and then use these affective responses to change or stabilize the existing distribution of power" (483).[15] He concludes with a call to study the affective component of democratic style more fully in order to "recover [its] primal bodily and emotional force" (488). But, of course, the body is no more the site of emotion than it is of reason as the two are inseparably entangled within our habituated motivations. Thus, this ideologically weighted view of affect would benefit from positioning the emotional alongside the rational and making both derivative of the bodily filtration of affect, which could be studied as its own rhetorical terrain of invention.

Known for his foundational essay on critical rhetoric, Raymie McKerrow nudges us in this direction with his less celebrated article on corporeality. Part of the materialist wave that swept through the 1990s, his "Corporeality and Cultural Rhetoric" offers several provocations to study the body as a template for a different rhetorical sensibility. Rather than view rhetoric as democratic negotiation, he proposes a materialist perspective of rhetoric as "the force behind the impulse to give voice to one's condition" (320). An energetic compulsion to voice one's lived experience, this "rhetorical impulse," McKerrow asserts, cannot be stifled (320). Defining rhetoric as a force that obligates one to speak, McKerrow's argument resonates with George Kennedy's earlier essay, "A Hoot in the Dark," which conceives rhetoric as an energy moving through all living things.[16] If we locate this fundamental urge as the site of rhetoric, the material terrain opens itself up to bodily affect at the smallest, most imperceptible level. So positioned, rhetorical theory might focus on what Brian Massumi calls "bare activity" or, recalling Spinoza, "naturing nature's own ontopower" (Massumi, *Ontopower* 44). In other words, Kennedy and McKerrow both embrace the premise that an unnamed power—the passion gnawing within the rhetorical tradition—works materially at the level of the body to predispose audiences toward specific tendencies and not others. Understanding this rhetorical energy is key to analyzing and intervening into the contemporary political economic moment, one in which capitalism has deepened and strengthened is biopolitical reaches.

Affect as Capitalist Being in the Contemporary Political Economy

As I have explained, this book characterizes affect as a force that travels through material environments, shaping individuals and the spaces in which they operate. It moves through bodies, influencing their biochemical composition, but it does not reside in the body. Moreover, as a semiautonomous force, affect circulates apart from conscious designs even though it can be modulated within specific encounters. This definition relies on several theorists who hypothesize that affect moves among people through their sensuous experiences, including their communicative practices. Across a wide range of approaches and objects of study, these scholars intersect in their belief that affect—a material entity that propels the sociocultural life of a particular milieu—accounts for the unaccountable ties and divisions among people, things, and spaces.[17] For them, seemingly irrational behaviors cannot be explained fully through psychological identification, partial knowledge, or particular worldviews but must be studied with an eye toward the material forces motivating such behaviors. In short, affect describes a thing that travels through our material world, reconstitutes divisions as mutually imbricated relationships, and opens the door to understanding phenomena that have been previously inexplicable.

A turn toward affect burgeoned in the 1990s at a time when scholars were increasingly frustrated with the inability of ideological analysis to prevent the increasing spread of capitalist power into our everyday lives.[18] The shift from an industrially based, nationally organized economy to a knowledge-based, globally organized one, along with the accompanying change from analogue to digital communication, enabled decentralized mechanisms of control to replace apparatuses of discipline as the dominant mode of power. Biopolitical society, as Foucault has termed it, balances disciplinary power by encouraging the proliferation of individual difference while regulating population metrics at the impersonal, statistical level.[19] The multiplication of identities and different life practices, however, has done little to challenge the vast cultural and political economic inequities at play in our contemporary moment. Faced with this apparent contradiction, scholars have returned to Marx's critique of capitalism in an effort to update it for the contemporary moment.

Marx imagined the rough contours of our current capitalist stage as the real (or total) subsumption of life to capital as opposed to the formal (or limited) subsumption operative during the mid-nineteenth century, when he was writing. For Marx, the formal subsumption of labor to capital took place as soon as the labor process became mediated by employment and wages. This entailed state and juridical interventions that privatized the land and other means of production, enabling the conditions whereby free workers entered into contractual obligations with employers. In this formal space of capitalist subsumption, work continued much as it did before except that "the capitalist intervenes in the process as its director, its manager" (Marx, *Capital* 1019). After this initial period, manufacturing becomes industrialized through technological development, and constant innovation introduces ever-new products into life experience. Ultimately, as we are now witnessing, these technologies bleed so seamlessly into everyday activities that we find ourselves unconsciously working on behalf of capital and its interests during all parts of our day. The pervasiveness of this capitalist influence obscures its exploitative powers. As Marx envisioned it, "the mystification implicit in the relations of capital as a whole is greatly intensified here, far beyond the point it had reached or could have reached in the merely formal subsumption of labour under capital" (1024). Capitalism no longer stops at economic production or even cultural consumption but seeps into what Michael Hardt and Antonio Negri call "the social bios itself" (*Empire* 25). Because its power dynamics have rooted themselves deeply into all aspects of our lives, capitalism has become coextensive with our rhetorical being, directing our orientations in the world. Capitalism, that is, has fused with the energetic power of affect, which invisibly compels our instinctual ways of being, thinking, and acting.

To reiterate, in the contemporary political economy, affect, an organic power circulating throughout the world and its inhabitants, has become inseparably bound up with capitalist valuation as the central manufactured power of our world. The production and circulation of value are central to Marx's assessment of the capitalist system. For Marx, the value of things derives from the fact that "human labor is accumulated in them" (*Capital* 128). Rather than describing laborers as autonomous bodies strategically positioned for capitalist exploitation, Marx conceptualizes workers as creative beings who transfer their life energy into the commodities of their production. Their work, a concrete "expenditure of human brains, muscles, nerves, hands," produces commodities that have, in addition to their material qualities, an invisible value that measures the social energy necessary for their production (163).[20] Consequently, the table Marx famously discusses at the end of *Capital*'s first chapter becomes humanized: "it stands on its feet" and evolves ideas out of "its wooden brain" (163). The table's ability to move and to think indexes the affective transfer of life energy through labor. Because the things we produce contain our physical and psychic energies, they connect the human beings who create them with those who consume them—commodities, producers, and consumers become coextensive through a material process that facilitates energetic or affective flows.[21]

Although the value theory of labor has been criticized for its transcendent quality, the insertion of affect in the place of value reasserts the materiality of these encounters. Affect is not a theoretical abstraction or an illuminating metaphor but a concrete, physiological force circulating into and out of bodies through their sensuous interaction in the world. Teresa Brennan, for instance, conjectures that affect hangs in the air and moves between individuals. It produces a sense of belonging through a "process that is social in origin but biological and physical in effect" (3). Articulating this theory through Marxist terms, laborers transfer material vitality (through mental and physical exertion as well as their accompanying affects) into the commodities they produce. Recipients of these things consume not only their use values but also their affective values—energies taken in through our sensuous interactions with these products.[22] As theorists such as Brennan, Bennett, and Massumi emphasize, affective vibrancy circulates among all things—human and nonhuman as well as animate and inanimate. From this perspective, the elusive thing that haunts commodities, the surplus value that represents the excess or remainder of exploited labor, may be invisible to our eye's perception, but it is neither immaterial nor transcendent. Its materiality transforms concrete existence, manufacturing what Diane Davis calls affectability and Thomas Rickert identifies as rhetorical being.

Just as the labor theory of value can be represented through a shorthand circulation process, so too can the affective theory of value.[23] For Marx, the key to capitalist profit—the ability for money to make more money—occurs in the productive sphere where laborers transfer value into commodities by means of their working bodies without being fully remunerated by the value of their wages. This surplus value enters commodities that are then sold in the marketplace. They are sold according to their total value—both the value paid to workers in wages and the surplus value not paid. Once sold, the surplus value created in production becomes actualized as profit. These profits are distributed among several places, but a significant chunk goes back to production to further the process. This is described, in the figure below, alongside a parallel process wherein affect, similarly invisible, begets more affect through its circulation. The increase in affect—signaled, for instance, when a word carries significance beyond its referential capacity—can be represented in much the same way as the increase in economic value. As a physical energy, affect moves into signs, spaces, and bodies. Affect multiplies as these things repeat, its intensity increases with improved visibility, and the qualitative experience of our interactions with these things adjusts accordingly. This affective process creates a rhetorical predisposition that affects how one engages as a speaking and acting subject. Carrying affective weight, these engagements feed back into and further modify the circulating affect. The two circulations explain the creation of value in its economic and affective forms. They circulate through environments, people, and things, but in the process a residue adheres to those objects and constitutes their affectability.

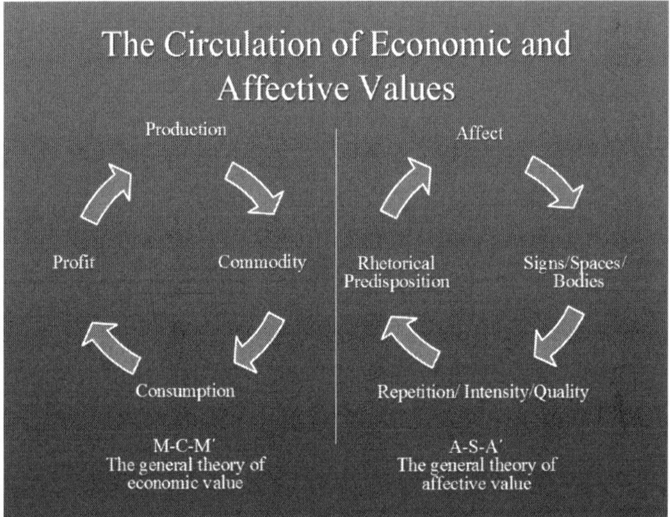

Of course, in reality, the circulation of affect does not run parallel to the capitalist circulation of commodities. We do not have two lives—one that taps into capitalist production through work and consumption and one that senses and interprets the significance of those things. On the contrary, our affective realities come with us as we work, during our leisure time, and in our public engagements. Our affective lives, circulating through the bodies we can never leave behind, are thus subsumed by capital, requiring that we imagine the circulation of affect as embedded within the process of commodity circulation. In other words, affective circulation overlays capitalist circulation such that commodity production transmits affect and consumption practices repeat, intensify, and qualify that affect. Consequently, the valorization of commodities into economic profit is also the valorization of an affective subject with his or her own rhetorical predisposition. The current political economic milieu is at once crafted for the optimal circulation of capitalist value and its affective being: the air we breathe is redolent of competition, the clothes we wear cover us in the microelements of global exploitation, the food we eat nourishes us with its bioengineered calories, and the culture we consume patterns our imaginations with the banalities of violence.

Yet it is not a total colonization of our rhetorical being inasmuch as other possibilities lie in excess of the hegemonic pathways. As Nathan Stormer and Bridie McGreavy suggest, agency names an individual's capacity and that capacity develops through one's history and experience with a given ecology wherein bodies, environments, and things become capacitated through a dynamic and evolving structure of connectivity produced from the circulation of affective energy. From this perspective, twenty-first-century capitalism exists as an ecological environment to nurture particular affective capacities. Like any ecosystem, it needs to be nurtured and maintained, or it becomes susceptible to the encroachment of other forms of engendering life. Because capitalism maintains itself through its constant production of affective being, affective production offers an important site for those rhetorical engagements aimed at alternative political economic modalities.

If the circulation of affect is both an independent process that predisposes individuals to rhetorical practices and a process that intersects with and is ultimately subsumed by capitalist flows, then our rhetorical inquiries must pay attention to both affective and capitalist circulations. Jenny Edbauer Rice's taxonomy for what she calls critical affect studies points us in that direction. Her review of several important affect-related books postulates four topoi from which to launch affective investigations: the physical life of social bodies, the political life of social bodies, the economic life of social bodies, and language beyond official accounts. As the first three topoi indicate, affect travels through space to enliven its possibilities and animate its collective spontaneities. Any discrete place or moment of affectability derives from the movement, flows, and pathways of a transsituationally and transhistorically circulating affective energy. By rethinking affect as a circulating force, we have a material entity through which theories such as Davis's notion of affectability or Rickert's ambient rhetoric can calibrate to the dynamics of political economy.

Toward a Method of Affect-Oriented Rhetorical Criticism

From vibrant materiality to actor-network theory to object-oriented ontologies, new materialist scholars explore the power of inanimate things to persuade and motivate.[24] The perspective of affect I have been outlining suggests that this is a physical power that moves seemingly uncontrollably through human beings and other things to produce preconscious readiness. It is a power that has been at the center of a deep uneasiness about rhetoric since the classical era because it points to the radically incomplete nature of human beings, their knowledge, and their agency.[25] Affect, that is, highlights a hole in our rhetorical theories—one occupied by what Denise Riley calls "impersonal passion" or nondesiring agency. Affect has objectivity and purpose (it is a physical entity that connects with and predisposes), and yet it has no motivation: energies capable of effecting change circulate but do not have independent designs on the world. This autonomy notwithstanding, affect remains essential to the practice of rhetoric because it exerts influence, procures the capacity for action, and prescreens our perception of the world and its possibilities. Although this automatic, instinctual, and often unconscious bodily orientation precedes conscious rhetorical decision making, it is not beyond the purview of rhetoric; on the contrary, the human being has perpetual access to the heterogeneous ontologies shaping the inclinations of its bodily reason. Consequently, it is imperative that we learn to discern and negotiate these affective forces as part of our rhetorical practices—a project explored in more detail in the conclusion. Here I offer a method for tracking this pervasive power by attending to the theoretical intersections between affect theory and materialist rhetoric.

Affect theorists make a compelling case, one of importance to rhetoricians, for how experiences not only train our thinking but also familiarize our bodies and our sense of being along particular trajectories. In such a conception, one Plato long ago called the habitude of rhetoric, the mind/body divide collapses, blurring the distinction between the epistemological and the ontological as well as between the agentive subject and the passive object. Thus, when Sara Ahmed contends that "the significance of things is not simply 'in' the thing but a 'characteristic of being,'" she points to the way that being is held in common ("Orientations" 550). Being does not adhere to a body or form to produce its stable capacity, but evolves and unfolds in relationship to its historical situatedness. Ontologically multiple and in constant flux, affective energy shapes being through the repetitive pathways of its connections. Both lived and inherited history singularize affective multiplicities through what Ahmed calls "straightening devices" (562). Such devices, built from the residue of repeated experiences, enable one to fit unfamiliar encounters into familiar ones in order to maintain a coherent picture of the world. These alignments do not result from conscious design but from affectively inspired bodily charges. Ahmed gives the example of a heterosexual woman living next to her and her female partner. The heteronormativity shooting through the neighborhood and entering the neighbor's body like hidden barbs, as Renaissance rhetoricians might say, compels the woman to realign the couple as either sisters or as husband

and wife. This incident shows the persuasive power that habituated being has on meaning making: affect literally rescripts the reality that is unfolding before one's eyes.

Given the way affect guides the collective thinking that orients communities (such as the neighborhood Ahmed joined), critical communication scholars have tended to study affect through group behavior. Julian Henriques, for instance, maps the affective forces that motivate behavior on an imperceptible level during dance night in Kingston, Jamaica. Borrowing from Henri Lefebre's rhythm analysis, he conjectures that affect travels through bodies, things, and sociocultural spaces; thus, its vibrations can be measured through frequency (repetition), volume (intensity), and timbre (quality). Frequency can be counted and volume can be measured according to the significance afforded to specific iterations, but quality, or "the way in which a fundamental frequency combines with its harmonics, resonances and overtones, to give rise to an infinite range of intimate and subjective sensations," must be experienced (81). Rhetorically, this means that we interpret a situation (the repetition of signs, things, people, and spaces); we feel its intensity (the significance of its impacts); and then we enter into the situation to become part and parcel of its vibrating quality. As Henriques's interview subject DJ Squeeze says, "you kind of fit, or melt, right into it" (67). He goes on to explain that the night's "vibes" permeate social spaces—markets, streets, and mass gatherings—until "your whole body transmits an energy that connects to another person's energy, so that . . . everybody is doing the same thing without even realizing" (69). Claiming not to understand these motivating forces, DJ Squeeze nevertheless directs them through his music selections. His song choices orient the crowd, increasing or decreasing its momentum. An energy that persuades without conscious determination, affect moves through the DJ, the song, and the audience to unite them all within the same sensed milieu. Music, which works through vibrations and seduces bodily movements, illustrates human sensibility for and negotiation with affective being particularly well, but affectivity saturates all environments, even those characterized by silence and inactivity or the supposedly logic-based transmission of information between screen and worker.

Take the workplace example from Karin Knorr Cetina and Urs Bruegger's participant-observation study of currency traders. Contrary to the frenzied stock-exchange floor that dominates popular images, contemporary trading typically takes place digitally with a broker tethered to a computer and a range of communication devices. The success of traders, according to those interviewed in this study, stems less from scientific algorithms and more from an ability to sense the market's affective rhythms. They describe the market as a dynamic life form—an entity that needs to be both intellectually assessed and physically intuited. Traders, they say, have to be skilled at merging professional reflection with sensuous engagement. They must keep abreast of the current climate by monitoring market indices, government policies, and social trends to discern how this information feels to the market. One trader explains that "you notice every small shift, you notice when the market becomes insecure, you notice when it becomes nervous. . . . All of this (amounts to a) feeling (for the market). When you develop this feeling, and not many people have it, the capacity to feel and sense the market . . . then [you] can anticipate (it) and can act accordingly. When you get away from the market, and you lack this feeling (for it), then it's incredibly difficult to find it again" (180). This individual combines observation and sensation to become consubstantial with the market. Participants, texts, and markets exist separately across time and space and are nonetheless materially connected. No one would mistake this trader for the market, and yet he feels what the market feels in the same way that Diane Davis tells us that individuals neurologically respond to observations of others' activities precisely as they react to performing those activities themselves.

Davis, of course, engages her notion of affectability through psychoanalytic Derridean, and Heideggerian theories, avoiding critical materialist traditions. Indeed, rhetoric's growing new materialist perspective generally operates outside traditional materialism's historical and political frames. Take Thomas Rickert, for example. In one memorable illustration, he explains how the Microsoft startup music positively disposes users to what might, on occasion, become a frustrating computer-user experience. Automatically playing when a person turns on his or her computer, this music functions as ambient rhetoric inasmuch as it "persuades us prior to symbolicity"; it "situates us differently in the world, evoking other ways of being" (33). To the extent that we allow ourselves to dwell in its affordances, we will be better enabled to navigate the computer-human experience. According to Rickert, this process "is not just a form of communication between entities but an ontological manifestation of their dynamic entanglement" (111). The music sweeps through the environment and its objects, reconstituting the computer and the listener as a human-machine dyad with its own capacities. The traditional materialist perspective missing from this account would likely note that this human-machine dyad is not raw, universal materiality but particular materiality with capacities that differ according to structural inequalities. Just as we have inherited a historically shaped world, so too have we inherited its affective modes of being. Moreover, that affectivity manifests in uneven and divergent modalities. Because we are not all affectively equal before the computer and its orienting sounds, we need theories that thread through preceding materialist insights so as not to lose sight of historical and institutional oppression.

One such stitch might locate itself in the resonances between affectability and the dialectical struggles that underscore political economic change. Marxist dialectics—negation of negation, unity of opposites, and quantity into quality—not only imply a permeable relationship between supposed counterparts, but they also imply an organic movement between these terms that accounts for historical progress.[26] Thus, to link affect with dialectics emphasizes the role of sociohistorical agency that exists both apart from and within people, motives, and intentional actions. As Dana Cloud explains it, the dialectics of historical motion imply *kairotic* knowledge of revolutionary potential: people discern the historical opening when numerous separate struggles snowball into an opportunity for a more broad-based qualitative change.[27] Rhetorical mobilization at such moments requires identification among people who rally around a particular issue, and dialectics, Cloud says, "reminds us that those identities and intentions can have a real basis in the existing antagonisms that move society forward" ("Materialist Dialectic" 299).[28] For Cloud, the *kairotic* moment, engendered through an accumulation of actions that paved the way for a transformative possibility, is at once rational (policy demands, for instance) and sensual (the bodily discernment of critically timed actions).[29] From this perspective, *kairos* can be understood as the moment when we feel ourselves propelled by multiple circulating powers and have a sensibility for how to modulate such forces, contributing quantitatively (adding oneself to the numerous other forces) toward a desired qualitative shift.[30]

This definition of *kairos* entails a relationship between subject and object such that the objective situation or historical milieu calls the agent into action, all of which could be understood to emerge through the habitation of affect that produces consubstantial identification among people as well as between them and their worldly milieu.[31] Compatible with new materialist thinking, the idea that the historical object, alive with possibilities, is every bit as much an agent as the revolutionary subject requires a world-animating power, one that I am calling affect. An individual senses an affective quality moving throughout the entire political economic landscape. Recognizing this force as it moves with and through a host of sites, including our own subjective ones, is an experience that is simultaneously epistemological and ontological. To modulate these forces without complete knowledge of the many unconscious bodily processes affecting our decision making means that we must learn to experience objects bodily as well as intellectually, opening ourselves up to the surplus of affective production.

Adding such historical materialist sensibilities to Henriques's vibration model, I propose a political economic schema (summarized in the table below) for assessing the materiality of affect and its rhetorical significance. The first column of the model identifies three material manifestations of affective energy, each serving unique functions.[32] The second column correlates each function with its material force: constructing identification, timing possibilities, and producing energy. The idea that affect pushes and pulls identification, opens and closes possibilities, and raises or lowers energy derives from the particular functions of affect. Those functions produce specific rhetorical effects; therefore, the third column extends this affective work to its rhetorical ends. Identification shapes ideology, calculating possible openings manufactures *kairos,* and energy enables action. Taken in its entirety, this chart categorizes the material work of an always circulating affect and its relationship to rhetoric in order to offer a framework for tracking such affectivity as it pushes or pulls identification, opens or closes affectability, and raises or lowers agentive energy. Creating rhetorical predispositions that influence the effectiveness of rhetorical exchanges, these three modalities represent the affective terrain that this book investigates.

Assessing Affective Movements

MATERIALITY OF AFFECT	MODALITIES OF AFFECT	RHETORICITY OF AFFECT
Frequency/Repetition	Push or pull identification	Shapes ideological context
Timbre/Quality	Open or close possibilities	Produces *kairotic* opportunities
Volume/Intensity	Raise or lower energy	Motivates action or inaction

This method could track affect through cultural events, workplace practices, and street protests, but it also works in ostensibly static textual artifacts such as the ones constituting the intellectual history of capitalist debates. With a focus on the key modalities of affect, this book studies the animating powers that push/pull, open/close, and increase/decrease material possibilities within various political economic arguments. Using this triple lens, it surveys how key economic theorists intuited and engaged the living power I am calling affect. It explores political economic texts spanning nearly 250 years of disciplinary reflection by utilizing an affective materialist lens built into the preceding materialisms that attempts to understand the motion of individuals and society as operating separately from individual agentive will. Examining pairs of political economic theorists—one who espouses capitalism and one who opposes it—this study excavates a theory of affect latent in each author's early theoretical and rhetorical work and uses this affectivity to reevaluate each thinker's official political economic propositions.

2 Adam Smith and Karl Marx

The Founding Fathers and Their Foundations

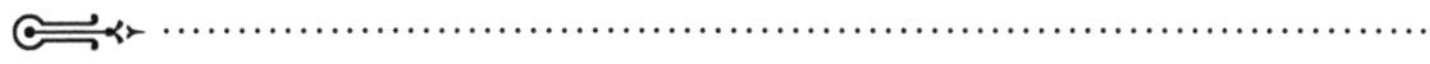

Marx is among those who discovered the fact that things live.

Peter Sloterdijk, *Marx Reloaded*

It is commonplace to pit Adam Smith (1723–1790) against Karl Marx (1818–1883), whose criticism of the capitalist mode of production emerged nearly a century after the publication of Smith's *The Wealth of Nations*, as "founding fathers" of two opposing political economic systems. Yet Smith, the progenitor of laissez-faire capitalism, and Marx, the philosophical bedrock of communist revolutions worldwide, are strikingly similar. Both men understood labor, rather than land (as did the physiocrats) or gold (as did the mercantilists), as the source of wealth within the capitalist system; both claimed that the division of labor was the condition for its possibility; both were concerned about the exploitation of laborers at the hands of profit-hungry capitalists; and both offered what they thought was a comprehensive and scientific explanation of wealth creation. Living in the first generation after Isaac Newton's groundbreaking theory of universal gravitation, Smith sought an all-encompassing principle like gravity to explain the connections among disparate economic and social phenomena. Indeed, physics-centered language such as energy and force pervade his account of political economy.[1] Marx, a contemporary of Darwin, was similarly enamored with the idea of a single overarching principle to explain the entire political economic terrain and its vast superstructure. Although the language of physics can be found in his texts, biological metaphors feature even more prominently. Situated within the Enlightenment tradition, both theorists based their scientific analyses in concrete empirical evidence and used inductive reasoning to make their claims.

Given the resonances of their respective economic theories, it is tempting to assume that Marx's critique of capitalism stems from an ethical position that Smith quarantined from his exploration of the marketplace; such a position, however, is difficult to sustain. Contrary to the so-called Adam Smith problem (the purported gap between Smith's early concern with moral sentiments and his later work on self-interested economic pursuit), *The Wealth of Nations* requires Smith's moral framework of institutionalized sentiment, imagination, and sympathy.[2] Smith characterized capitalists as greedy, conspiratorial, and in need of regulation—a task primarily accomplished through social convention and innate human tendencies, though also requiring political apparatuses that align with these processes. His schema certainly differs from Marx's account, which views institutional and social structures as corrosive to rather than cooperating with human freedom, but arguments about which philosophy is more ethical fail to get at the underlying difference in their theories.

The more crucial distinction lies in their differing conceptions of the power structure propelling human relationships. Human senses and their often unconscious receptivity motivate economic thinking and acting within both accounts, though in vastly divergent ways. For Smith, the ultimate empowering mechanism, the market's invisible hand, exists as an external entity that naturally connects, categorizes, and directs individuals according to the greatest social good. People are generally not conscious of this power even when they find themselves instinctually driven according to its directives. For Marx, the empowering agent exists internal to human species-being. The entire potentiality of the world exists within human beings who consciously direct this force for the collective social good. Capitalism disrupts this process by transferring a specifically human power into things, resulting in Marx's famous conception of commodity fetishism or the argument, as Peter Sloterdijk indicates in the epigraph, that people become thing-like while things become life-like.[3] Robert Bolz, in the same documentary, goes on to explain that commodities live because they possess not only the labor of another but also "a spiritual surplus value, and this value is the real reason for their purchase" (*Marx Reloaded*). If Smith theorized an external force motivating human beings for the good of society, then Marx countered that capitalism wrenched this powerful force from laborers and funneled it into nonhuman things. This dispute centers on the underlying forces animating materiality or what I have been referring to as affect.

To track this affective differentiation, we need to attend to how these thinkers conceptualize embodied capacities and their relationship to consciousness. Both scholars understood language production, the material form of consciousness, as exceptionally important. Indeed, Smith spent over fifteen years teaching rhetoric and *belles lettres* to students, first through his lectures in Edinburgh and later at the University of Glasgow. Like many Scottish Enlightenment rhetoricians, Smith focused on style and delivery with little regard for invention. The elimination of rhetoric's first canon and its attendant shift from the political to the artistic realm underscores Smith's thinking and epitomizes bourgeois consciousness, according to Marx. Although Marx did not offer an explicit theory of language, he spent a large part of his two-year exile in Paris embroiled in the study of political economy and its relationship to ideology. During this time, he produced texts that grapple with the relationship between political economy and consciousness. Marx believed that just as capitalism alienated people within the labor process, it likewise alienated them from their own thinking about the world. Within this space of alienated or false consciousness, the ruling ideas were simply the ideas of the ruling class made universal.[4] The widespread effects of alienation all stem from capitalist production in which an agentive subject and the object of one's creation in labor serve the circulation of value rather than the needs of a species-being in community with others. In different labor structures, Marx assumed, the relationship between subject and object shifts in such a way as to eliminate this alienation.[5] Describing a process whereby power moves among people as well as between people and things to create or not create alienation, Marx offered an unexpressed theory of affect.

This exploration of power as a circulating force moving through and orienting human decision helps explain why Marx came to such a different position on capitalism than Smith, even though they shared so many foundational beliefs about its structure and ability to produce innumerably more goods, greater scientific developments, and ever-newer technologies than did any previous economic structure. A theory of affect is implicit in each of these thinkers' early writing. For Smith, the crucial texts are *Theory of Moral Sentiments* and *Rhetoric and Belles Lettres,* the unpublished student notes from his rhetoric lectures. For Marx, the key texts are *Economic and Philosophic Manuscripts of 1844, The German Ideology,* and "On the Jewish Question."

Affect: Human Nature or Human Alienation

As a student of Francis Hutcheson and a contemporary and friend of David Hume, Adam Smith was well versed in arguments about the internal senses—the human capacity to take in sensory information and create reason. For such Scottish empiricists, knowledge entered the mind via the senses and therefore was not separate from the body but illustrative of the human faculty to mold passions into reasonable action. Although this capacity was understood to be innate, it needed to be cultivated and refined. As Harold Cook explains, "because the passions were products of body as much of mind, they could not be directly controlled by volition" but only by systemic or institutional structures within which individuals habituate themselves through repetition (38). This was the Enlightenment's response to the long-held belief that bodily passions are stronger than reason and unable to be controlled by mere arguments. In effect, what Enlightenment scholars did was to make reason a bodily passion.[6] Rather than counter passion with reason, this strategy suggested that bodies could be trained into correct practices through the institutional structures of education, democracy, and religion. Viewed from this light, the overarching goal of Smith's oeuvre is to uncover the natural power by which human beings function and ensure that their institutions are structured according to those natural inclinations: this search for systemic power serves as his implicit theory of affect.[7]

Smith surmises that a unifying power exists within nature that enables people and institutions to work for the common good. This power accounts for the fact that disparate and apparently unrelated phenomena work together to form an organized whole. The search for this kind of systemic power motivates modern scientific inquiry, as Smith discusses in "The History of Astronomy."[8] In addition to the invisible hand that guides actions, there are invisible chains that hold all those actions together. The goal of science is to explain the connecting principle that pieces together a unified whole from apparently chaotic individual phenomena. He says, for instance, that philosophy, "by representing the invisible *chains* which bind together all these disjointed objects, endeavours to introduce order into this chaos of jarring and discordant appearances, to allay this tumult of the imagination, and to restore it, when it surveys the great revolutions of the universe, to that tone of tranquillity and composure" (20).

This is not merely a rhetorical endeavor to calm the masses: these invisible chains exist, and to understand the rules by which they operate is to uncover the truth of our world. Characterizing Newton's theory as paradigmatic of this inquiry, Smith describes gravity as "the discovery of an immense chain of the most important and sublime truths, all closely connected together, by one capital fact, of the reality of which we have daily experience" (93). Just as Newton revealed the force that governs the everyday behavior of things, Smith aspires to disclose the force that governs the ordinary behavior of people—personally, politically, and economically. Recognizing this goal, Roger Frantz says that "sympathy for Smith played the same role in human society and moral affairs as gravity played in the physical universe: it held things together" (9).

Smith begins his inquiry in *The Theory of Moral Sentiments* with an everyday experience that illuminates those invisible bonds. He notices that when we imagine another's pain, "we then tremble and shudder at the thought of what he feels" (12). Or, more immediately, if we see an impending strike at another, "we naturally shrink and draw back our own leg or our own arm; and when it does fall, we feel it in some measure" (12).[9] So ordinary and perhaps timeless are these examples that they could be used today. We all wince when someone in view gets hurt—there is a physical reaction in us to another's pain as though we were tethered together, making one's bodily experience meld into another's. The first and second examples, however, address two slightly different phenomena. In the first description, we are affected by reflecting on someone's pain while the second has us reacting immediately without reflection. In both cases, claims Smith, we physically experience someone's pain because we are able to sympathize with that person. Sympathy results from the imagination or the faculty that allows us to enter into another's body, to "become in some measure the same person," and thus to see things from "the eyes of other people" (12, 128).

Whether we are conscious of it or not, sympathy results from some substance moving into the imagination. Although Smith is primarily interested in how sympathy enables moral action, his discussion of sympathetic behavior belies a richer, perhaps intuitive, understanding of the physiological work of affect. As he explains, sympathy allows one person to enter the body of another imaginatively in order to understand his or her sensuous experience of the world and is activated by an agent that physically alters one's body. For instance, sympathetic responses can be triggered from sound and language, the strength of which requires proximity between sender and receiver. For Smith, sympathy among those with whom we share spaces—family, friends, and colleagues—is nearly instantaneous, while it is more difficult to emerge when we do not know the person and did not witness the event in dispute. He contends that the happiness of a crowd "enlivens our own mirth" and that when we congratulate friends "their joy literally becomes our joy" (18, 57). He also explains that when people confide their troubles, the confidant "not only feels a sorrow of the same kind with that which they feel, but as if he had derived a part of it to himself, what he feels seems to alleviate the weight of what they feel" (18). Furthermore, he discusses "how uneasy" people feel upon entering "a house in which jarring contention sets one half of those who dwell in it against the other" (48). Not only does the sensory trigger of sympathy pass between individuals, it also saturates environments, orienting those within them.[10] It travels between people spatially and has a temporal shelf life: "the man of to-day is no longer agitated by the same passions which distracted the man of yesterday" (183). As an external circulating force, the substance must leave the body and the imagination just as it once entered it; the repetition of such flows leaves an accumulating trace that constitutes an individual's instinctual disposition.

In fact, Smith's explanation of the embodied responses to sympathy overlaps with the three key modalities of affect described earlier: to push or pull identity, to open or close receptivity, and to increase or decrease energy. His description of hearing the call of an individual in trouble exemplifies how sympathy increases our energy and motivates action. He says that "as soon as it strikes the ear, it interests us in his fortune, and, if continued, forces us almost involuntarily to fly to assistance" (45). Sentiments also predispose and orient our actions. Music, he contends, modulates our passions "or at least puts us in the mood which disposes us to conceive them" (45). The music makes individuals more open to particular ideas and feelings.[11] A third function of sentiments is to connect people to particular groups or ideas. Smith explains that when we are in sympathy with another who has been wronged, "we feel ourselves to be in a particular manner tied, bound, and obliged to the observation of justice" (93). Using sympathy, Smith connects a wide variety of phenomena suggesting that our human faculty for imagination allows us to understand and act in such a way as to construct a morally sound and organized society. In his estimation, nature "formed man for society" by giving him this faculty for sympathy (135). That nature imbues humanity with the imaginative faculty is crucial because it means that sympathetic practices ultimately enable the perfect functioning of society. Declaring that "what is agreeable to our moral faculties, is fit, and right, and proper," Smith not only naturalizes sympathy but also links those natural forces with the normative order (192). Reflecting its historical milieu, sympathy mobilizes bodies along various pathways and goes without question as it derives from the unfettered forces of human life.

The natural imaginative faculty positions individuals and their institutions, ranging from legislative and judicial bodies to political economic systems, within the social good. Smith argues that the "imagination expands itself to everything around ourselves" so that the luxury of the wealthy strikes "the imagination as something grand and beautiful and noble of which the attainment is well worth all the toil and anxiety which we are apt to bestow upon it" (214). He goes on to say that this is an ennobling attribute because "it is this deception, which rouses and keeps in continual motion the industry of mankind" (214). So conceived, the imagination allows us to see things from the eyes of the rich, and we are joined together with them in sympathy for their well-earned luxury. This sympathy does not simply allow us to judge their behavior as good but also "rouses" us toward such industry in hopes of receiving similar luxuries. As a natural system, sympathy, works to benefit all humanity. Consequently, the rich, despite their selfishness, "are led by an invisible hand to make nearly the same distribution of the necessaries of life, which would have been made, had the earth been divided into equal portions among all its inhabitants" (215). Moreover, we need not inquire into this guiding force as "the administration of the great system of the universe, the care of the universal happiness of all rational and sensible beings, is the business of God and not man" (279). People do not organize society according to a self-determined system; on the contrary, by following their natural instincts they unconsciously construct a society that accords with godly providence.[12]

In this regard, Smith advocates what Marx calls alienation—the process by which individuals externalize their own power into something else and thus engage each other through this fabricated concept.

Like most German intellectuals of the mid-nineteenth century, Marx was a student of Hegel, from whom he borrowed the concept of alienation.[13] Hegel understood history as the unfolding of a World Spirit that materializes in all individuals and their social structures. The World Spirit becomes alienated from itself when people relate to others as foreign beings. The political state as a site of national identification, however, transcends this alienation. Predictably, traditional Hegelians viewed contemporary political structures centered on democratic citizenship as the culmination of world history. The young Hegelians, a more radical faction made up of thinkers such as Bruno Bauer and Ludwig Feuerbach, used Hegel's theory to agitate for even greater political equity, including things like religious freedom. In either application, Hegel's World Spirit discloses itself through the institutional structures of the nation-state. Marx earned his political stripes and his life of exile by participating in this intellectual dispute—one embroiled in the critique of religious and of state institutions. Because he wished to liberate the whole of humanity and not just its religious or political aspects, he extended these critiques to another institution of oppression—a political economic system that treats the human being as "a working animal" or "a beast reduced to the strictest bodily needs" (*Economic and Philosophic Manuscripts* 73).

Marx articulates his position on the nation-state and capitalism as mediating forces standing between human beings and their authentic species capacity in an early essay that addresses religious freedom for Jews. Responding to Bruno Bauer's recently published *The Jewish Question,* which outlines the problem of religious identity in the secular state, Marx says that the fundamental problem is neither religious nor political; instead, it lies in the fact that "man leads, notably in thought, in consciousness, but in reality, in life a double existence" ("On the Jewish Question" 34).[14] Individuals imagine themselves as social beings through the abstract notion of citizenship, but they live their lives as egoistic beings in the private sphere. Worse still, people live an alienated existence in both aspects of their lives. As citizens they place their species-being in the state, and as members of civil society they place their species-being in commodities. The answer to the question of human emancipation, therefore, cannot be founded in an identity as either a free citizen or a free worker. Instead, it must be derived from the process by which individuals extend their social existence from the abstract realm of politics into their concrete lived experiences. In Marx's words, true freedom happens when "in his everyday life, in his work, and in his relationships, [an individual] has become a species-being; and when he has recognized and organized his own powers *(forces propres)* as social powers so that he no longer separates this social power from himself as political power" ("On the Jewish Question" 46). The key terms contributing to Marx's implicit notion of affect are all outlined here: alienation, species-being, and social power.

Marx developed these concepts more fully in *Economic and Philosophic Manuscripts of 1844,* written during his exile in Paris. To flesh out the ideas hinted at in his brief critique of Bruno Bauer's discussion of religious and political emancipation, he embarked on a systematic investigation into the political economy of the French physiocrats and the English mercantilists. It was at this time that he encountered Adam Smith. Smith's version of political economy, he says, functions on the one hand as "a product of the real *energy* and the real *movement* of private property—as a product of *industry*—and on the other hand, as a force which has quickened and glorified the energy and development of modern industry and made it a power in the realm of consciousness" (128). In a footnote to this passage, Marx suggests that these ideas have created "modern industry as Self," suggesting that bourgeois political economy and its institutions privatize the social power that rightly belongs to human beings. Marx refuses to follow this move, one crucial to Smith's sense of affect, because it contributes to alienation by upholding industry as the source of power and wealth. Under such a system, he posits, the individual "yield[s] his inner wealth to the outer world" (139). This inner wealth of individuals, their affective power, manifests in all activities as a complex whole rather than as an individual faculty.

Like Smith, Marx does not offer a conscious theory of affect even though one can be teased from his early writing, which emphasizes embodied engagement with the world as the collective expression of life value or affective energy. For Marx, "the forming of the five senses is a labor of the entire history of the world down to the present" (*Economic and Philosophic Manuscripts* 141). This statement (and his argument more generally) establishes stasis with Adam Smith and other bourgeois political economists around the fact that knowledge derives from sensuous engagement with the world. From this point of agreement, he critiques Smith and others for having left the realm of empiricism by placing agency within other entities—God, the market, or the invisible hand, for instance. Rather than going back to "fictitious primordial conditions" as do theologians and political economists, he proceeds from "the economic fact of the present" (*Economic and Philosophic Manuscripts* 107). Capitalism, he argues, alienates people from their species-being by creating man as an individual who works only as a means to life and in that labor transfers his own powers into the commodity world. To put it differently, the problem with capitalism is that it impedes the natural circulation of affect by inhibiting the free expression of productive human activity. The abolition of this process means, for Marx, the implementation of authentic species-being in which one's ontology becomes resocialized and reconnects humanity with its own potentiality.

Marx spends a great deal of time explaining species-being in its authentic or unalienated form. Species-being, the thing that makes us uniquely human, resides in the free development of our conscious physical and mental labor. The value-adding power of life, what Marx calls passion, emerges in labor wherein "all the natural, spiritual, and social variety of individual activity is manifest" (66). In language that strikes critics of his early work as dangerously Hegelian, Marx explains that "the dominion of the objective being in me, the sensuous outburst of my life activity, is *passion* which thus becomes the *activity* of my being" (144). Later he contends that "passion is the essential force of man energetically bent on its object" (182). This object is "the life of the species. It is life-engendering life" (113). For Marx, affect is that which adds value to life, and it is the essence or the core of our being as humans to participate in such value-adding activities. Whereas Smith makes reason an embodied passion through institutionalization, Marx makes labor the natural expression of passion and does not pose an external regulating force beyond humans and the world they inhabit. The source of passion, or affect, is the human being as a social being and not some transcendent force. As Marx contends, the individual is "endowed with *natural powers of life*" and "these forces exist in him as tendencies and abilities" (181). The origin of affect is not mysterious, nor is it beyond human reason; on the contrary, affect resides in the human being and emerges in his or her conscious efforts to construct society from the natural world.

So conceived, affect circulates through the constitution of human society, engendering life along its pathways. The human species and its powers evolve through this affective relationship with nature. Both our physical and mental senses emerge from our relationship to the world: "not only the five senses but also the so-called mental senses—the practical senses (will, love, etc.)—in a word, human sense—the human nature of the senses—comes to be by virtue of its object, by virtue of humanized nature" (141). The concrete, empirical reality of his description faces off against the more abstract notions of political citizenship or economic transcendence. What is particularly prescient in this description, however, is the suggestion, clearly opposed to Smith's view, that the senses are not evidence of a perfect transcendent order. For Marx, the senses help us discern the movement of passion or affect, and in so doing, they are the "*ontological* affirmation of being" (165).[15] Our bodily senses, rather than our sympathetic capacity, diagnose being and its affective possibilities.

From Marx's perspective, an individual exists in the world only to the extent that he or she can perceive the world. Those perceptions differ according to our different relationships to the world. Capitalism, because it alienates man from himself by virtue of commodity production, changes man so that his sensuous life is mediated by money. This change is ontological: "the senses of the social man are *other* senses than those of the non-social man" (141). Man no longer has innate powers but becomes a being whose powers derive from commodities. Instead of individuals capable of exerting innate human capacity to express passion through labor, individuals derive their powers from an external entity. In capitalism, Marx claims, "the extent of the power of money is the extent of my power. . . . Thus, what I *am* and what I *am capable* of is by no means determined by my individuality. I *am* ugly, but can buy for myself the most beautiful women. Therefore I am not *ugly*" (167). Because money is the result of collective labor and collective efforts, it is "the alienated ability of *mankind*" (168). In proper affective relations, "man appropriates his total essence in a total manner—that is, as a whole man. Each of his human relations to the world—seeing, hearing, smelling, tasting, feeling, thinking, observing, experiencing, wanting, acting, loving—in short, all the organs of his individual being" work simultaneously to further both individual and social life (138–39). Capitalism reduces all of this sensuous experience to one sense—the sense of having. Whereas Smith begins by unearthing the natural match between human potential and its reality, Marx begins by premising a mismatch between human potential and human reality. Not surprisingly, their respective theories of language reinforce these positions on how well individuals do or do not align with natural processes.

Language: The Carrier of Affect
or the Bearer of False Consciousness

Adam Smith discusses language production, at least peripherally, in all his writing, but the most thorough explanation of his ideas can be found in the student notes of his rhetoric lectures published as *Lectures on Rhetoric and Belles Lettres*. Smith focuses primarily on style as rhetorical form properly calibrated to the affective frequency of a given situation. Correctly gauged, language enables a moment of sympathetic alignment between reader and writer; rhetoric is the art of perfecting this alliance between the distinctive spirit of the author and his or her audience. In this sense, language serves the faculty of imagination and functions as a vehicle for the transmission of affect—the connective force among individuals.

Language, like sympathy, functions physiologically and naturally, but can be trained through habit and education. Thus, Smith's lectures instruct students to choose the correct form, develop a coherent arrangement, and use language that most clearly represents one's ideas. If all of this is accomplished, he conjectures, it will make "the sense of the author flow naturally upon our mind"

(6). When we are passionate about a subject or, as Smith says, when we "are affected with any thing some one or other of the Ideas will thrust itself forward and we will be most eager to utter what is strongest" (18). The author needs to be trained to recognize these inclinations and habituate him or herself into social conventions; that author, however, is not the originating source of communicative language. There is instead a natural power that flows through individuals and imprints itself within their minds. When the author writes clearly and when "the passion or affection he is possessed of and intends, by sympathy, to communicate to his hearer" finds its match in language, then the expression has its force (25). Affect comes into bodies from an outside force and rhetoric helps us place it with the appropriate language. This well-chosen language carries one individual's affect into another individual so that they might be aligned through sympathy.

The alignment of author and audience, the sympathetic state, further requires congruity between the author and his or her language. Smith emphasizes, for instance, that it is only "when the expression is agreeable to the sense of the speaker and his affection that we admire it" (34). Assessing the work of Lord Shaftesbury, whose writing he admires, Smith says "every circumstance, every word, has an energy and force in displaying" his self and his argument (61). He concludes that style should change according to the character of the writer as well as his or her psychological state. Implicit in this suggestion, and reinforced by an emphasis on energy and force, is the notion that bodily passions attach themselves to and travel with language. As words leave one person by way of the imaginative faculty and the physical work of writing or speaking, they enter another's body through the same faculty. Although this is an embodied activity related to the work of the imagination, the skilled author can enhance this natural process through rhetorical instruction. As Smith explains, "the more lively and shocking the impression in which any phenomenon makes on the mind the greater curiosity does it excite" (93). Presumably the impression on the mind will exist regardless of how well the description is crafted, but appropriately chosen language closes the spatial and temporal gap that stretches the boundaries of sympathy.

A clear indication that language transmits affect is its ability to move people along the three affective vectors outlined in Smith's *The Theory of Moral Sentiments*. As a carrier of affect, language enters into and changes the body such that it can push or pull identification, open or close receptivity, and increase or decrease energy. Beautiful objects, for instance, draw in spectators: a viewer "leans forwards and stretches out his neck, with his eyes fixt on the object and his mouth a little open" (68). In front of ugly objects, "he rather inclines to draw back" (69). Proper language composition, dedicated to vivid descriptions of cause and effect, produces similar bodily responses that pull people together or push them apart. Thus, when the skilled historian writes about human tragedy, audiences are interested because of the "sympatheticall affections they raise in us. We enter into their misfortunes, grieve when they grieve, rejoice when they rejoice, and in a word feel for them in some respect as if we ourselves were in the same condition" (90). This rhetorical ability highlights, like my earlier reading of Burke, the fact that identification works through bodily processes and is therefore not simply a psychological alignment. Smith references another aspect of affect when he instructs writers to choose actions that "are most apt to draw our attention and make a deep impression on the heart" (85). This deep impression, if it produces "uneasy sensations" on the reader, will rouse one to action while easier sensations tend to be less powerful incentives toward action. He goes on to say that some sentiments tend "to soften and humanize [readers], whereas the others would rather tend to make the heart insensible to tender emotions" (88). Language predisposes one to hear an argument or prevents one from hearing that same argument. The right language for any given rhetorical situation is the language that matches the affective energy of the moment, a force that comes from outside and need not be questioned.

Not surprisingly, Marx finds this conception of language to be another iteration of alienation stemming from the externalization of human powers. Unlike Smith, who offers a rhetoric in the handbook tradition, Marx problematizes contemporary consciousness and its language practices.[16] *The German Ideology*, for instance, focuses on the transcendent thinking—reasoning that separates consciousness from lived experience and fights ideas with other ideas while leaving the existing conditions untouched—practiced by the young Hegelians.[17] These German intellectuals, says Marx, theorize in isolation from the material world, creating the illusion that consciousness exists separate from its concrete, experiential nature. To understand the function of language, Marx makes the opposite move: he begins with "real individuals, their activity and [the] material conditions under which they live" (42). For Marx, language is part and parcel of material existence. It not only represents material realities but lives an embodied existence as well: "the element of thought's living expression—language—is of a sensuous nature" (*Economic and Philosophic Manuscripts* 143). Consciousness and language, residues of the social labor of the human species as it has evolved with the world, are every bit as intertwined with the material world as the production of physical communities, and yet they appear as otherworldly forces acting on and through human beings.

The Hegelian tradition and its speculation about the World Spirit constitute what is, for Marx, a false consciousness, wherein theorists imbue ideas with the material powers that rightly belong to people. According to Marx, language is a social product—it exists wherever human relationships exist. As these relationships change along with sociohistorical development, so does language and thus consciousness. From this perspective, language and consciousness are "the result of the activity of a whole succession of generations" and not in any way outside of human experience (62). The capitalist division of labor, however, breaks this symbiosis between experience and language as it produces ideologues. Practicing a specialization, language experts such as priests, legislators, and professors cultivate consciousness as something distinct from the world of lived experience (51–52).[18] In this world—the one in which Marx lives—"abstract ideas hold sway, i.e., ideas which increasingly take on the form of universality" (65). For example, the capitalist world is awash in the discourses of freedom, equality, and self-determination, and while the ideas are firmly rooted in the democratic consciousness, they have little material connection to lived experience.

From this perspective, Marx makes what will become the often-repeated refrain that the ruling ideas are in every epoch the ideas of the ruling class. He outlines the process by which this takes place in three steps that lead to the colonization of thought: (1) separate the ideas from the empirical reality of the rulers who espouse them, (2) create an order to the ideas, ensuring that they explain disparate phenomena, and (3) transform the ideas into a person or some agentive force. Although this critique is aimed at a particular thread of German intellectualism—Hegel and his disciples—it fits political economic thinking equally well. True for both is that the material world undergirding hegemonic opinion "cannot be dispelled by dismissing the general idea of it from one's mind" (83). Marx asserts material change as requisite to any change in consciousness. Stated differently, consciousness must be reabsorbed into the material world in order to align with its affective realities. This critique has inspired a long history of ideological criticism that has disclosed the complicity between language and capitalism; ultimately, however, such work has failed to substantially change capitalism. This limitation does not derive from the fact that language cannot change materiality but from the false division between language and materiality. As long as language and consciousness remain quarantined from material practices—as long as we write about rather than participate in—social life, such language will be impotent no matter what it says. Frustrated with the separation between lived experience and intellectual pursuits, Marx boldly states in his eleventh thesis on Feuerbach that "philosophers have hitherto only *interpreted* the world, in various ways; the point is to *change* it" (Marx, *German Ideology* 123).

Marx no doubt separates himself from the philosophical tradition in which thought and language are independent of lived experience in the material world. For him, both thinking and speaking are embodied activities that arise from material necessity. They are similarly tethered to labor—alienated labor produces false consciousness while nonalienated labor (passionate, free labor) allows individuals the liberty to explore all their affective possibilities. Consonant with this theory, Marx predicts that in a communist society "it is possible for me to do one thing today and another tomorrow, to hunt in the morning, fish in the afternoon, rear cattle in the evening, criticize after dinner, just as I have a mind" (53). Although this paints an idealized picture, the main point is worth emphasizing: human beings are meant to engage in diverse labor practices without being defined by any one individual activity. The mental work of language production, criticism functions alongside other physical labor practices, all of which create the social world rather than the individual being. As Marx imagines it, the individual never becomes any one thing tied to these practices but lives, works, and thinks in his or her concrete material world. The production and circulation of affect emerges in labor regardless of whether one produces language, dinner, or the table at which one reads and eats, but the capitalist mode of productivity limits this potentially open-ended process within its routinized forms of being. Thus, affect and language provide the edifice of his (and Smith's) political economic system.

Political Economy: The Invisible Hand
or the Commodity Fetish

Adam Smith makes it clear that language provides the foundation for the commercial system he outlines in his most famous text, *The Wealth of Nations*.[19] Although beyond the parameters of his study and thus not fully developed, the fundamental role of language is discussed early in the text. His argument hinges on two crucial assumptions. First, the division of labor, which enables one person, who could make only twenty pins working alone, to produce forty-eight hundred pins while working in collaboration with others, results, he says, from "the necessary, though slow and gradual, consequence of a certain propensity in human nature which has in view no such extensive utility: the propensity to truck, barter and exchange one thing for another" (19). His second point suggests that this propensity is likely "the necessary consequence of reason and speech" (19). In this explanation, language, which—as we know from his rhetoric lectures—serves the imagination as a conduit for the exchange of moral sentiments, also functions as the base of exchange. Yet, as both his explicit discussion of language and his theory of moral sentiments contend, sympathetic alignment results from a source beyond human agency— the invisible hand. Sentiments function unconsciously in close proximity as they transfer from one person to the next physiologically; at greater distances, however, they must be carried by means of conscious, often habituated, cultural and linguistic practices. Commercial exchange necessitates and to some degree mimics speech precisely because it must take place across distances and among strangers.[20] While one may expect benevolence from friends, capitalism requires the cooperation of a "great multitude" with whom one is unacquainted. In the exchange transaction, one party says: "give me that which I want, and you shall have this which you want" (20). An economic transaction, from this viewpoint, functions as a mutually agreed-upon conclusion among bartering parties. The fact that money mediates this exchange is mere convenience and in no way foundational (38).

Given that language carries affect, the proposition that economic exchange takes place through communicative labor is tantamount to arguing that economics is the exchange of sentiment. Indeed, Smith's treatise highlights the sentiments in his exploration of economic activities. For instance, the economic principle of hard work and frugality, which counteract our slothful tendencies, are themselves embodied passions. Smith says that "the principle which prompts to expense, is the passion for the present enjoyment; which though sometimes violent and very difficult to be restrained, is in general only momentary and occasional. But the principle which prompts to save . . . comes with us from the womb and never leaves us until we go to the grave" (282). Because these sentiments are regulated by some natural propensity toward order, "the number of the frugal and industrious surpasses considerably that of the prodigal and idle" (292). In Hobbesian fashion, this natural political economy operates as a single entity made up of a multitude of independent individual bodies. According to Smith, the individual body contains an "unknown principle of preservation, capable either of preventing or of correcting, in many respects, the bad effects of a very faulty regime" (458–59). This principle is extended to the political body in the form of the nation-state as well as to the political economic body in the form of capitalist exchange. As he explains it, "the natural effort which every man is continually making to better his own condition, is a principle of preservation capable of preventing and correcting, in many respects, the bad effects of a political economy" (459). The market as the collective work of individuals is as natural as human beings themselves.

Smith repeatedly emphasizes this natural process—a synonym for beauty throughout Enlightenment thinking—and ultimately gives it shape through the invisible-hand image. The motor of the whole system is not agentive individuals but a transcendent force that Smith refers to as the invisible hand. From my perspective, the invisible hand acts as a placeholder for a much larger theory constructed layer by layer throughout Smith's entire career. This overall scaffolding suggests that what Smith calls moral sentiments, the entities that bind people together, corresponds to what I call affect. Like affect, the sentiments function along a tripartite pathway that includes the push and pull of identification, the opening and closing of receptivity, and the increase or decrease of energy. Economics, fundamentally a language, puts this functionality into practice. Thus, *The Wealth of Nations* illuminates an affective structure that motivates capitalism such that market freedom opens one's receptivity to capitalism, while participation pulls one toward particular identifications within the system and the supply and demand of exchange mobilizes the fluctuating energies of specific actions. Each of these affective modalities can be discursively tracked throughout his account of capitalism.

For Smith, the affective charge that opens people to the vast possibilities of capitalism circulates as a consequence of a free environment. In choices as well as exchange, freedom lays the foundation for much of Smith's economic system, and this opens people to the opportunities afforded by a thriving market economy. In particular, liberty predisposes individuals to the unregulated nature of capitalism (105), allowing an individual "to cultivate and bring to perfection whatever talent or genius he may possess" (21). So important is freedom that it needs to be extended even beyond the reaches of capital. Agricultural and service workers, laborers not directly relevant to the production of industry, should have an open environment in which to pursue or not pursue work as they please. "The greater the liberty which this unproductive class" is granted, explains Smith, the greater the competition and the better for the other two classes (454). Of course, this freedom needs to be extended to the circulation of products as well as their production. As long as there is confidence in the financial system and the government, there should be few regulations preventing the sale of goods domestically or internationally (241, 578). "The natural business of law [is], not to infringe, but to support" freedom, says Smith (263).[21] Fulfilling human needs, commodities self-regulate according to those needs (332). Furthermore, these goods gravitate toward their "natural" levels, and so their quantity and price need not be legislated (61). The organic forces of supply and demand regulate production, and the sentiments regulate the movement of goods. Given this perfecting structure, individuals should be free to hire and work or buy and sell as they please.

While freedom primes the pump that opens people to the possibilities of exchange, participation in the marketplace pulls them into identification with capitalism.[22] According to Smith, just as nationalism transforms one into a citizen of the nation-state, capitalism makes one a citizen of the world. As he sees it, everyone lives through exchange, and so everyone identifies with and "becomes to some measure a merchant" (29). Consubstantial with the merchant, the citizen of the nation becomes a "citizen of the world" who exchanges with others across the globe (520).[23] Yet, as I noted earlier, sentiments work strongest within spatial proximity. Therefore, one will identify with those around him or her and will want to do business locally more than internationally, tempering one's international perspective as a merchant with national identification. As Smith explains it, "home is in this manner the center, if I may say so, round which the capitals of the inhabitants of every country are continually circulating, and towards which they are always tending, though by particular causes they may sometimes be driven off and repelled from it" (350). Although the natural ebb and flow of supply and demand may require one to produce or sell at a distance, generally one feels uneasiness when investing precious capital in distant locations. This results in the great majority of business taking place with those nearby, culminating in an affective pull toward urban centers.

If everyday market activities maintain identification with capitalism, the energy required to keep pace with its ongoing evolution places an affective stress on opulence, according to Smith. The wealth and prosperity of others "animate more or less the eagerness of the competition" (59). This process derives from the natural sentiments that Smith characterizes as pervasive among individuals of all classes. Specifically, it results from "the over-weening conceit which the greater part of man have of their abilities" and "the absurd presumption in their own good fortune" (113). People are energized to action—moving into a burgeoning business pursuit, for instance—because the "chance of gain is overvalued" (113).[24] Such sentiments dictate our life pursuits and enable us to take risks that may not pay off individually but do pay off collectively.

Sentiments propel individuals toward their own self-interest and not the interest of society; nonetheless, society benefits even when the individual does not. This serendipitous result emerges from the fact that the invisible hand (not individuals) regulates society and its sentiments. As an organizing principle, the invisible hand occupies the metaphorical and physical center of Smith's most famous text.[25] Specifically, he employs the invisible hand to discuss the uneasiness (or natural sentiment) a merchant feels when investing capital in distant locations and the inclination to invest in domestic industry. This sensibility inclines every individual to work toward the greatest revenue of the nation even though he "neither intends to promote the public interest, nor knows how much he is promoting it" (351). On the contrary, "he intends only his own security; and by directing that industry in such a manner as its produce may be of the greatest value, he intends only his own gain, and he is in this, as in many other cases, led by an invisible hand to promote an end which was no part of his intention" (351–52). Although the explicit content of this passage is the risk-taking behaviors of merchants, Smith broadens this reference by including the phrase "as in many other cases." Thus, the invisible hand guides investment decisions as well as employment, price, and distribution decisions. Making order out of the thoroughgoing chaos of exchange, the invisible hand serves as the connecting principle that explains the whole system. It guides individuals, groups, and nations; it ensures a morally, politically, and economically fair society; and it has all the information that fallible human beings do not. The invisible hand allows people to follow their natural instincts, even if they have to be cultivated through education, without giving any further thought to the cause and effect of those instincts. The invisible hand has endured centuries of critique precisely because, as the affective epicenter of capitalism, it functions in synergy with pervasive instincts, inclinations, and myths.

Espousing a very different theory of affect, Marx does not share Smith's faith in the natural regulating force of an invisible hand even as he builds from many of Smith's economic concepts. For instance, Smith notes that the value of an exchangeable good stems from the labor that went into procuring that object—what he calls the commodity's natural price (*Wealth of Nations* 58). A commodity's price gravitates toward that natural mark, but increases and decreases along with supply and demand, resulting in a market price (59). This fluctuation in price gives the illusion that profit may be derived from buying low and selling high. Such profits do exist, but they are anomalous; in general, products sell at their natural price or according to the amount of labor that went into their production. While Marx agrees with this entire Smithian description, he investigates the unexplained contradiction that silently sits at the heart of this theory: from where does profit derive if everything sells at its natural value?[26] To study this question, Marx's *Capital* proceeds on a careful investigation, lingering mostly in the realm of production and focusing on the value-transferring mechanism of labor.

He begins his study by inquiring into the question of the commodity. What difference, Marx asks, does it make that man produces commodities for sale rather than for use? For Smith, the main difference is that commodity production is more efficient and leads to greater national wealth, which is divided up among all citizens such that the lowly peasant in a capitalist nation lives better than an African prince in a noncapitalist society (*Wealth of Nations* 18). Marx's *Capital* directly addresses this conclusion in its opening sentence: "The wealth of societies in which the capitalist mode of production prevails appears as an 'immense collection of commodities'; the individual commodity appears as its elementary form" (125). Marx does not disagree with the appearance of greater wealth—capitalist societies do produce more goods—but this appearance, he says, is not the full story. The difference between commodity and noncommodity production cannot be measured adequately in quantity (how much wealth exists) but must also address quality—what the production process does to both the producer and the object of production. The issue of quality refocuses attention on how labor functions within the capitalist mode of production.

In Marx's view, labor is crucial to all societies because it is the activity that circulates the passion and energy of life—what I call affect. For him, labor is "a process by which man, through his own actions, mediates, regulates, and controls the metabolism between himself and nature. He confronts the materials of nature as a force of nature. He sets in motion the natural forces which belong to his own body, his arms, legs, head and hands, in order to appropriate the materials of nature in a form adapted to his own needs. He develops the potentialities slumbering within nature, and subjects the play of its forces to his own sovereign power" (283). In this passage, as well as throughout *Capital*, Marx refers to this relationship between humans and nature as a metabolism. It is a living and breathing symbiosis in which the forces within individuals cooperate with the forces of nature to create social life.[27] This power to create life is what Marx calls labor power—the potentiality that is "possessed in his bodily organism by every ordinary man" (135). While labor power exists in humans of all societies, it is only within capitalism that this potential becomes commodified. It is this labor power—the potential for acting on nature, for creating life, and for creating society—that a worker sells in exchange for his or her wages. During a contracted time, that power belongs to the capitalist to mobilize however he or she pleases. Under capitalism, one's labor power exists for another's use; it is a commodity designed for exchange and not spontaneous use.

Exchange values, as Smith noted earlier, sell according to the labor used up in their production. For Marx, this means that commodities are the bearer of value for that labor; they are "congealed quantities of homogenous human labor" (128). Marx uses a range of terms to denote this important concept: congealed, embodied, objectified, and crystallized labor, among others. Viewed from the perspective of value, commodities are "the visible incarnation, the social chrysalis state, of all human labour" (159). As bearers of this invisible labor power—one that cannot be located as a physical property of any product—commodities contain a "phantom-like objectivity" (128). In addition to characterizing the invisible property of labor power as phantom-like, Marx calls it suprasensuous, fantastic, magical, and supranatural.[28] Such language calls attention to the intangible and yet consequential fact of labor shifting from the spontaneous and creative property of social beings into a quantifiable property sold on the market. This property contained within all exchangeable commodities represents, for Marx, the imprisonment of life potentiality or the stagnation of a fluid species-being.[29] The reason for this stagnation can be found in the capitalist form of wage labor that extracts a surplus value from the purchased labor power.

The bare bones explanation of profit for Marx is that all commodities exchange according to the value transferred into that product—all things are fair equivalents—except for labor power. The price of labor power is determined by the average cost of reproducing the laborer who possesses that power (an individual's food, housing, education, and so on.). Because this commodity is sold for a time period, the purchaser of labor power has the opportunity to use it more rigorously, increasing what Marx calls the rate of exploitation. Profit derives from utilizing this labor power beyond the cost of its reproduction. By extracting more labor power from workers than the value of their wages, commodity production "has acquired the occult ability to add value to itself. It brings forth living offspring or at least lays golden eggs" (255). The worker's daily wages, sufficient to reproduce the labor power depleted in a day's work, are less than the value that the worker transfers into products during that day. The value difference between daily wages and the daily transfer of labor power results in the surplus value that produces profits. In other words, the source of profit is the uneven exchange of the worker's labor power. Framing this in terms of value rather than money, Marx highlights the depletion of affect through exploited labor. At the end of the day, the worker has exerted more energy and more of his or her life potential than can be replenished through one's wages. The worker dies a slow death (not metaphorically but literally) so that commodities might live long enough to actualize profits from the surplus value bequeathed to them. In short, capital "sucks up the worker's value-creating power" (716). It is not just that the working class produces wealth for other people; it is also that it sacrifices its own life potential in doing so.

To be clear, this discussion of value is not a rhetorical form but an abstraction as Louis Althusser defines it in his "Preface to *Capital*": a concrete though invisible reality (77). Human life potential has been extracted from workers and transplanted into the objects of their production. Whereas Smith sees commerce as an ongoing process of persuasion that circulates affect along three related pathways invisibly mobilizing people into the proper activities that produce and distribute the correct number of products, Marx sees capital as a process of coercive labor that traps naturally fluid life energies, or affect, within the commodity form. Capitalism changes useful objects into exchangeable values and thereby changes creative, energetic social beings into mechanical, lifeless, individual beings. Marx's perspective on commodity production—a life-depleting transfer of value from humans to products—envisions the various pathways enabled by the Smithian perspective as dead ends. For Marx, capitalism closes people off, making them less and less receptive to social potentialities; it repels or pushes away identities other than capitalist and worker; it depletes life energy of both identities, making them mere caricatures of capital. When labor power is sold as a commodity, some piece of one's life-creating potential is transferred to the commodity, adding to the commodity not an essential component of its existence as a useful object but a "purely social" characteristic that allows exchange to create profit (139). Wage labor and commodity exchange appear as equally fair economic conversions even while the only possibility for profit stems from an uneven exchange with workers.

The idea that life potential moves fluidly through individuals and bursts forward in conscious labor practices—both physical and mental—suggests that for Marx affect in its ideal state circulates through people and their environment. Capitalism interrupts this ideal state by funneling a fluid process into commodity form, where it becomes ossified and impotent. Human labor power is the affective force that creates value—it is living labor and living capital—whereas the commodity is the container that traps this value—it is dead labor and dead capital.[30] As Marx explains it, the labor "process is extinguished in the product" such that "labour has become bound up in its object: labour has been objectified, the object has been worked on. What on the side of the worker appeared in the form of unrest *[Unruhe]* now appears, on the side of the product, in the form of being *[Sein]*, as a fixed, immobile characteristic" (287). The fluidity of a life as an open and evolving becoming acquires a fixed being in its commodity form. Workers abdicate the fundamental nature of their species-being as they pass their life energy into commodities without the possibility of adequately reproducing that potential. This process results in the commodity fetish. As long as this process of affective transfer exists, human beings and commodities are functionally transformed.

Human beings within the capitalist political economy live an existence in which they are slowly divested of their potential. Under the prevailing structures of capitalism, human beings adopt the characteristics of things. These traits dwell so deeply within our bodies that they appear to us as natural instincts even though they are the qualities adopted through the capitalist mode of production. The worker, who must live the life of a commodity by continually selling his or her labor power in order to live rather than exert labor creatively and differentially in response to the dynamics of being-in-the-world, turns into a static being. The wage worker becomes fixated within his or her role as the conduit for value production, and the worker's labor, the source of life power, "constantly undergoes a transformation, from the form of unrest into that of being, from the form of motion into that of objectivity" (296). The entire range of possibilities open to a given life narrow within wage labor until one is just a worker replaceable by other workers. The owners, though they reap material rewards, are equal victims of capitalism's dehumanization. Driven by well-honed instincts, the capitalist, as long as he or she remains a capitalist, has no choice but to act according to the logic of capital. As Marx says, "the imminent laws of capitalist production confront the individual capitalist as a coercive force external to him" (381). Put more directly, "his actions are a mere function of capital—endowed as capital is, in his person, with consciousness and a will" (739). Rather than indict a few capitalists who over-step their boundaries, Marx suggests that a capitalist becomes as much a part of the machinery of capital as does a worker.

Whatever ideas and potential a worker has must be funneled into products for another's use and profit. Because "the capitalist incorporates labour, as a living agent of fermentation into the lifeless constituents of the product," things acquire social life whereas people lose their sensual being and become mere things (292). When a product is made within the structure of capitalism, when it becomes a commodity, it takes on a new life undetectable by human senses: "not a fiber of it is changed, but a new social soul has entered into its body" (909). The social soul, the collective labor of the species, goes into every product of labor; in the process of commodity production, however, that labor limits the life possibilities of its creators. Things take part of workers' species-being, leaving them less well prepared to fulfill their own potential as a species. Consequently, the species power—its sensuous ability to interact with nature and with others—does not function properly within the structure of capital. The senses of capitalist beings, for instance, cannot detect the living labor trapped within the commodities they engage with on a daily basis. Marx stresses this point, stating that "the taste of porridge does not tell us who grew the oates" (290). Just as consumers are unable to sense the particularities of the labor process, capitalists are unable to discern that process within their profits: "neither seeing nor smelling will tell us that this sum of money is surplus-value" (725). Human beings cannot see, smell, hear, touch, or taste the value produced within this system.

So diminished are human beings under capitalism that they simply cannot trust their sensual experience with the world. Jettisoning the empiricism of sensory experience, Marx concludes that capitalism must be subject to "scientific" investigation (433). This embrace of scientific abstraction is less a break from his earlier work—in the preface to *Economic and Philosophic Manuscripts of 1844*, Marx tells readers that "my results have been attained by means of a wholly empirical analysis based on a conscientious crucial study of political economy"—than a consequence of his theory affect (63). Rather than viewing the human being's sensory capacity to evolve with their life practices and environmental emplacement in the world, he understands their sensory capacity as lost within capitalism; consequently, he must utilize a different method for discerning and engaging the world. Because this scientism, and not the sensual world of dancing tables and social souls, marks so much of the political economic work produced in his name, the persuasive potential of anti-capitalist affect has indeed been ceded to the inferior potential of syllogistic logic.

Our Affective Investments:
Why Smith's Mysticism Trumps Marx's Scientism

The admittedly broad strokes with which I characterize Smith and Marx nevertheless indicate that each of these theorists possessed an implicit theory of affect that informed his political economic arguments. Each of these affect theories points to a circulating power within and among human communities that enables them to live in fluid relationship to the world. For Smith, a market economy allows the individual to pursue his or her self-interest, and the good of the community follows. This is a predominantly positive process: it opens people, pulls them in, and gives them energy. Such life potential ossifies within the Marxist tradition. No doubt, Marx's writing marvels at the world of possibilities opened through human species-being. Nonetheless, his critique of capitalism puts a pall over this enthusiasm, emphasizing a scientism that extinguishes hope from capitalist life. Even though Marx understands human value as an affective potential, his political economic theory leaves little room for accessing that potential before the fall of capitalism. This places critics in the difficult position of waiting for the revolutionary moment as everything less than complete transformation becomes mere accommodation—a likely reason for the upsurge in alternatives ranging from the Italian autonomists to the Laclauian post-Marxists to the Althusserian-inspired postcapitalist theorists. Marx stages his argument as an intervention that requires unraveling the capitalist structure in order to allow for the free flow of affect. Smith's affect theory, which leaves its ultimate origins to the mythical invisible hand, trumps Marx's affective account, which requires not natural instincts but arduous propositional thinking and scientific reason, forcing a reconsideration of critical political economic theory.

Smith offers a complex notion of sympathy, illustrating multiple pathways that replicate much contemporary work on affect. Marx, on the other hand, provides a relatively monolithic understanding of life potential—it either exists or it does not. Under capitalism life potential is trapped within the commodity, and the human becomes a kind of shell of an existence. In the Marxist account, human beings—particularly the capitalist workforce—have both the potential and the responsibility for changing their dismal existence under capitalism. Such change, however, requires a worldwide revolution, which amounts to a titanic undertaking. Even if one favors Marx's critique of capital, such a position is difficult to sustain without sufficient energy, hope, and possibilities for intermediate victories. Alternatively, neither the worker nor the owner is required to do anything more than follow what Smith says are their natural instincts. In Mark Longaker's reading, economic decision making in Smith reveals that "people neither calculate their personal interests nor consider the community's welfare. In the moment of decision, people follow their ingrained habits and their psychological impulses" (66–67). Responsibility for the larger, social wellbeing rests on the mythical shoulders of the invisible hand. In crude terms, capitalism may be slowly killing the natural environment and its inhabitants, but we are happily oblivious to that death.[31] Marx, whose arguments are as carefully crafted as Smith's and who undoubtedly engages a broader and more documented set of literature than does Smith, who falls back on anecdotes, generalizations, and mythologies, remains the underdog in this dispute.

A nascent theory of affect for each of these theorists offers a tentative explanation for why this might be the case. The answer, I contend, is that Smith has a richer and more fluid sense of affect than Marx has, and that this bolsters his account of capitalism. Smith endows humans with sympathy or the instinctual capacity to attune themselves with their environments and align themselves with others. Human beings unconsciously adjust to the circulation of affect. According to Marx, human beings are similarly capacitated by nature via their labor power, but the capitalist structure decapacitates these individuals. With their affective sensibility numb, anticapitalist subjects must rely on the cold rationality of science. In the long tug-of-war between reason and passion, Smith chooses passion (sympathy) while Marx chooses reason (science). Not only do I think Smithian sympathy trumps Marxian science, but I also believe that this advantage carries through other theorists who build on each of these foundational thinkers. The subsequent chapters explore this proposition by tracking the afterlives of Smith and Marx through key economic debates, focusing particularly on how theorists deal with these initial, though implicit, theories of affect in the capitalist political economy. This intellectual genealogy ebbs and flows according to the value extended these foundational affective propositions.

3

John Maynard Keynes and Thorstein Veblen

Reimagining the Founding Legacies

To convert the businessman into a profiteer is to strike a blow at capitalism, because it destroys the psychological equilibrium which permits the perpetuance of unequal reward.

John Maynard Keynes, "Means to Prosperity"

[In capitalism] there comes an irrepressible—in a sense, congenital—recrudescence of magic, occult science, telepathy, spiritualism, pragmatism.

Thorstein Veblen, *The Instinct of Workmanship*

Opposed in their conception of capitalism's social value, John Maynard Keynes (1883–1946) and Thorstein Veblen (1857–1929) shared many perspectives on contemporary society and the role of economics in it.[1] Both, for instance, believed in the interconnectedness of the world market; both focused on aggregate consumption rather than local production (as Smith and Marx did) or individual freedom (as the Freiburg and Frankfurt schools would do later); both valued economic liberalism historically but felt it no longer reflected capitalist practices; and both contended that World War I was an imperialist struggle that required a new economic order for its resolution. Most important, both men argued that such economic stability rested on a rational understanding of apparently illogical human behavior. For Keynes, this meant studying mass psychology; for Veblen, it meant analyzing the evolution of human instincts. These theories—mass psychology and biological instincts—aligned themselves with the intellectual zeitgeist of the early twentieth century. Sigmund Freud recently popularized the psychological method and was well read among the Bloomsbury group so important to Keynes's early intellectual development; William James's theory of instincts, associations, and emotions influenced many American intellectuals, including Veblen; and Gustave Le Bon's *The Crowd*, Walter Lippman's *Public Opinion*, and Edward Bernays's *Propaganda* all speculated that collective action produced a heightened sense of urgency, bordering on the irrational, that could be manipulated if understood properly.[2]

Although there are significant overlaps in their thinking, these economists by no means shared a common vision. Keynes spent his career trying to preserve capitalism against what he believed to be the oppressive system of socialism, whereas even a peripheral reading of Veblen betrays his animosity toward capitalism and the classes that benefit from it. In many ways, these two men could not be more different. Born in Cambridge, England, to an upper-middle-class family, Keynes grew up among a privileged group of intellectuals: his father was an economist, and his mother was a social reformer. One could argue that Keynes was the synthesis of the two, as his economic pursuits were always tethered to larger moral and social questions. As a member of the Bloomsbury group, he was part of a loose set of artists and writers dedicated to overturning contemporary conventions and exploring the relationships among individuals, society, and institutions.[3] Across the ocean in the still relatively distant United States, Veblen was born to Norwegian immigrants in the farm country of Wisconsin. He later moved to southern Minnesota, where he spent most of his childhood and early adulthood. His formative experiences were rural, pragmatic, and more isolated than those of Keynes. But, as Douglas Dowd attests, his family "was anything but typical" ("The Theory of Business Enterprise" 196). At home Veblen spoke Norwegian, German, Latin, and Greek, engaged in intellectual inquiry, and learned to be extremely self-reliant. He entered Carleton College, earned a doctorate from Yale in philosophy, and studied economics as a postdoctoral student at Cornell before landing his first academic position in the newly established Economics Department at the University of Chicago. His rocky career, sometimes attributed to his unorthodox thinking and sometimes to his nonconformist behavior, suggests that Veblen continued to be slightly out of step with other economists throughout his lifetime.[4]

What unites Keynes and Veblen across these divergent histories is that they were born in the late nineteenth century and experienced major productive advances from capitalism, as well as significant volatilities that derived from a shift toward greater financialization and increased dependence on consumerism.[5] Unlike so many of their contemporaries, these men understood that the answers to economic crises lie not only in mathematical models but also in the much less clear psychological and instinctual makeup of human beings. For them, new solutions lay in the tensions between the emotional and the rational. As the epigraphs to this chapter assert, both theorists sought answers to economic questions in the deep precipice between reason and emotion. Seeking a rational framework for what often appears as irrational behavior, Keynes and Veblen approach the political economy of capitalism through one of rhetoric's ongoing struggles—the desire to reconcile the human proclivity toward and the persuasive mechanisms of both *pathos* and *logos*. At the heart of this dynamic is the question of affect or the role of bodies influencing the behavior of other bodies.

Keynes, for instance, uses the term "animal spirits" to describe how passions take over the body of reasonable human beings.[6] Briefly mentioned in his important economic treatise *The General Theory of Employment, Interest, and Money,* these animal spirits, it is often assumed, separate Keynes from the tradition of Adam Smith.[7] This chasm is narrowed, however, by attending to their similar affective sensibility. Keynes subscribes to Smith's theory of affect outlined earlier with one crucial caveat: he opposes the idea that an infallible invisible hand guides the sympathetic process; instead, in his view, sympathy is contextual and nationally bound. This difference means that locally circulating affect often runs at cross purposes with the needs of an international and interdependent capitalist economy. For Keynes, the split of the propertied classes into investors (with international interests) and business owners (with local interests) interrupted capitalism's psychological balance. As he puts it, "to convert the business man into a profiteer is to strike a blow at capitalism, because it destroys the psychological equilibrium which permits the perpetuance of unequal reward" (*Tract on Monetary Reform* 24). Investors who are physically distant from the means of production and its affective circulation can only respond to market indices that reference mass and not individual psychology. Consequently, affect operates on two different registers, and the alignment of these circuits requires structural intervention. Seeking to manage capitalism through state policy making, Keynes rationalizes or at least puts a rational harness on Smith's process of affectivity.

Veblen offers an alternative route from affect to language to economics. His explanation centers on a theory of instincts outlined in *The Instinct of Workmanship* but present throughout all his published work. For him, the instincts are biologically innate—they are part of what Marx calls our species-being—and in keeping with Marx, the most important of these instincts is the drive toward workmanship. Natural instincts manifest in socially constructed environments, and as they do, they adapt to the cultural and habitual exigencies of those material realities. These habituated instincts have a tendency to change their innate purposefulness—a process Veblen names corruption. Cultural values evolve along with changing institutional structures, and as they do, they feed back into a group's biological makeup so that the corrupted instincts feel natural to those who practice them. From this evolutionary perspective, Veblen extends Marx's arguments about ideology into cultural artifacts, particularly consumer goods, which serve the same semiotic function as language.

For Veblen, institutions and the habits they engender stifle the social and productive instincts of human beings. Like Keynes, he offers what he believed to be a rational account of the problems of capitalism as opposed to Marx, who in his view sublimated the rational operations of materiality beneath "the dominating presence of the conscious human spirit" ("The Socialist Economics of Karl Marx" 415). To be clear, he interprets Marx's labor theory of value as no more real than Hegel's World Spirit, whereas the biological instincts at the heart of his theory are for him both physiologically real and historically traceable. The divergent economic theories of Keynes and Veblen are undergirded by variations on the affective theories of Smith and Marx. Both Keynes and Veblen, explored from this angle, attempt to rationalize the affective arguments of their predecessors, shifting the foundations from ontology to epistemology.

Affect: Mass Psychology or Innate Human Instincts

In *The Economic Consequences of Peace,* his first and highly influential book critiquing the Treaty of Versailles, Keynes offers a case study for his theory of affect. Although many have commented on his dramatic portrayal of these negotiations, his highly stylized psychological investigations represent more than rhetorical flourish.[8] They betray a deep sense of affect inherited from Adam Smith as well as an evolution of that schema. For Smith, affect moves bodily from person to person and can, as Keynes so often says, remain "in the air" of a given environment to align sympathetically among individuals on behalf of a particular orientation toward the world. Keynes develops this theory in two significant ways. First, he contends that the circulation of affect through the intimate, person-to-person transmission of sympathy produces the mass psychology of nationalized sentiment. Second, and consequently, he conjectures that our faculty of imagination, the physiological mechanism that enables sympathy, runs up against the historical, cultural, and spatial limitations of its habituation, preventing affective alignment among diverse nation-states.

More specifically, Keynes argues that capitalism has become increasingly global in its operations, but individual sympathies have remained national. Situating the exigency of contemporary economics as one of psychological adjustment to a new stage of capitalism, he asserts that economic foundations are not "natural, permanent, and to be depended on," as is frequently assumed, but are "complicated, unreliable, [and] temporary" (53). He goes on to say that the immense wealth produced over the half century preceding the First World War "depended on unstable psychological conditions" that held consumption in check and encouraged continual reinvestment (69). Those who negotiated the Versailles Peace Treaty not only failed to restore that psychological order but also failed to create a new affective state consonant with the altered capitalist landscape. As Keynes explains it, the powerbrokers at Versailles—who acted as national representatives—drafted a treaty based on domestic interests without regard to the global interdependencies inherent in the latest stage of capitalism.

According to his account, the Parisian environment charged negotiators with an outdated sentiment that reinforced their separate interests. Put differently, the peace deliberations took place within an affective milieu—what Rickert calls an ambient rhetoric—of national identification, thwarting new allegiances within the international structures of capitalism. Keynes's report on the 1919 Paris Peace Conference dwells on this affective mismatch between the nationalist negotiators and the larger global context, concluding that "the word was not flesh, that it was futile, insignificant, of no effect, dissociated from events" (56). Certainly, this phrasing exemplifies his characteristically robust style. Yet it also indicates that the postwar atmosphere affectively displaced negotiators from the material realities of global capitalism. Framed this way, the problem with the Paris talks is that the world leaders who sat at the discussion table, the nations they represented, and the entire ambiance of the city were calibrated according to an affective environment that came to an end before the war.

Keynes's depiction of the treaty's negotiators underscores the difficulty for a nationalized affect to solve international problems. Prime Minister Georges Clémenceau, who secured French interests by appropriating resources from Germany, symbolizes the self-contained nature of this affective sensibility. He would "close his eyes with an air of fatigue when French interests were no longer" center stage and later reawaken with a "sudden outburst of words" that "produced their impression rather by force and surprise than by persuasion" (78). On the other hand, Prime Minister Lloyd George had multiple "senses not available to ordinary men, judging character, motive, and subconscious impulse, perceiving what each was thinking and even what each was going to say next, and compounding with telepathic instinct the argument or appeal best suited to the vanity, weakness, or self-interest of his immediate auditor" (86). This skill notwithstanding, George was at the mercy of his constituents, who wanted significant reparations returned to England. From Keynes's perspective, such "grosser effluxions of atmosphere" surrounded the prime minister, who could not afford to ignore this "psychological reaction" (167). Whereas George was hindered by the lingering sentiments of English nationals, President Woodrow Wilson was crippled by the absence of American affect. Wilson "stood in great need of sympathy, of moral support, of the enthusiasm of masses" but was "stifled in the hot and poisoned atmosphere of Paris, [where] no echo reached him from the outer world" (92). Uprooted from the nourishments of his national soil, Wilson's sympathies failed to forge allies. More than depicting simple caricatures, Keynes paints a picture of progress muted by "the morass of Paris" and "hopelessly befogged" by outdated nationalized sentiments circulating within the city and through these leaders (105, 174).

Although several reviewers take Keynes to task for his emasculating representations of these leaders, it is clear that for him agency and historical authority lie elsewhere. The world he describes is not managed by a handful of powerful individuals "but by the hidden current, flowing continually beneath the surface of political history" (296–97). If one intends to shape history, one must change that current by unleashing "forces of instruction and imagination which change opinion" (297). The capitalist world needs, Keynes says, to promote a current of collectivity, what he calls "the universal element in the soul of man" (297). Unfortunately, the sedimentation of national affect and its attendant faith in the self-made individual piles up against the floodgates and prevents this alternative current. To open that gate, economic theorists would need to replace the affective pull of laissez-faire individualism with faith in the ability of elected representatives to determine international economic policy.

For Keynes, laissez-faire represents a disposition with specific origins that has outlived its economic utility even as it continues to exert psychological influence. As he explains in *The End of Laissez-Faire*, Locke and Hume founded capitalist individualism by linking property rights to political equality. This doctrine merged with Bentham's utilitarianism and Darwin's competitive spirit to forge the platform from which to understand and engage nascent capitalism (14). This historically specific sensibility inhabits "the air we still breathe" and permeates "our atmosphere of thought" (7, 9). Consequently, people feel "a strong bias in favour of *laissez-faire*" and respond to government intervention with "passionate suspicions" (15).[9] The economic battle against laissez-faire is, argues Keynes, first and foremost one of aligning the "psychological" attitude with the material currents of the historical moment (51). In other words, the problem concerns a mismatch between affect accumulated in our bodies and the changing political economic landscape; thus, "our sympathy and our judgment are liable to be on different sides" (53). Acclimated to the sentiment of national landscapes and local populations, individuals mire economic progress by misidentifying their instinctual desires as the needs of a globalized political economy. This error necessitates the circulation of different affective sensibilities. The solution, therefore, requires "a new set of convictions which spring naturally from a candid examination of our own inner feelings in relation to the outside facts" (54). Without this new affective terrain, even the most earnest individuals will reformulate the evidence to conform to their bodily dispositions.

Keynes exemplifies the difficulty of escaping the embodiment of capitalist affects in his struggle to understand state communism. As outlined in "A Short

View of Russia," he attempts to align his feelings about communism with the facts of Bolshevism, a movement situated in a country geographically, culturally, and economically distant from the capitalist epicenter of Western Europe. Given that imagination works by proximity to enable sympathy, the case of Russia represents a challenge. Keynes concedes that "matters, which are often palpable at close quarters, are hard to distinguish at a distance," and thus he shares with his readers what he learned from his 1925 trip to Russia "and could not have learnt elsewhere" (90). Even after firsthand experience, however, this endeavor to intellectualize his feelings remains difficult. Keynes candidly expresses appreciation for those who want the Russian experiment to succeed but declares that "brought up in a free air undarkened by the horrors of religion, Red Russia holds too much which is detestable" (98). Characterizing the political economic dogmatism of Russia as religious zealotry while understanding laissez-faire as a legitimate philosophy in need of update, he unwittingly performs his argument about the rigidity of national sentiment. Russian air, absorbed temporarily, cannot penetrate the lifelong affective inhalation of capitalist individualism.

Affect does not work individually on a case-by-case basis but collectively, over time, and often along national lines, predisposing people to a particular psychology. Keynes notes, for instance, that "the moral atmosphere of Russia is a very different compound of emotional chemistry" than the often-praised American "air of liberty" (141). This different compound is the weight of seriousness. As he says, "there never was anyone so *serious* as the Russian of the Revolution"; "the tenseness of the atmosphere" leaves him desiring "the frivolous ease of London" (142). The gravity of this social project depletes Keynes, and thus he longs for a different, more energizing atmosphere. In Russia, "the chemicals are being mixed in new combinations" that simply do not align with the collective psychology of capitalism (144). Nonetheless, he suspects that if placed in the position of a Russian, "I should feel that my eyes were turned towards, and no longer away from, the possibilities of things; that out of the cruelty and stupidity of Old Russia nothing could ever emerge, but that beneath the cruelty and stupidity of New Russia some speck of the ideal may lie hid" (144). This purported alignment requires Keynes to sympathetically inhabit the body of a Russian—a position he can only vaguely imagine after visiting the country, walking on its soil, and breathing its air. Implicit in this account is the fact that Keynes both endorses Smith's position on affect and illuminates its limitations for the early twentieth century, a moment in which capitalism is globally embroiled but during which individuals are mostly limited to their national, if not local, conditions. Affect circulates locally while capitalism functions globally, forging a gap between our inner feelings and the outer reality of economic operations.

Whereas Keynes seems to accept Smith's notion of a bodily affect as the inherent motivating force passing between individuals but finds its operations compromised at a larger scale, Veblen's theory of human motivation as instinctual aligns with Marx, who understood labor to be the core of our species-being. Veblen derived his theory of instincts from the psychological work of Jacques Loeb, William McDougall, and William James. Providing an especially important platform, James's schema ties the instincts to the nervous system and asserts that they function through an impulsive reaction to the stimuli of a given environment. According to his *Principles of Psychology,* reasoned behavior reflects the *"tendency to obey impulses"* (389). Such compulsions do not operate in a vacuum but combine with "memories, associations, inferences, and expectations" (390). This impulse-environment relationship means that instincts work through habit, which, "once grafted on an instinctive tendency, restricts the range of the tendency" (395). After habits have been naturalized, the responses "fade away" from consciousness (402). Veblen narrows the wide range of instincts discussed by James to a determinant four. What James calls parental love, curiosity, constructiveness, and appropriation become, under Veblen, parental bent, idle curiosity, workmanship, and the pecuniary instinct. Of these four instincts, Veblen emphasizes two in particular: the parental bent and the instinct to workmanship, which for him are the fundamental human motivations. Veblen's overall theory suggests that workmanship asserts itself through practical tasks on behalf of the community-oriented parental bent; idle curiosity, the desire to narrate human experience, functions as a corrupting force; and the pecuniary instinct is the habituated result of such corruption.

The Instinct of Workmanship, Veblen's detailed explanation of these biological propensities, tells a selective anthropological narrative wherein individuals are by nature social beings whose work is directed toward the community.[10] Earliest history is peaceful, and its technological advances serve the common good. Once subsistence is surpassed, enabling surplus, a predatory phase establishes itself wherein groups pillage and display their exploits as a sign of status. The predatory phase evolves into the handicraft stage and then into the industrial era of capitalism, which, like all epochs, creates new sociopolitical and economic structures that pervert the original purpose of our biological instincts. According to this narrative, the predatory, and later the pecuniary, instinct is not one of the main ingredients of human behavior; it is, rather, the result of a cultural or institutional intervention. Moreover, the shift from handicraft to industry precipitates the corruption of workmanship (practical labor) into sportsmanship (a false sense of purposeful activity). As its main drive is not to create sufficient goods for the community but to amass wealth for the individual, business falls under the umbrella of sportsmanship. Thus, Veblen's trajectory moves from instinct to habit to corrupted instinct to arrive at a position of false affect. Just as Marx asserts that life power stems from the human capacity to labor and that humans became alienated when this power is externalized, Veblen argues that humans have an instinct toward practical work but that when this instinct is redirected from the collectively useful to the individually profitable, sportsmanship or a false instinct toward work emerges.[11]

In addition to cultural institutions misdirecting innate human capacities, the intersection of instincts can also result in contamination. Continuing to use workmanship as his example, Veblen explains that the instinct of idle curiosity mythologized capitalism, allowing its practices, which are at odds with practical labor and the common good, to go unchecked (49–50).[12] Theorists and institutions that conflate capitalism's culturally and historically specific practices with universal human nature disorient the instinctual drives of human beings by privileging business practices over the common good.[13] By the close of the eighteenth century, idle curiosity's desire to impute meaning into cultural activities solidifies self-interest as natural rather than cultural. According to the best thinkers of this age, there is a "beneficent order of the universe [such] that in the end, in the finished product of its working, it would bring about the highest practicable state of well-being" (258). The external ordering mechanism was so tied to profit making that "habituation to the sentiments, ideals, standards and manner of life suitable to a state of predation had swamped the handicraft spirit" (273). Under capitalism, the industrial workers and their technologists are at cross purposes with the absentee owners who finance the system and rule it by statistical cause and effect divorced from actual serviceability to the community (348).[14] In short, the instinct of idle curiosity splits workmanship into two categories—the absentee owners who function according to a received theory about natural forces and the industrial workers who follow a habituated matter-of-fact reasoning.

A fuller articulation of this process is outlined in *Vested Interests and the Common Man,* a collection of popular essays first published in the *Dial.* Veblen begins with the basic premise of his instinct theory by stating that "the changeless native proclivities of the race will assert themselves in some measure in any eventual revision of the received institutional system" (11). Rather than revise the native proclivities to meet the changed institutional form of capitalism, the postwar negotiations simply affirmed the same point of view inherited from the mid-eighteenth century. As he sees it, the principles of natural order "have been enabled to stand over unimpaired into the present" (19). In the system Adam Smith so richly celebrated, the owner hired workers and managed them on site. He relied on his "skill, dexterity and judgment" to produce profit; indeed, capital resulted from "savings parsimoniously accumulated out of the past industry" (28). Veblen repeatedly cites this notion of the skilled craftsman to indicate the difference between the economic structure

Smith describes and its twentieth-century offspring, which relies heavily on the financial manipulations of owners, who are often physically and intellectually distanced from the means of production. In the new economic order, it "is no longer the workman and his manual skill, but rather the mechanical equipment and standardised processes" that drive the system (37). The industrial process "embodies not the manual skill, dexterity, and judgment of an individual workman, but rather the accumulated technological wisdom of the community" (37). Contrary to Smith's natural order, which presupposes equilibrium to be achieved through free bargaining between "man and man on a footing of personal understanding and equal opportunity," the new order operates through "absentee ownership of anonymous corporate capital" (43, 44). Not only is the employer-employee relationship significantly altered, so too is the notion of a self-sufficient industrial enterprise. Each member of the industrial community is now dependent on the "industrial community as a whole" (52). The affective principles of self-help, equity, and freedom are, for Veblen, the historical residue of eighteenth-century institutions, ones that do not reflect the practices of an industrial world.

Like that of Marx, Veblen's formula puts the focus squarely on the instinct of workmanship (practical labor) and the parental bent (the common good) with idle curiosity, or the desire to add meaning to life and the world, as a secondary and often corrupting force. In his theory, it is irrational to attribute human characteristics to things, as it only serves "to hinder and deflect the agent from effectual pursuit of mechanical design" (74). This critique of anthropomorphism comes very close to Marx's notion of alienation—the externalization of human functions into metaphysical entities. Viewed from this perspective, Veblen offers a rationalized account of Marx's theory of value inherent in human labor and its alienation under capitalism. He does so by citing the instincts as a biological basis for the human drive toward work. In fact, citations to McDougall and James are among the very few sources that Veblen references in any of his books, underscoring their scientific importance for him. This rational account of affect feeds into an equally rational theory of language for Veblen every bit as much as it does for Keynes.

Language: Rational Persuasion or Life Habits

An answer to the problem of transmitting proper affectivity raised in Keynes's popular texts of the 1920s can be found in another of his early works, *A Treatise on Probability.* Published in 1921, the *Treatise* explores probability as the process of rational decision making. Probability does not deal with certainty to separate truth from falsehood; it deals with uncertainty, which distinguishes stronger and weaker arguments in order to determine better actions from worse ones. As opposed to logic, its syllogistic method, and its faith in absolute positivism, probability focuses on "arguments [that] are rational and claim with some weight without pretending to be certain" (3). As he argues, probability functions as a relationship among factors such as the available information, individual experience, and cultural contexts. More specifically, it concerns the negotiation between our beliefs or "primary propositions" and their supporting evidence or "secondary propositions" (11). It is difficult, however, to determine the origin of these secondary propositions as "it is not easy to draw the line between conscious memory, unconscious memory or habit, and pure instinct or irrational associations of ideas" (14). Even though Keynes suggests that the boundaries of these different forms of evidence—direct experience, inherited practices, and instinctual motivations—blur, they are fundamentally separate. Crucially, Keynes divides experience and custom, which he sees as rational, from instincts, which he identifies as irrational, stating that knowledge has a direct element, while the instinctual takes place without any clear experiential foundation (15). Experience gives one a rational basis for probable expectations and makes for stronger arguments, whereas the irrational evidence of one's instincts weakens an argument because it lacks concrete empirical data. Nevertheless, almost all judgment includes at least some irrational evidence. So defined, affect functions irrationally in the sense that it requires no warrant for its validity; yet, to repeat, that irrational stigma does not disqualify its evidentiary function.

According to Keynes, judgments of probability derive from direct experience as well as from indirect experience in the form of argument. Arguments work through induction, a summation of like examples, or through analogy, a linking of one example to a different one. Rational argumentation requires extended examples or analogy, while irrational argumentation relies on deductive reasoning from universal first principles. For example, it is logical to attribute some probable cause between different parts of a given relationship and illogical to attribute a causal agency to an unknown external force because an analogy can always be assessed by looking at two tangible examples, whereas a deduction depends on an unverifiable conclusion (300). As an analogy, it is contingent on situated evidence, and this contingency precludes the invisible hand from serving as evidence—such an inductive conclusion has no experiential foundation.

From this perspective, Smith's concept of an invisible hand serves not as an empirically verifiable fact nor as a metaphysical proposition beyond interrogation, but as an argument that can be assessed as strong within its eighteenth-century context and weak within the Keynesian context. As Keynes makes explicit, new evidence can "modify the force of subsequent inductions. But the force of the old induction *relative to the old* evidence is untouched"

(221). This is what he means by probability being subjective: it changes with changing circumstances. It is also what makes his theory of probability rhetorical.[15] Just as rhetoric encompasses deliberation about the best course of action in uncertain circumstances, Keynes defines the probable as "the hypothesis on which it is rational for us to act" (301) and says that "probability is to us 'the guide of life'" (323). This methodology shifts Smith's invisible hand from an inductive certainty to an analogy that can be assessed and measured according to the given circumstances. If Keynes is read as taking what was previously certain and opening it up to probable argument, then his economic and polemical writing begins to look less like blasphemy against the tried and true doctrines of capitalism and more like an attempt, as he claimed, to help capitalism accord with the exigencies of a changing political economic terrain.

The *Treatise* highlights Keynes as a theorist who believed in rational argumentation as the way to rehabituate behavior that had been ossified into affective habits. By redefining affect as an uncertain form of evidence that must be assessed, Keynes replaces the perfect invisible hand with imperfect visible arguments and grounds the need for greater economic deliberation among the public at large.[16] As explained previously, Keynesian affect functions along the lines of mass psychology—it is the habituated instincts of people who share a common history and collective experiences. This massified form of affect, what he often calls "public opinion," maintains institutional structures and influences individual behaviors. Argument, though an imprecise tool, is the means by which one intervenes in this alliance between mass psychology and the structures of material existence. It is the way one mobilizes and redirects the currents of history.

Given this theory, it should not be surprising that Keynes was as tireless a critic of those policies he opposed as he was an advocate for those he favored. His argumentation took two forms—one for the larger lay public and one for his fellow economists. A survey of the former can be found in *Essays in Persuasion,* a collection of articles written, as he explains in the preface, "in an attempt to influence opinion" (v). Keynes defines public opinion as "the mysterious entity which is the same thing perhaps as Rousseau's General Will" (60). Mysterious because it is so often illogical, the general will governs a democratic society through the consent of its members.[17] People consent though embodied and affective encounters (the production of which is difficult to authenticate, track, or change) even as they participate in and are moved by rational deliberation. Whether called the general will or public opinion, purportedly unreasonable beliefs function, often unconsciously, through an affective circulation with its own history but are managed, says Keynes, through logical critique.

Keynes's critique of government-enforced austerity exemplifies this symbiosis between discourse and affect. As he tells it, the fiscal restraint advocated by England's conservative postwar government fails to facilitate economic recovery because it produces a suffocating environment.[18] Such policies, he says, "compress our lungs. Fears and doubts and hypochondriac precautions are keeping us muffled indoors. . . . We need the breath of life" (133). The conservative government that encourages saving—consumer, corporate, and governmental—as the cure for the economic slump manufactures an affectivity inattentive to the contemporary context. By inhabiting this space, people are sealed into a depleting affective atmosphere. Beyond these boundaries, however, different affective energies circulate. Economic recovery, Keynes emphasizes, necessitates different sensibilities: we must "feel ourselves free to be bold, to be open, to experiment, to take action, to try the possibilities of things" (133). Unlike Smith, Keynes asserts the possibility of incorrect affective responses to empirical stimuli and conceives argument as the main apparatus for their correction. As he says, "the moral energies of the nation are being directed into the wrong channels" and should be redirected through rational persuasion (280). We must "bend our wills and our intelligences, energized by a conviction that this diagnosis is right" (146). Once this happens, the public will be "energized by a confident conviction," and that energy will bolster new policies that reinvigorate the stalled machinery of capitalism (147). To summarize: for Keynes, early twentieth-century affectivity, cultivated through the habits of an older form of capitalism, is misguided; the new structures of capital require an affective adjustment and the leverage for such reorientation is rational argument.

Argument serves an equally important, but less explicit, role for Veblen, who posits consumer behavior as a form of logical disputation.[19] If Marx gives us a method for understanding how language produces dominant ideology, Veblen extends that assessment to commodities in general. In fact, he rationalizes Marx's commodity fetish, suggesting that the power of market goods lies in their ability to convey arguments rather than in their role as bearers of human value. This process is nowhere more clearly evidenced than in Veblen's most popular work, *The Theory of the Leisure Class*.[20] According to this text, conspicuous consumption impedes the instincts of workmanship and parental bent by delimiting the consuming public within a predatory culture of emulation. These cultural habits represent an atavistic institutional framework that not only corrupts what are, for Veblen, basically altruistic instincts but also advocates for its own reproduction through the visible display of wealth. The central feature of Veblen's theory is that consumer goods indeed can make arguments—in fact, they signify meaning in addition to whatever utility they might have.

The Theory of the Leisure Class identifies a shift in human instinct toward persuasion, wherein argument takes place through the display of concrete items. Each human being is, Veblen says, "a centre of unfolding impulsive activity" and is thus "possessed of a taste for effective work, and a distaste for futile effort" (15). Yet predatory culture and its inherited traditions have enforced a habit of comparison so that "visible success becomes an end sought for its own utility as a basis of esteem" (16). In such a situation, one he identifies as institutionally habituated rather than natural, human communities divide into two classes: industry and exploit. Those in the industry class make useful things through their own labor; those in the exploit class appropriate the "energies previously directed to some other end by another agent" (13). Both, however, use consumer goods to display their position in society. Thus, for Veblen, status is on the one hand "an expression of the instinct to workmanship," which for him is an innate human characteristic and also "an expression of men's animistic sense of a propensity in material things," which he sees as a corruption of instincts by cultural habit and idle curiosity (292). In other words, people instinctively find things useful and, by way of inherited culture, they also find things capable of speaking for and about them.

Both the language and function of argument pervade Veblen's analysis of conspicuous consumption. As he says, once we exceed a level of necessary sustenance, things such as homes, food, clothing, and furniture, as well as behaviors such as proper speech, good manners, and fine tastes derive their value not in utility but as "a voucher of a life of leisure" (48). "Wealth or power must be put in evidence" through the display of things or visible activities (30).[21] Items that are not necessary and do not explicitly ease our lifestyle function primarily as an argument of status directed toward the peeping eyes of neighbors. For Veblen, the only practical means of "impressing one's pecuniary ability on these unsympathetic observers of one's everyday life is an unremitting demonstration of ability to pay" (87). Additionally, he notes, these ends can be achieved through the consumption practices of those close to you. If one's wife and children are well-dressed, it reflects on the husband; or, if one's hired staff is properly attired, it reveals something about the employer. Such consumption serves "to enhance, not the fullness of life of the consumer, but the pecuniary repute of the master for whose behoof the consumption takes place" (121). Like Marx's notion of ideology, conspicuous consumption creates surface-level identifications that cover over structural and material divides. Marx argues that the ideas of the ruling class are presented as universal truth in order to persuade individuals into a state of false consciousness, and Veblen speculates that things similarly coerce individuals into a tradition of class status contrary to the instinctual community and work-oriented teleology of human beings.[22]

In keeping with his theory of instincts as motivations in play with each other and with the cultural environment, Veblen posits that the economic subject is inseparable from the community and its idle curiosity. He says clearly that "economic interest does not lie isolated and distinct from all other interests" (116). Personal consumption, an economic habit developed through repeated material exposure, creates habits of thought that help individuals assess value beyond the economic. For instance, one finds beauty in certain objects to "which long and close habituation has made the mind prone" (151). This extensive habituation not only determines cultural norms, it also trains the body, adapting its "physiological structure and function" (151). Consumer habits argue on our behalf—what Veblen calls "a suggestion or expression of adequacy"—but they also change our physiological makeup so that we are hardwired toward specific things (151). In this way, the cultural practice of emulation so crucial to the industrial era has "invested consumable goods with a secondary utility as evidence of relative ability to pay" and affectively shifted our innate human propensity toward these objects (154). Or, in Veblen's terms, "so thoroughly has this habit of approving the expensive and disapproving the inexpensive been ingrained into our thinking that we instinctively insist on some measure of wasteful expensiveness in all our consumption" (155). Because his theory of instincts fundamentally informs his economic thinking, it is difficult to read his choice of "instinctually insist" as anything other than biologically driven, arriving at the conclusion that institutional environments change bodily drives.

This physiological habituation shapes our consumer choices and informs our larger worldviews. For instance, Veblen argues that the leisure class develops its conception of the world from its lived experience in the world. That lived experience predominantly takes place in isolation from the everyday existence of the working population. In this sheltered environment, "the exigencies of the general economic situation of the community do not freely or directly impinge upon the members of this class" (198). Rather than view the wealthy as consciously protecting their fortunes from another class, Veblen argues that, on the contrary, "the opposition of the class to changes in the cultural scheme is instinctive" and reflects its isolation from the material difficulties of other classes (199). Given the distinct material settings and their class habituation, social change will require "a greater expenditure of nervous energy in making the necessary readjustment than would otherwise be the case" (203). For Veblen, material life persuades, and the constant habitation to our material setting makes individuals physiologically predisposed to arguments in ways that align with those settings. Cultural and material habits of class antithesis imbue humans with new propensities so that the economic dialectic acquires "the tenacity of transmission that belongs to the hereditary trait" (222).

Rehearsing the pervasive rhetorical debate between *pathos* and *logos*, Veblen positions himself in the realm of the body and its passions: "an hereditary bent of human nature is not to be put out of the way with an argument showing that it has difficulties" (73). Change, that is to say, requires material reconditioning of bodies and not just persuasive lines of argument.

This somewhat sterile assessment, which attributes so much that falls under the umbrella of the aesthetic to the corruption of human instincts by cultural habits, ends on a note of cautious hope. The way out of this unnatural social state might be achieved through workers whose daily material reality trains them into a matter-of-fact way of thinking that will not tolerate the make-believe of conspicuous consumption. The exploit class will not lead the way toward social change because this "class is sheltered from the stress of economic exigencies, and is in this sense withdrawn from the rude impact of forces which make for adaptation" (336–37). Consequently, it is up to the working class, cultivated by its industrial habituation, to discover new pragmatic solutions. Although this position contains echoes of Marx, Veblen does not agitate for the overthrow of capitalism. In part, such political economic differences stem from the way that Keynes and Veblen rewrite the affective theories of Smith and Marx.

Political Economy: Taming the Animal Spirits
or Institutionalizing the Instincts

Keynes spent most of his career criticizing mainstream economic theory for its inability to adjust to the changing capitalist landscape.[23] For him, classical economics assumes that equilibrium occurs naturally and maintains itself permanently. This position, as his *Treatise on Probability* implies, stems from the feeble grounds of inductive argumentation. The natural regulating order of capitalism is an imagined conclusion based on eighteenth-century examples that crumbles under the evidentiary weight of early-twentieth-century practices. Keynes takes this position as early as his 1921 *Economic Consequences of Peace*, which argues that because equilibrium comes and goes it requires regulation (53). *A Treatise on Money* (1930) further explains that his overarching goal is "to find a method which is useful in describing, not merely the characteristics of static equilibrium, but also those of disequilibrium, and to discover the dynamic laws governing the passage of a monetary system from one position of equilibrium to another" (v). *The General Theory of Employment, Interest, and Money,* published six years later, is a treatise on precisely those governing laws.[24] Viewing Keynesian economic theory through this history and especially through the lens of affect reveals a clear revision of Smith's three affective modalities. Keynes argues for an open disposition toward free economic activity but says it must be managed; he calls for a disidentification with classical theory in order to accept his new interventionist strategies; and he suggests that the ebb and flow of market action gets distorted by twentieth-century financialization, requiring rational manipulation to ensure steady equilibrium.

In *A Treatise on Money,* his first attempt at an overall political economic theory, Keynes establishes that the entire banking and securities system works on the expectation that people can convert their representative wealth (stocks, bonds, deposit slips, and other papers of ownership) into actual money whenever they wish. Although the system requires that people be assured in this ability, it also relies on the fact that they will not all do so at once. This gap between possibility and actuality requires individuals to orient their dispositions toward saving, consuming, and investing toward long-term market needs and not the short-term fluctuations of economic indices. Happily, this need matches affective training: steeped in history, tradition, and national culture, people "do not shift, as a rule, rapidly or widely" (120). However, this is not always the case, and based primarily on affective habituation, the system provides "no possibility of intelligent foresight designed to equate saving and investment" (279). Thus, Keynes argues for semiautonomous regulating bodies that work on behalf of the public good rather than private or national interests (*The End of Laissez-Faire* 41). He agrees with Smith that people ought to have freedom—inviting an open disposition toward capitalism—but tempers this position with the repeated suggestion that such liberty must conform to rational policies.

Because we cannot know about the future with certainty, we are left in the position of having to make predictions based on probable evidence. Such evidence derives from empirical experience as much as from affective intuition— our past and present encounters within a given environment as well as our conformity with the going belief. This temporally and spatially limited information fuels our economic decisions. As Keynes explains in an essay responding to critics of his *General Theory,* "there is no scientific basis on which to form any calculable probability whatever. We simply do not know. Nevertheless, the necessity for action and for decision compels us as practical men to do our best to overlook this awkward fact and to believe exactly as we should" if the future were certain ("General Theory of Employment Summary" 214). At best, this rhetorical practice works most of the time. The brutal reality that Keynes highlights like cold water to the face is that our form of economic decision making lacks firm grounds; consequently, he wants "the game to be played, subject to rules and limitations" (*General Theory* 163). This is hardly the kind of open affective modality of Adam Smith; indeed, it is more like a half-ajar doorway with a lukewarm invitation.

Keynes encourages disidentification from the classical principles of natural equilibrium as a precondition for the possibility of regulation. His *General*

Theory explicitly addresses this shift, telling fellow economists that the difficulty of the text will not be its new ideas but "in escaping from the old ones, which ramify, for those brought up as most of us have been, into every corner of our minds" (5). Writing the book was, Keynes confesses, a struggle to "escape from [the] habitual modes of thought and expression" that define classical economics (5). Like him, readers must disarticulate themselves from earlier identifications before they can forge new ones. Thus, a significant part of his book is dedicated to persuading readers to turn their backs on the foundational tenets of their identification as professional economists. He does this by logically undermining the classical belief structure, arguing that its principles "have been applied to the kind of economy in which we actually live by false analogy from some kind of non-exchange Robinson Crusoe economy" (13).[25] Keynes works arduously to pull his readers along the same intellectual path he has taken so that they too see that the natural order argument assumes self-sufficiency and independence out of step with the cooperation and interdependence required of the twentieth-century economy.

This affective pull of identification, lodged within rational disputation, functions overwhelmingly as an attempt to logically dissuade readers away from classical economics and its natural-equilibrium assumption. Rather than attack Adam Smith, who remains unscathed throughout all his writing, Keynes attributes the recalcitrance of the natural equilibrium belief to David Ricardo. Offering a careful intellectual history, he concludes that the professional dialogue about aggregate consumption simply stopped with Ricardo's proposition that demand takes care of itself, naturally and inevitably adjusting with supply. This theory not only became dominant, according to Keynes, but "the other point of view completely disappeared; it ceased to be discussed" and simply "vanished from economic literature" except for such unsanctioned spaces as "the underworlds of Karl Marx" (18). Emphasizing that equilibrium cannot be taken for granted, Keynes offers an inefficient version of affective identification as he relies too much on persuasion and not enough on the human capacity to synergistically combine around similar experiences. Indeed, Ricardo's position—that balanced exchange is natural, inevitable, and perfect—maintains a stronger pull of identification with less effort precisely because it does not ask readers to think but only to identify.

More contentious than this change in identification that Keynes advocates is his discussion of the role collective psychology plays as the animating force inflating and deflating the activities of individuals within the capitalist system. For Keynes, disequilibrium results when affect in the aggregate (the psychology of the community, as he calls it) does not match current economic experience (16). According to his theory, people do not respond to a natural force raising and lowering their energies, but respond to each other as well as to the information available to them. The material state of capital and its systemic operations are a manifestation of both rational and embodied expectations. Trouble arises when the market provides unexpected feedback in the form of dramatic shifts. These anomalous market responses alter expectations—making them greater than before—and those altered expectations circulate to others, changing the aggregate psychology based on limited evidence disconnected from the longer trend of experience. Just as inductive reasoning, which jumps to rationally indefensible conclusions, results in potentially weak arguments, the escalation of affective energy based on the normalization of unusual market activity produces similarly poor decisions. The result is mass affective practices untethered to concrete material realities.[26]

The distance between the affective environment of investors and the industry in which they invest reinforces this instability. From Keynes's perspective, "real knowledge" of financial valuation "has seriously declined" as investors no longer have on-site experience nor detailed business knowledge (66). Without the appropriate grounds to make probable decisions about the economic future, these investors rely on collective feeling and this "conventional valuation which is established as the outcome of the mass psychology of a large number of ignorant individuals is liable to change violently as a result of sudden fluctuations of opinion . . . the market will be subject to waves of optimistic and pessimistic sentiment, which are unreasoning and yet in a sense legitimate where no solid basis exists for a reasonable calculation" (66). Thus, the market fluctuates "under the influence of mass psychology" (66), compelling investors to anticipate "what average opinion expects the average opinion to be" (67).[27] Individual decision making gets filtered through economic apparatuses that spatially distance its affective foundation and thus weaken its rationality. In this situation, people respond to "animal spirits" more than to logical deliberation. Keynes summarizes that "it is our innate urge to activity which makes the wheels go round, our rational selves choosing between the alternatives as best we are able, calculating where we can, but often falling back for our motive on whim or sentiment or chance" (69–70). Financial uncertainty propagated through impersonal market apparatuses contorts the natural affective energies that underpin the entire economic system, making exceptional market moments appear indicative of a new reality as opposed to an unexplainable blip.

Keynesian economics, the need for state intervention to maintain an ongoing balance between production and consumption, does not hijack capitalism on behalf of an entirely different affective agenda but updates its principles for the twentieth-century marketplace. Understanding the need for individual freedom, Keynes argues for the regulation of financial mechanisms and not of people. Defending this position, he maintains that "the task of transmuting human nature must not be confused with the task of managing it" (163). He wants, as he puts it, to "cure the disease whilst preserving efficiency and freedom" (166).[28] Unfortunately, within the dominant imagination, freedom operates as a zero-sum game so that its management defaults into simply restriction.

Rather than transmitting human nature or regulating it, Veblen simply charts the evolutionary relationship between humanity and its institutions. That evolution includes capitalism's division into business (finance capital) and industry (productive capital) as his *Theory of Business Enterprise* (1910) and his later *Absentee Ownership and Business Enterprise in Recent Times* (1923) both outline.[29] Veblen's fundamental position is that business enterprise, "through the mechanism of investments and markets," drives industrial capitalism (*Theory of Business* 2). This driving force is not, however, accounted for in the philosophical justification of capitalism inherited from the eighteenth century and mythologized in the doctrine of Adam Smith. Neither is it adequately theorized by Marx. For Veblen, Marx's critique represents "a romantic school of thought" that works through make-believe every bit as much as classical economics does ("Socialist Economics" 434). From his perspective, Marx wrongly asserts that workers will recognize capitalist exploitation through consciousness of their common class interests. As Veblen sees it, collective thinking is not rational and "men's reasoning is largely controlled by other than logical, intellectual forces" (441). Those other forces include the instincts, institutional habituation, and material environments. Although his theory of political economy has many similarities to the one put forward by Marx, Veblen insists that his method subscribes to a literal account of materiality rather than the metaphorical one he believes characterizes Marx's value theory.

Building on Marx, who argued that commodities impede the free flow of human passion, Veblen says that institutions—particularly their mental and material infrastructures—corrupt the innate human instincts, resulting in a palpable mismatch between natural human inclinations and the enforced practices of capitalism. This revision of Marx suggests an alternative framework of affect's three modalities. Veblen claims that the dominant economic predisposition of capitalism relies on an animating myth that closes off the community orientation of workmanship; contemporary capitalism, he says, splits identification into business enterprise and matter-of-fact thinking; and he contends that the energies activating capitalism come from the goodwill and salesmanship of business rather than the transfer of value.

The capitalist predisposition stems fundamentally from a belief in the naturalness of its economic structure. Just as eighteenth-century philosophy declared human beings to be innately free, it suggested that production and exchange were equally intertwined in this liberty. For Veblen, humans instinctually desire an organizing myth, and capitalism's natural-order doctrine serves that purpose. According to it, one's natural right to property derives from the fact that the owner mixed his labor with raw materials to produce an object, and thus "he has extended to the object of his labor that discretionary control which in the nature of things he of right exercises over the motions of his own person" (*Theory of Business* 72).[30] The natural-rights doctrine justifies ownership by virtue of the fact that one "embodies the work of his brain and hand in a useful object" (77). This theory positions a particular type of owner—one who designs, manages, and produces goods—as naturally entitled to the profits derived from those goods (78). Tradition imports this belief system, which properly belongs to the handicraft era, into the twentieth century. Indifferent toward tradition and impatient with unsubstantiated arguments, Veblen finds this natural-order doctrine irrelevant to modern capitalist processes in which profits derive less from production than from the ability to manipulate the market from a distance.

The reality of capitalism, especially apparent in the early twentieth century, is that owners do not produce products; in fact, they have little knowledge of the production process. Owners have the right to products because of legal contracts and not because of any material relationship to the product. This is, for Veblen, a tautology: they "own these things because they own them" (*Theory of Business* 51). Stocks, titles, and other documents lack the material relationship supposed in the natural-rights doctrine. As capitalism progressed, "the visible relation between the owner and the works shifted from a personal footing of workmanship to an impersonal footing of absentee ownership" (*Absentee Ownership* 59). The twentieth-century economy, Veblen maintains, thrives on "competitive selling" and thus focuses on salesmanship (advertising and packaging) and sabotage (limiting production so as to drive up the market price). Such practices take "effect in an impersonal and dispassionate way, as a matter of business routine" (215). It does not matter whether workers need jobs or consumers need products; what does matter is that profit can be derived from employing workers and selling products. This process is quite simply "immune from neighborly personalities and from sentimental considerations" (216). Fueled by a residual myth, contemporary capitalism keeps participants open to its structures through faith in its natural, inevitable, and human capacities, affectively closing off critique of its more malignant forms, such as the legal structures empowering absentee ownership at the expense of the material interests of the larger community.

This split between absentee owners and industrial producers conditions two different modes of receptivity, according to Veblen. The business class "proceed[s] on metaphysical grounds" (*Theory of Business* 238), while the working class functions according to "measurable cause and effect" (310). The matter-of-fact practices of industrial workers, he says, do "not lend themselves to statement in anthropomorphic terms of natural rights" (318). On the contrary, their habitual training in brute matter as well as cause-and-effect logic predisposes them toward arguments that rely on material evidence. Receptivity to new economic ideas is determined by their proximity to the material habits of industrialism: consequently, "the line of demarcation between those available for socialist propaganda and those not so available is rather to be drawn between the classes employed in the industrial and those employed in the pecuniary occupations" (348). It is for these material reasons, he argues, that socialism has its greatest chance in urban industrial centers (349). The willingness to engage new economic proposals—being open to a certain line of argument—stems not from one's economic interests but from the cultivation of one's natural instincts within the concrete material reality of an immediate environment. As human instincts become habituated in specific ways, they enable people to be open to those ideas that comport with their surroundings and closed to those that deviate from them. Veblen reads Marx as proposing a revolution of consciousness wherein workers rationalize their exploitation and he saw himself as offering a concrete material ground for that shift in thinking.

Not only does the physical reality of people's work and everyday lives condition their openness to different interpretations of the world, but it also affectively ensures their identification with others who share the same reality. Thus, for Veblen, there are two main identifications—those who are pulled toward the business class and those who are drawn toward the working class. People are motivated by instincts, and those instincts manifest in relationship to material frames of reference. Accordingly, absentee owners are not motivated by a desire to exploit workers, who do not exist in their material world, but by a desire to be of service to the other business people who do make up their world. In addition to being a material theory, this is an argument for the pull of affect. Affect, which mobilizes the instinct of workmanship, "touches primarily the dealing of man with man" (43). The absentee owners of this stage of capitalism are "commonly removed from all personal contact" with employees as well as with customers, delimiting their material reality to interactions among business people and members of the leisure class (52–53). Because employees and consumers are at a distance from the locus of economic decision making and belong to another class, "personal contact and cognizance of them is not only not contemplated, but is in a sense impossible" (53). The people of this class understand themselves as aligned with other members of their class simply because those individuals populate their day-to-day reality. This is not a conscious decision but the literal retraining of innate human instincts or affectivities through the material feedback loop.

The other primary form of identification takes place within industrial spaces. As already mentioned, these individuals are trained in a matter-of-fact logic that, according to Veblen, resists both "an uncritical acceptance of institutional truths," and "the construction of new myths" (352, 358). By virtue of their initiation within mechanical processes, workers learn to view the world as a complex and "delicately balanced interplay of forces that work blindly, insensibly, heedlessly" (368). From this perspective, the affective identification of the industrial class and its attendant "machine discipline acts to disintegrate the institutional heritage" (374). That this identity counters the inherited openness toward capitalism is not, for Veblen, the final word. Business principles penetrate the worker's matter-of-fact world through print media and educational training, which work toward "the maintenance of archaic ideals and philistine affections" (381). In Veblen's view, those in power "bend their energies to the preservation" of the system through "indoctrination of the young by undeviating habituation in word and deed" (*Absentee Ownership* 426, 427).[31] This propaganda machine serves the same material function as all other material artifacts, and so capitalism's future, for Veblen, remains uncertain.

Regardless of one's identification, the key factors energizing individuals toward action or inaction in this system are the goodwill and salesmanship of business. Salesmanship includes an array of advertising, product presentation, and social emulation. What Veblen calls goodwill is the immaterial portion of a company's valuation that "depends from hour to hour on the quotations of the stock exchange" (*Theory of Business* 131). These valuations fluctuate "on variations of confidence on the part of investors, on current belief as to the probable policy or tactics of the business men in control," and mostly "on the indeterminable, largely instinctive, shifting movements of public sentiment" (149). In this schema, what appears to be natural affective energy transfer is actually a manufactured energy supported by various financial apparatuses and advertising mechanisms. For instance, because companies borrow money, stock market evaluations of those companies may be well beyond their tangible assets (*Absentee Ownership* 357). Thus, "the fabric of credit and capitalization is essentially a fabric of concerted make-believe resting on the routine credulity of the business community at large" (383). Like Keynes, Veblen argues that such a structure is "always in a state of unstable equilibrium, liable to derangement and extensive disintegration in case of an appreciable disturbance at any critical point" (383). Economic activities operate through "a confidence game" that is "played according to the rules governing games of that psychological nature" (384). The energy transferring between people gets redirected through market institutions, detaching it from human experience and its authentic pathways. Thus, people act or fail to act according to their psychological instincts, but those instincts do not accurately reflect reality as they are habituated through the business institutions of goodwill and salesmanship. Ultimately, for Veblen, product design and market psychology motivate people to behave at odds with the collective and pragmatic ends of human nature.

The Futility of Rationalizing Affect

Keynes and Veblen offer alternative affective understandings of capitalism that derive from and rationalize the foundational affective terrain of Adam Smith and Karl Marx. Keynes accepts Smith's claim that affect transmits by proximity but emphasizes that modern capitalism works through global rather than local spaces. Thus, affect becomes skewed. Likening this to any other problem, Keynes suggests that affect can be amended through correct probabilistic thinking. His solution enlists professionals to regulate the economy so as to ensure balance between individual affect and its broader refractions. Stray or misguided affect can be pulled back into alignment through rational thinking and its attendant institutional interventions. Veblen also attempts to ground the metaphysical aspect of affect within a rational scientific explanation—the instincts. Veblen simultaneously sheds Smith's invisible hand and Marx's value theory of labor in favor of what he calls matter-of-fact thinking. Humans do not mysteriously transfer energy among themselves and the things they produce but are energetically motivated by the biological predispositions of human instincts, which transform through institutional habits. As materially determined, human beings have little capacity to consciously outwit capitalism; so, unlike Keynes, Veblen does not promote public deliberation as an interventionist strategy but does position workers, who he contends are materially habituated toward real-world problem solving, as potential agents of change.

Although Keynes and Veblen offer two contrary accounts of capitalism, both theories suffer from an inflated valuation of rationality. In their desire to update foundational economic claims, they tend to underestimate the need for untheorized affective attachments or the role of organizing myths within economic structures. There is no disputing that the core mythology animating both capitalism and its Marxist critique tends to disconnect reality from a theoretical ideal. On this account, both Keynes and Veblen are wholly correct, and yet many of their readers bristle against their economic theories. Indeed, Keynesian economics is often maligned as communism in disguise, while Veblen's economic theories are nearly invisible to readers who position him as a sociologist or cultural satirist. The uneven reception of these economic theories might very well stem from affect rather than any particular misstep in their logic. Exploring these divergent theories through the lens of affect teaches us that rationality is not always persuasive—a lesson of as much significance for rhetoricians as for economists.

The argument here has been twofold. First, I have proposed that Keynes and Veblen reimagine the affective structures of Smith and Marx. Second, I suggest that these alterations, especially the rationalization of affect, weaken their persuasive power and thus the receptivity of these thinkers. By calling affect into question, these theorists have compromised the structural integrity of the foundational arguments for and against capitalism. To escape this economic limbo, one will likely need different affective accounts of Smith and of Marx, such as those variants found in the post–World War II scholarship of Friedrich Hayek and Theodor Adorno.

4 Friedrich Hayek and Theodor Adorno

Reactions from Displaced Capitalist Subjects

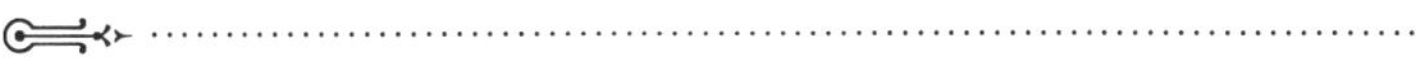

Something which may be worth studying more closely . . . is the curious closeness and parallels between what we call the Freiburg School or ordoliberals and their neighbors, as it were, the Frankfurt School.

Michel Foucault, *Birth of Biopolitics*

At first glance, it may seem strange to explore Friedrich Hayek (1899–1992) and Theodor Adorno (1903–1969) for a comparative study of economics. Neither was an economist by training—Hayek received degrees in juridical and political philosophy while Adorno studied to be a philosopher and musical composer. Yet, as the epigraph to this chapter asserts, there is something curious about the pairing of a Freiburg ordoliberal such as Hayek with a Frankfurt social theorist like Adorno. Both lived and worked during roughly the same periods in central Europe, England, and the United States.[1] For both, scientific rationality ends in totalitarianism and Hitler's regime is paradigmatic of this trajectory. In fact, a critique of rationality serves as the bridge that surprisingly connects their divergent positions on capitalism. In Hayek's view, a rationally managed capitalist state, such as the kind supported by Keynes, achieves the opposite of its intentions—it creates poverty rather than wealth and serfdom rather than freedom.[2] For Adorno, managed capitalism is symptomatic of the larger Enlightenment project, which attempts to regulate nothing less than nature itself. The encroachment of this rationality on the political economic and cultural spheres, according to Adorno, drains individuals of the freedom to think for themselves. Thus, the goal for both scholars and their attendant schools of thought is to counter the problematic extension of scientism into the social sciences, including economics, with a form of rationality that takes the limits of calculable experience seriously.[3]

Each theorist offers a negative methodology for securing such rationality. Hayek endorses the rule of law—a state in which government actions are strictly delimited by a few universally agreed-upon rules. Adorno proposes negative dialectics—a critique that never culminates in a final equilibrium but transgresses all points of stasis. Both methods privilege micropolitics over macropolitics and take difference rather than identity as their starting point. Neither retreats into an assumption of the natural state of being nor proposes a rational means of controlling the irrationality of individual or historical behavior. Instead, they psychologize rationality in a way that each deems more appropriate to the sociological study of economic and cultural behavior than scientific rationalism.

Opposed to Keynesian-style economic management, Hayek goes back to Adam Smith's classic description of the market as an invisible hand that enables spontaneous, self-regulating order.[4] Unplanned order, he argues, results from both freedom and rules. People must be free to make their own choices within a rule-governed terrain that clearly defines the limits of governmental action but makes no positive assertions that dictate individual behavior. Within this worldview, it is unnecessary, and indeed impossible, to regulate the market because no one person or group of people possesses sufficient knowledge of its innumerable and always-changing contingencies. While Keynes uses reason to extend Smith's notion of affect into the diverse global economy, Hayek allows affect to transcend the limits of space and time through his carefully crafted and rigorously defended spontaneous order. In similar fashion, Adorno pushes back against the scientific version of Marxism inherent in state formation, arguing that communism suffers from the same crushing administration as its capitalist counterpart. Unlike his colleagues in the Frankfurt School, who embrace Marx's newly available early writings to lodge a critique against the scientific reading of his work that had prevailed throughout the late nineteenth and early twentieth centuries, Adorno refuses to let Marx's idealist humanism escape critical analysis.[5] Relying on Freud's sense of a double instinct to create and destroy, Adorno resists translating the positive affective position of species-being in Marx's early work into a program for state communism. Instead, he puts humanity under the lens of Freudian psychoanalysis, suggesting that individuals who strongly identify with either the capitalist or communist ideology sacrifice their egos and thus their ability to experience and reflect on the world for themselves. What is needed but lacking is the kind of reflexive action that only comes from critically examining one's instinctual passions and then consciously reacting to the world. Freedom, for Adorno, emerges from the interplay of embodied spontaneity and rational self-reflection, but decidedly not through rules.

This post–World War II moment in the intellectual and political discussion of capitalism is a crucial fork in the road as Hayek's capitalist advocacy extends Smith's theory of affect in the invisible hand, while Adorno, opposing capitalism, abandons Marx's attunement to affect in species-being. Hayek, like Keynes, recognizes the geographical and cultural limitations of an invisible hand based on the alignment of sympathy among members of a self-identified community. Unlike Keynes, he finds futile the rational scientific approach of managing national and international economic data. Hayek's *The Sensory Order* provides a theoretical apparatus, as opposed to a scientific one, for transcending these limitations.[6] The mind, he explains, creates global order out of chaotic individual experience, and the market, as a complex order, works the same way as the mind but on a larger and more intricate scale. Creating an analogue between market and experiential life, Hayek effectively theorizes Smith to go beyond Smith. By disarticulating Marxism from the revolutionary praxis of state communism, Adorno represents a similar theoretical recuperation. Adorno asserts an antagonistic relationship to state capitalism as well as its communist counterpart but reminds us that Marx, whose critique gestures at a relationship between human beings and the world that is creative and empowering rather than alienating, never provides a blueprint for producing that world. For him, the failure of Marxism begins with a rush to practice that erases the spirit of its theoretical underpinnings. The only viable goal is to create and then undermine always-evolving constellations of reality that might indirectly advance material changes without calling for any specific action.[7] Adorno argues for a Marxist theory that escapes doctrine, but also introduces a destructive instinct into that theory. Adorno's use of Freudian psychology insists on the double instincts of creation and destruction, leaving his critique of capitalism bereft of the idealized human relations that underpin both Marx's and Veblen's critical assessment of capitalism.[8]

A brief excursion through each scholar's inaugural lecture highlights these curious similarities as well as their underlying differences. "The Actuality of Philosophy," a lecture delivered on May 7, 1931, to the philosophy faculty at the University of Frankfurt on the occasion of his appointment, outlines several of Adorno's key methodological tenets. He begins with a critique of rationality as insufficient to an understanding of "the totality of the real" (120). Yet, he says, philosophy tends to unfold along two unifying rationalities: an idealism that espouses "illusory transcendence" and an empiricism that grants "validity only to the natural sciences" (121). Phenomenology, he says, attempts to straddle this intellectual divide, but it too suffers from the same problematic. On the one hand, phenomenologists who remain exclusively in the scientific sphere leave only "the weakest trace of hope" for social connectivity; on the other hand, those who abandon the material for the metaphysical perpetuate fictions "against which [phenomenology] originally declared battle" (123). Adorno stakes out a new position—one based in a Freudian critique of capitalism that premises a dialectical relationship between the transcendental and the material realms that can only be consciously mediated by a strong individual ego.

His methodology takes localized phenomena, organizes them within a larger picture of reality, and then, surprisingly, pokes holes in that picture.[9] The point, he says, is not to create order but to point out the limitations of any one construction of reality: philosophy "must proceed interpretively without ever possessing a sure key to interpretation" (126). Such a practice can illuminate possible paths toward social change, and yet it can never spell out a program for comprehensive change. Instead, Adorno calls for the theorization of underexplored material elements of contemporary life so as to enact an unceasing negation of the social order that organizes and reorganizes material reality in a constant display of its unintended failures.[10] Against the presumption of complete knowledge, Adorno asserts that "the mind *(Geist)* is indeed not capable of producing or grasping the totality of the real, but it may be possible to penetrate the detail, to explode in miniature the mass of merely existing reality" (133). His method critiques the whole by exploring the particular, even as it refuses to provide the basis for a future society such as a capitalist or communist utopia.

Thirty years later, when Hayek assumes a faculty position at the University of Freiburg, he delivers an inaugural lecture on many of these same themes—the failure of science to capture the totality of experience, the perversity of rational intentions, and the role of individualism within material reality. In his 1962 lecture, reprinted as "The Economy, Science, and Politics," Hayek argues that Max Weber's critique of personal values slipping into scientific work has been overstated. In economics, as in other social spheres, rationality appears to work well within localized contexts in which individuals are able to know all the relevant information; but, he interjects, that does not mean individuals make rational decisions. Even though individual economic decision making seems to operate according to the facts of the matter, people simultaneously and unconsciously use nonrational, cultural rules in their economic choices. Economic judgments never operate without personal and cultural values, and, therefore, their determination cannot be scientifically managed because they are simply beyond the human mind. Like Adorno, Hayek explains that the limitation of rational economic prediction derives from "the fundamental difficulty of any complete explanation of highly complex phenomena" (259). The shift toward larger economic scales does not require greater rationality. On the contrary, such macroeconomic narratives, as he sees it, result from "the erroneous belief that theory will be useful only if it puts us in a position to predict particular events" (262). Opposed to exacting scientific thinking and its economic prophecies, he advocates a value-rich theory based on "schematic orders or patterns" derived from successful past experience that can be used to establish a rule-governed society (260). In short, Hayek contends that unforeseen costs, at least on a large scale, can be avoided by economic and political liberalism, which function through the rule of law.

In his defense of theory as the articulation of nonrational structures invisibly organizing human activity, Hayek borrows heavily from his work in cognitive psychology. As he says, "the problems of the formation of our civilization and institutions are closely connected with the problems of the development of our mind and its tools" (267).[11] Just as our minds spontaneously order information derived from patterns of experience, so does the invisible hand of capitalism. We do not know all the particular features of a given material form, and yet we instinctively know how to fit things into our life activities. Similarly, "we know the general character of the self-regulating forces of the economy," and yet "we do not know all the particular circumstances to which they bring about an adaptation" (263). In lieu of falling down a mathematical rabbit hole, Hayek suggests that aspiring economists go outside the discipline to round out their study with social theory.[12] Disciplinary knowledge, he maintains, is only "the beginning of a struggle for achieving a comprehensive philosophy of society" (268). This statement—that economic study requires a larger philosophy of society—closes the curious circle between these two very different thinkers: they both position capitalism within a psychological theory of society even as they assume divergent philosophies of how affect moves through individuals to hold the world together.

Offering two accounts of affect, their initially similar positions opposing scientific rationality move in drastically different directions. Hayek strengthens the role of intuition in his vindication of the self-regulating nature of capitalism, while Adorno weakens the role of nonrational motivation in his relentless critique of administrative society's ability to manufacture its own "second nature." For Adorno, Enlightenment rationality has seeped into our psyches, mediating our bodily instincts and impulses, which need to be more critically examined in order for a truly free will to emerge. Commensurate with these affective theories, each thinker espouses an implied understanding of rhetoric. Hayek argues for a persuasive agenda that aligns instinctual thinking within the liberal order while Adorno cautions against persuasion because of its complicity in group identification; in turn, these two accounts advocate different political economic systems wherein Hayek envisions a political structure under the rule of law while Adorno refuses to advocate for any structure whatsoever.

Affect: Dispositions and Rules or Group Identification

The success of capitalism, for Hayek, results from its ability to organize society without any plan to do so: a self-generating complex—what he calls spontaneous order—simply emerges through acquired dispositions and unconscious social rules.[13] His most in-depth exploration of this process is found in *The Sensory Order,* which explains how an individual mind categorizes phenomenal experience and creates a propensity to adjust to new empirical data. According to this theory, a mind is not an external, rationalizing apparatus that tells a body what to do. On the contrary, a mind is the product of bodily experience in the world and its neurological cataloguing of that experience into particular orientations toward new information (112). These dispositions motivate individual behavior on a level distinct from rational explanation. Staking its ground in unconscious, intuitive, and ultimately unknown processes, this position returns to Adam Smith's *The Theory of Moral Sentiments* and replaces imagination and sympathetic alignment, which work via proximity, with personal disposition and unwritten rules. Unlike other psychologists who raise what Hayek calls "a phantom-problem" by listing and describing immutable human instincts, the agentive force of individual action is, according to him, "an order of events" in the neurological firings of our brains and thus an evolving pattern of associations (35).[14] For Smith, the mind's imagination allows it to align with others because sympathy moves between people who physically encounter one another. For Hayek, the brain constructs individual and social dispositions that align with the unconscious rules of successful action. These dispositions develop into social rules that organically transcend the boundaries of local mores without the imposition of rational calculation.[15] The local and proximate form the limits of Smith's theory for both Keynes and Hayek, but while Keynes takes recourse in the logical management of economic behavior, Hayek relies on the evolution of the human mind to bolster Smith's theory beyond its internal boundaries.

There are two axes to the mind's order that cooperatively forge individual and social progress. Hayek uses the metaphor of a map to explain the repeated historical patterns—the semipermanent order built up through past experiences—and references the model to describe the sensory order evoked by a moment in time. The map and the model work together so that one's behavior derives from the historical experience encoded into the map as well as the immediate sensory data of the model. Insofar as dispositions derive from an ongoing catalogue of experience, they are not biologically or culturally permanent but evolutionary: they endure within individuals and are mimicked by others as long as the behavior produces successful outcomes (128–29). Our understanding of the material world is thus a function of individual and social experience with the world, which, although imprinted onto our brains, is under constant development.

This evolution takes place within the individual as well as the species, making disposition both ontogenetic and phylogenetic. Individual experience links to human evolution through social rules. Those experiences that form successful dispositions translate into rules that inform the experience of the entire species (52). More important, both individual dispositions and social rules emerge spontaneously and, for the most part, tacitly. Our actions are more deeply informed by the mind's unconscious sensory order than by our conscious interpretation of reality. Knowledge, Hayek says, "rests on a much more extensive basis of less fully conscious or subconscious images" (138). In other words, the sensory order highlights a profound ignorance that for Hayek is foundational to human beings. He concludes that even though we can understand the principles by which unconscious dispositions emerge and evolve, "we shall never, by means of the same brain, be able to arrive at a detailed explanation of its working in particular circumstances, or be able to predict what the results of its operations will be" (188–89). This principle— that an evolutionary apparatus of which we have limited knowledge organizes society—asserts that human beings implicitly follow the rules of successful evolution and ought not attempt to intervene in those rules.[16]

Unconscious dispositions regulate society according to similarly unarticulated community norms. Hayek develops this point in *Rules and Order,* a book dedicated to the claim that both individuals and society follow rules through unconscious imitation of productive activities. Human society, he says, self-organizes; it "constantly adapts itself, and functions through adapting itself, to millions of facts which in their entirety are not known to anyone" (13). In this evolutionary process, the successful spontaneously rise to the top, and others emulate their actions through the unconscious ordering process of the mind.[17] As "unconsciously held ideas about what is right and proper," social ordinances "are observed in action without being known to the acting person in articulated form" (69, 19). A rule manifests as customary practice, gets imprinted into our bodily memories, and is passed along through the generations (75). Thus, social order is held together by the power of rule-bound dispositions. Because human beings intuitively follow such directions, they need not be regulated by external organizations that create rules through deliberation. The only legitimate regulation is one that makes those tacit rules explicit but does not attempt to supersede them.

Returning to his sensory-order thesis, Hayek's "Rules, Perception, and Intelligibility" outlines the mechanisms by which individuals unconsciously conform to unwritten social rules. He begins by stating that human beings have a "rule-guided perception" that includes the ability to unconsciously read "gestures and facial expressions" (46). Human beings, he says, possess some unspecified "mechanism of sensory pattern transfer" that instructs them to mimic behaviors (49).[18] Evidence for this mechanism of imitation can be found in the brain's neurological structure. Unconsciously identifying different entities as part of the same class of phenomena happens because the different events trigger neurological complexes that contain "some identical elements among the 'following'" or the staccato-like pattern of brain firings triggered by a particular incident (50). Repetitive firings of the same following "provide master moulds" through which to perceive future phenomena. Reasonable conduct thus follows rules "with which we are acquainted but which we need not explicitly know" (55). In short, we are directed by patterns that follow "a superconscious mechanism which operates upon the contents of consciousness but which cannot itself be conscious" (61). The final causal agent for Hayek is a process taking place beyond consciousness that we can recognize, but cannot manipulate. Nearly synonymous with Adam Smith's invisible hand, the spontaneous order is Hayek's term for this mysterious mechanism.

Although Hayek cites the invisible hand throughout his discussion of these spontaneous orders, his more limited references to Smith's *The Theory of Moral Sentiments* are instructive for understanding the origin of this self-organizing force. For instance, he recalls Smith's metaphor of the "great chessboard of human society" to explain unconscious collective action (*Rules and Order* 35). According to Smith, individuals correspond to the different pieces on the chessboard with each having "a principle of motion of its own" (*Theory of Moral Sentiments* 275). The pieces only move according to those distinct rules, unaware of how they work together under the external guidance of the invisible hand, which alone can calculate in advance all the moves needed to succeed. *The Theory of Moral Sentiments* pegs sympathy to morality and argues that the habit of imagining ourselves in another's experience constitutes sympathetic alignment between ourselves and another. Smith uses the imagery of the invisible hand to explain how something like what I have been calling affect organizes all these different elements. Based on the enumeration of multiple examples, Smith's theory remains speculative, while Hayek's model stems from concrete neurological evidence.[19] In other words, Hayek's theory of sensory order provides the scientific backing to support what Smith understood yet could not adequately explain. Indeed, Hayek says that contemporary research has "taught us much more than Adam Smith knew" ("Rules, Perception, and Intelligibility" 47–48). Adding cognitive psychology to Smith's theory of moral connectivity, Hayek replaces sympathy with disposition and refines morality as political and economic liberalism.

Similarly interested in freedom, as opposed to the human suffering that seems inseparable from Western history, Adorno uses Sigmund Freud's depth psychology to rethink Marx's classic formulation of alienation and thus indicates a nascent theory of affect. Freud's structural model of the mind famously postulates three competing forces: the id, the ego, and the superego. The id, which demands instant gratification of its need for love (libido) as well as destruction (thanatos), and the superego, or socially sanctioned morality of the outside world, are regulated by the ego—the only part of an individual's psyche to have access to conscious reflection. In group psychology an individual displaces one's ego ideal onto a leader and identifies with other group members, who achieve a derivative form of that ideal by following the leader's authority (*Group Psychology* 80).[20] This process strips an individual of the ability to self-manage his or her instincts but compensates for that forfeiture with group membership. Consequently, there develops a herd instinct in which one conforms to group standards and projects anxieties onto out-groups that are then persecuted.[21] Just as a real-life leader quells anxieties that arise from an uncertain world, so too do the myths, such as the invisible hand of capitalism, that secure group identification.

Following Freud, Adorno assumes human beings are motivated by both positive and negative psychological drives, that these drives are socially mediated, and that a healthy society requires individual self-reflection on this process. This has two important implications for the role of affect in political economic discussions. First, unlike both Marx and Veblen, for whom the human being is a creative force opposed to the corrupting powers of capitalist society, Adorno posits human beings as equally productive and destructive. Second, the historical movement of the species is neither driven by its exclusively biological basis (Marx's ontological perspective) nor the corruption of those instincts (Veblen's epistemological thesis); instead, it proceeds through self-reflection on the dialectical relationship between instinctual drives and their socialization. For Adorno, previous understandings of species-being tend to reify one of the twin poles of human instinct—Smith's notion of self-interest or Marx's unfettered creativity. His intervention suggests that true knowledge (freedom) unpredictably erupts from the friction between biological instincts and the material society in which they exist. This requires a psychologically healthy individual with a strong self-reflective ego. The primary problem with contemporary society, from Adorno's perspective, is that the ego has been separated from the individual and displaced onto the capitalist spirit, leaving people under the spell of capitulation and conformity.

In further alignment with Freud, Adorno emphasizes the central role that the family has played in the reproduction of society's tacit rules. In the shift from liberal to monopoly capitalism, however, the family cedes its power as the seat of authority to the regulating institutions of state capitalism.[22] Capitalism assumes the family's function as caretaker: in addition to satiating our physical needs, it shapes our leisure culture and soothes our anxieties about life's uncertainties through its totalizing narrative. Encapsulating this change as "the liquidation of the self," Adorno argues that the human being is no longer an individual and cannot be expected to act within the liberal tradition of bourgeois subjects who forge society in their own interests. Capitalism regulates our instinctual drives, or affect, because we have displaced our egos onto the administered world of exchange. Rather than distancing us from ourselves as the alienation thesis asserts, capitalism functions as a surrogate for the self we no longer possess. Under the psychological hold of capitalist identification, we quite simply do not have the internal ego necessary to reassert the individual back into history.

As monopoly capitalism creeps into all life activities, human beings lose their ability to experience themselves outside of the system—both their sensual and rational capabilities filter through the social ether of monopoly capitalism. These capacities, however, are integral to Adorno's understanding of affect, which begins from the premise that "there is no immediacy which is not at the same time mediated" (*Metaphysics* 29). Enlightenment theorists who place total knowledge in the sensory capacity mistakenly fold the transcendental realm into the material world. For instance, in Hume, as in Hayek's recuperation of this tradition, the habitual associations of sensory data acquire the stature of complete reality (30). Kant and the rationalist school, which does not allow for the mediation between reason and embodied sensation, suffer from the opposite problem. Whereas Scottish Enlightenment thinkers limit the external world to the embodied experiences they privilege, the speculative philosophers radically separate the two realms and privilege reason. Critical of both explanations, Adorno looks to Aristotle, who maintains a duality between material matter and the metaphysical "power center which moves matter" (36). The motivating force—affect—is nonidentical with individuals at the same time its animating power moves through and "sticks" to them, as Sara Ahmed says. Although separate from the individual, the external engine of history only exists concretely "from the touching of matter and form" (85). According to this schema, knowledge is neither exclusively identical with individual experience nor the domain of an external power, but emerges from the dynamic struggle of the two, wherein both are affecting and being affected.

Material reality and the embodied experience of that reality represent two separate existences that stand in dialectical relationship to each other, and only the egoistic self is capable of critically reflecting on that relationship. Unfortunately, capitalist identification psychologically subverts the individual ego. As Adorno explains it, "the mechanisms of identification have stamped themselves on people's characters to such a degree that they are quite incapable of the spontaneity and the conscious actions that would be required to bring about the necessary changes. This is because, by identifying with the course of the world, they do so in an unhappy, neurotically damaged way, which effectively leads them to reinforce the world as it is" (*History and Freedom* 76). He admits that freedom cannot be formulated without "recourse to something prior to the ego, to an impulse that is in a sense a bodily impulse that has not yet been subjected to the centralizing authority of consciousness" (213); but, if such spontaneity "split[s] off from reason" and operates unchecked, it holds the individual captive to its agentive authority (217). For Adorno, completely unconscious decisions are nothing more than reflexes or ventriloquism determined by the social order. Freedom requires conscious reflection on the relationship between those instincts and the larger socio-material world. Ostensibly combining Hayek's intuitive order with Veblen's rational order, Adorno argues that freedom is "both somatic and mental at the same time" (235). He says that "what is needed for a willed act or for practice in general is the coincidence of two antagonistic elements that do not become completely fused" (239). Free will necessitates both bodily impulse and critical reflection. Such freedom, he laments, "ceases to exist the moment an act becomes dependent on anything other than subjectivity" (*Problems of Moral Philosophy* 83). If psychological identification with the administered life distorts instincts, disidentification enables one to combine instinct with rational reflection in order to engender free will.

Adorno uses two anecdotes to exemplify free will as the conscious alignment of affect and rationality. The first centers on the indecision of Shakespeare's Hamlet, who "is incapable of performing an action that he believes to be right" (*History and Freedom* 231). Hamlet has the facts of the case (his uncle killed his father, married his mother, and took the throne), which, according to social mores, justify an act of revenge, and yet he is not able to move from this knowledge to action: bodily disposition confronts reason and he hesitates. While Hamlet represents the refusal to act, Fabian von Schlabrendorff represents the compulsion to act. As Schlabrendorff relates the story of his unsuccessful plot to kill Hitler, there was overwhelming evidence of both its futility and the disastrous personal results of that failure; yet, he could not stop himself from acting (*Problems of Moral Philosophy* 8–9). In both stories, the men are instinctually unable to follow the rationally demarcated path from knowledge to action, and in this refusal they exhibit free will. Resistance necessitates that rational thought grapple with bodily compulsion through a strong ego and not an external authority, rendering the persuasive realm, to which I now turn, problematic for Adorno and crucial for Hayek.

Language: Public Opinion or Aesthetic Expression

Language, for Hayek, functions as a complex order that emerges and evolves spontaneously. Consequently, unlike Keynes, who contends that rational argument based on probabilistic thinking could be waged through public deliberation in an effort to influence the general will, Hayek subscribes to a nonrational notion of public opinion. Individuals have opinions about the world and how to act in it, but those views are not the result of a logical process; instead, opinions represent the conscious residue of a larger unconscious ordering process that aligns with Hayek's notion of the sensory order. In his explanation, dispositions and tacit rules trump conscious reason. Yet, because dispositions form through repeated experience and exposure to phenomena that reconstruct our mental maps, they are vulnerable to conscious manipulation.[23] Based on the sensory order, his theory of affect thus results in a two-fold conception of language. First, he defends the empirical schema identified by the Scottish Enlightenment against the encroachment of scientific rationalism, arguing against popular extensions of liberal discourse. Second, he advocates the translation of such political economic liberalism into popular discourse that can be circulated to nonexperts in order to influence their opinions and dispositions. Whereas Keynes collapses public opinion into the general will, Hayek separates the two realms of persuasion, seeking to maintain affectively produced public opinion by interjecting in the general will through selective messaging rather than reasoned argumentation.

Throughout his long career, Hayek returned again and again to the task of enforcing correct political economic terminology. For instance, his 1945 "Individualism: True and False" complains that terms like liberalism, democracy, capitalism, and, particularly, individualism have succumbed to the ambiguities of contemporary usage. He argues that the Scottish Enlightenment thinkers (John Locke, David Hume, Adam Ferguson, and Adam Smith, for instance) hold the key to true individualism, whereas French scholars (Jean-Jacques Rousseau and the physiocrats, more generally) subscribe to one that maintains "an exaggerated belief in the powers of individual reason" (8). In the liberal conception of individualism, people serve the interests of society voluntarily and without conscious intent; in contrast, a rational notion of individualism allows society to plan for predetermined ends. The former protects individual freedom through liberal democracy, while the latter inevitably falls into some version of social democracy that curtails freedom. True individualism, he says, is "opposed to the most fateful and dangerous of all current misconceptions of democracy—the belief that we must accept as true and binding for future development the views of the majority" (29). The underlying assumption of this lecture is that our language practices determine our social realities, implying that correct terminology will reorient our dispositions within the proper structure of capitalism.[24]

This agenda of policing liberal thinking and its accompanying political economic order against rational thinking and its desire for economic planning especially stands out in Hayek's paper *The Confusion of Language in Political Thought.* The explicit goal of this piece is to separate correct terms from common ones so as to properly illustrate the spontaneous organization of capitalism.

Hayek does this by exploring pairs of terms that illustrate the difference between the spontaneous order of capitalism and the rational order of planned economies. To begin, he distinguishes *taxis,* an intentional organization, from *cosmos,* which establishes itself through unplanned events.[25] Contrary to the conscious human intention that motivates *taxis,* the organization of a *cosmos* results spontaneously from "knowledge dispersed among and accessible to thousands or millions of separate individuals" (14). The operating power of a *cosmos* extends beyond the limits of conscious knowledge because it takes its cues from unconscious and unarticulated rules of order. Two different kinds of rules correspond to each of these orders: *thesis* and *nomos.* A *thesis* is an articulated rule that must be enforced to secure specific ends, whereas *nomos* is an often unarticulated rule of thumb that derives from customary behavior. Continuing with this division, he says that *nomos* describes opinion and focuses on values while *thesis* describes the will and focuses on ends. The difference between public opinion and the common will, therefore, rests on the nonrational versus the rational. Individuals hold opinions according to the dispositions they have developed from the traditions cultivated within their society. To preserve capitalism, which thrives within the liberal political economic order, these opinions and not the general will should determine the rules that govern society.

The crescendo of this discursive taxonomy arrives with Hayek's distinction between an *economy* and a *catallaxy.*[26] He limits economy to "the deliberate arrangement or organization of resources in the service of a hierarchy of ends" and suggests *catallaxy* to describe "the structure of many inter-related economies" (28).[27] An economy is a planned exchange and belongs properly to *taxis.* It functions at the level of the individual or the small organization but loses its administrative ability at larger scales, which is where *catallaxy* takes force. Borrowed from ancient Greek, *catallaxy* means "not only 'to exchange' but also 'to admit into the community' and 'to change from enemy to friend'" (*Mirage of Social Justice* 108). The second meaning here is crucial, as it suggests that mere exchange is not sufficient to the organization of capitalism. It further requires the sharing of social values—*nomos*—found in friendship or, as Adorno maintains, in group identification. To summarize, an *economy,* narrowly limited in the sense of a household budget, can be made to follow a predetermined logic, but a *catallaxy,* such as the capitalist marketplace, requires the freedom to follow the nonrational order of its *cosmos*—an order in which human relations evolve organically rather than mechanically.

As these articles, separated by almost a quarter century, imply, Hayek believed the job of an academic is to get the scholarship straight and not to engage the public directly. Consequently, the second part of his language theory, outreach to the masses, requires groups of nonexperts who specialize in speaking to general audiences. Such people are responsible for serving complicated ideas to the public in easily digestible doses.[28] Contrary to these vocational distinctions, Hayek did write directly to the public in *The Road to Serfdom,* and although it was a popular success, he understood it as a professional mistake.[29] *The Road to Serfdom* addresses the general reader in an attempt to counter the prevailing economic beliefs of the time (37). Much is made of his main premise—that totalitarian regimes represent advanced forms of democratic state planning—and yet it is important to underscore that this argument discounts democratic deliberation.[30] Here, as elsewhere, Hayek fears any government based on the general will derived from public discussion. Even a cursory reading illustrates his dismissal of public governance. He asserts, for example, that the "docile and gullible" will believe anything "if it is only drummed into their ears sufficiently loudly and frequently" (160). He goes on to say that "the great majority are rarely capable of thinking independently, that on most questions they accept views which they find ready-made, and that they will be equally content if born or coaxed into one set of beliefs or another" (179). The socialist thesis prevails, he concludes, not because it is a stronger argument but because it is the repeated platform served up to the unthinking masses. For liberalism to reclaim its rightful position, its theorists must learn to counter the general will by adjusting public opinion. This means working with the intellectual class of nonspecialists.

"The Intellectuals and Socialism," written in 1949 for an academic audience, functions as a call to arms for the purpose of such engagement.[31] According to Hayek's definition, the intellectual is an "intermediary in the spreading of ideas" and includes "journalists, teachers, ministers, lecturers, publicists, radio commentators, writers of fiction, cartoonists, and artists," among others (107). Intellectuals use language to sway the currents of popular dispositions and their attendant rules of order. As long as representational democracy abounds, liberal theorists have no choice but to influence these "second-hand dealers in ideas" (205). Advocates of liberal capitalism must learn to translate the nonrational order into the language of public opinion. Achieving what Hayek calls "a liberal Utopia" requires the creation and circulation of liberal sound bites capable of encapsulating its complex concepts (128). Just as adherents of the planned economy make "shibboleths of abstractions" (such as the concept of social justice he so despises), so must liberal-minded economists (116–17). Abstractions, he says, are crucial to how human beings process information because they "enable it to deal with a reality it cannot fully comprehend" (*Rules and Order* 30). Thus, as opposed to Keynes's famous adage about the importance of a philosopher's ideas, Hayek contends that "the influence of the political philosopher may be negligible" except "when his ideas have become common property, through the work of historians, publicist, teachers and writers" (*Constitution of Liberty* 179).[32] Adhering to this philosophy, Hayek ingeniously absorbs this intellectual class into his conversations—inviting them to key meetings of the Mont Pèlerin Society, for instance—and gives them the language—spontaneous order, economic freedom, and the corruption of big government, to name a few—with which to influence public opinion. His goal is to better inform the well-meaning, but misinformed, intellectual class so that they might persuade the masses.

Adorno, like Hayek, insists that the persuasive field of democratic deliberation be viewed skeptically—not because individuals are incapable of careful thinking but because their egoistic selves have been ceded to the administrative order of capitalism. Theorizing during the explosion of mass production, Adorno must make sense of a persuasive terrain only glimpsed by Veblen and barely imagined by Marx. In such a landscape, it is no longer sufficient to unveil capitalism as the manipulation of class interests in the productive sphere and commodity fetishism in the consumer sphere. With an abundance of products confronting individuals from morning to night, the post–World War II world seems impervious to these arguments. As Adorno says, the veil has been lifted, and we are confronted with a situation in which we decide "in favour of a thing even though [we] know perfectly well that it is a swindle" (Adorno and Horkheimer, *Towards a New Manifesto* 54). This predicament does not reveal consumers as passive dupes who must be retrained but as liquidated subjects—empty conduits for the agentive power of capitalist affect—who must be shocked out of their malaise so that they might reclaim their individual agency. Adorno, therefore, shifts the focus from making arguments to inciting the possibility of free will. He does this in two parts: first, he disassembles the argumentative sphere, and second, he emphasizes the importance of the aesthetic sphere, simultaneously critiquing the culture industry (the site, says Veblen, of capitalist argumentation) and embracing avant-garde alternatives.

Although Adorno undermines the deliberative sphere, he does not do so by retaining philosophy as a privileged space for accessing truth. He equally indicts rhetorical *doxa* and dialectical *theoria,* which share the same problematic position vis-à-vis thought and experience. Characteristic of Adorno's general perspective, he contends that philosophy's degradation of rhetoric is psychologically motivated. As he tells the story, Plato severed the ideal realm from everyday life and thus initiated an anxiety that philosophy displaced onto rhetoric, which it ridiculed as a mechanical shortcut to truth. Yet philosophers, he says, "did just as much for the technification of thought, for its potential abolition, as did those who cultivated rhetoric" (*Negative Dialectics* 55). To the extent that philosophers translate negative criticism into positive assertions, they present critique as scientific certainty and thereby enter the realm of domination. In opposition to Plato's suggestion in the *Phaedrus* that philosophy first finds truth and then uses rhetoric to disseminate that truth, Adorno contends that "the rhetorical element is on the side of content" (56). To be clear, the supposedly rhetorical crime of representing possibility as certainty (and thus foreclosing further inquiry) lies at the heart of philosophy's dialectical thinking and its claim to absolute truth.

Adorno continues this reflection on rhetoric and dialectics in his short essay "Opinion Delusion Society," which makes the case that both opinion and rational argumentation are susceptible to the pull of psychic needs. He contends that it is not a misunderstanding of material interests that compels people "to cling to [an] opinion" and "invest it with affect" (107). On the contrary, we hold opinions dear because they calm anxieties and organize a disorganized world. To maintain that sense of security, we defend these opinions through logic. As Adorno explains, "reason in the service of unreason—in Freud's language, 'rationalization'—rushes to the aid of opinion and so hardens it that nothing more can affect it or reveal its absurdity" (*Current of Music* 108). The capitalist political economy, awash with opinion, cannot be countered with rational argumentation—not because emotions inevitably trump reason but because society lacks egoistic individuals capable of rational deliberation. Reasonable debate "posits society as composed of free, equal, and emancipated people, whereas society's actual organization hinders all of that" (119). The distinction between mere opinion and well-reasoned argument is therefore "rendered untenable" (112). Although persuasion cannot penetrate the capitalist spell as long as the egoistic individual has been supplanted by collective psychological identification, the negative impulse of critique offers the possibility of lifting capitalism's enchantment, if even momentarily. This is not so much an unveiling as a puncturing, thinning, weakening.

Countering the affect circulating through mass-produced culture, critique serves both a critical and an affirmative role—it demonstrates the limitations of the object at the same time it recuperates the transcendental ideal to which that object aspires. A thinker must search out both the limitations of its object and the underlying value that gave life to the object in the first place, even if such value is psychologically warped. In this way, the critic hopes to pry open a closed world so that something might emerge that has not yet been cultivated and catalogued within the unifying logic of capitalism (*Metaphysics* 141). To do this, the critic distinguishes "between language as a means of communication and language as the precise expression of the matter under consideration" (*Critical Models* 28). Whereas communication settles the question of social import, expression leaves it open-ended so as to provide a glimpse into the affective energy animating the material world. Negative dialectics, Adorno's privileged mode of inquiry, provides this redemptive glimpse but does not fix it into a totalizing position.[33]

In many ways, this method flips the coin of Veblen's rationalized commodity fetish—wherein commodities speak on behalf of their owners—to explore its psychological copresence as the vantage point through which one might access affective energy, nonidentity, and the essence of the material world. As Adorno explains in "Veblen's Attack on Culture," the conspicuous consumption argument identifies the communicative aspect of culture, but fails to see its humanist side. For Veblen, he says, culture is exclusively "a display of power, loot, and profit. With splendid misanthropy he ignores everything that goes beyond this" (79). What does not come into focus through this lens is "the distinctly modern character of regression," which Adorno explains as "the futile but compulsive attempt to avoid loss of experience involved in modern modes of production" (85). To recall Marx's commodity fetish, the worker transfers his value into the commodity; the labor process, in turn, transfers to the individual a nonhuman, mechanical, pragmatic element that replaces the egoistic, human self. Thus, a desire for commodity goods may signify class status—as Veblen illustrates—but it also reflects an unconscious desire for a more human social existence. As Adorno puts it, "those features of luxury which Veblen designates as 'invidious,' revealing a bad will, do not only reproduce injustice; they also contain, in distorted form, the appeal to justice" (87). Culture's psychological functions—helping us identify and conform, soothing our anxieties, and orienting us to appropriate modes of behavior—at one and the same time ensure our alliance with administered capitalism and bely our enduring desire for the spontaneity of species-being.

Although the culture industry, which Adorno differentiates from spontaneously produced culture, primarily serves a negative role, its products reveal a desire to escape and illuminate the potential to break through the haze of administered life (*Culture Industry* 98). For example, popular culture colonizes individual sensory capacities and yet indicates the desire for a more sensual life. Occupying people's "senses from the time they leave the factory in the evening to the time they clock in again the next morning" (Horkheimer and Adorno, *Dialectic of Enlightenment* 131), the affective energy of the culture industry "multiplies within [a] person" and alters "the most finely-nuanced emotions of the individual, in his voice and gestures" (*Culture Industry* 122). As one's sensory organs are infiltrated by this all-embracing milieu, which tunes human instincts to capitalist frequencies, individuals, for instance, lose their capacity "for conscious perception of music" (46). So accustomed to the background music of stores, waiting rooms, and cars, people no longer know how to fully attend to music. Instead, they embrace the culture surrounding them, adjust to its influences, and undergo bodily changes: an "inability to hear the unheard-of with their own ears, to touch the unapprehended with their own hands" (Horkheimer and Adorno, *Dialectic of Enlightenment* 36).

Biological mimicry, facilitated by group identification, "determines the sense, even before perception occurs" (84). Consequently, individuals learn to react automatically or semiautomatically, and thus "impulse, subjectivity, and profanation, the old adversaries of materialistic alienation, now succumb to it" (*Culture Industry* 32). The critic who demonstrates that our instinctual "second nature" represents a reality filtered through the totalizing landscape of capitalism also reminds us that human sensual capacity might be different. The pervasive sounds, smells, and sights of manufactured culture betray the human craving for a sensual connection with the world. This possibility, one that cannot be translated into concrete action, nonetheless offers hope for redeeming the ideal that has been lost to its material manifestation.

Just as criticism of the culture industry pursues the possibility of a different human experience, so too does avant-garde art. Consequently, Adorno embraces the Austrian composer Arnold Schoenberg and what he more generally calls the "new music."[34] Such music, characterized by its atonality, shocks its listeners and thus invites them to look at the world outside its familiar terms. From Adorno's perspective, the music maintains "hostility towards the administered society" ("Music and New Music" 263) and a "rebellion against the illusion implicit in such second nature" ("Commodity Music" 2). Contrary to the communicative impulse, art should have no unifying organization (neither *thesis* nor *nomos*) but should have a disruptive one: authentic art highlights human destruction to redeem its more positive productive drive. Disoriented by the artwork, the individual is forced to either reject the piece or to think beyond the socially cultivated collective identification. Establishing an almost Herculean task for the artist, Adorno suggests that authentic artworks express "the fullest experience of horror, and there is scarcely anyone, except Schoenberg or Picasso, who can depend on himself to have the power to do this" (*Essays on Music* 200). Such art stimulates its audience into thinking without making overt arguments of its own. It is for this reason that Adorno favors Samuel Beckett to Bertolt Brecht and prefers the mysticism of Walter Benjamin to the realism of Georg Lukács.[35] Authentic culture creates the possibility of socioeconomic and political change without any specific advocacy. Not surprisingly, this desire to aesthetically interrupt organized affective experience also differentiates Adorno's account of political economy from Hayek's, which organizes society to maintain the unconscious transmission of affect.

Political Economy: Spontaneous Order of Competition or Spell of Monopoly Capitalism

Hayek worked with Ludwig Mises as the director of the Austrian Institute for Business Cycle Research in the late 1920s before joining the London School of Economics in 1931. During these early years he identified the problematic that motivated all his subsequent research: macroeconomics, such as the general theory put forward by Keynes, errs because it "substitutes quantitative for qualitative" analysis (*Prices and Production* 3).[36] Engaging the same economic turmoil as Keynes—declining profits, a dearth of private investment, and increased unemployment—Hayek concludes that mathematically based market intervention contributes to rather than solves these problems. Market disequilibrium, he says, occurs when the political sphere impedes the market's ability to communicate properly through prices. Prices organize individuals on a local scale so as to construct a global order; thus, we ought to "leave it to time to effect a permanent cure by the slow process of adopting the structure of production to the means available" (99). Viewed through an economic lens, the Keynes-Hayek debate represents a dispute over whether capitalism functions through crises in need of management or through a market order in need of free competition.[37] If we observe this iconic argument through the lens of affect, however, a different picture emerges. Keynes, for whom affect loses traction at large scales, relies on expert calculation to determine appropriate interventions, while Hayek, for whom affect (as long as it operates within a liberal political economy) scales up according to its own impersonal forces, subjugates policy deliberation to market forces.

In this way, Hayek's sensory order bolsters capitalism's three affective modalities by advancing Smith's own terms rather than, as Keynes does, by managing them. Whereas Smith argues that liberty inevitably opens individuals to capitalism, Hayek asserts that this liberty stems from market competition—a communicative process that displaces rhetorical deliberation from representative democracy onto the capitalist marketplace. Smith further suggests that individual participation and everyday activities facilitate capitalist identification. Hayek adds that even though this process is evolutionary, it is vulnerable to conscious manipulation and needs to be institutionalized through the rule of law. Finally, Smith claims that the equilibrium of supply and demand calibrates individual energies and activities. Hayek recuperates this idea by embracing Smith's invisible-hand metaphor, shedding its transcendental implications and aligning complex market order with the affective function of the individual mind writ large. Spontaneous order, Hayek's shorthand for the unconscious and impersonal organization of political economic reality, facilitates each of these affective modalities.

Functioning as a discovery process that communicates information and forms opinions through prices, market competition affectively predisposes individuals toward capitalism without any conscious determination on their part. Prices act as signals that tell people what they should and should not do. The mind's sensory order builds up dispositions for dealing with these signs so that individuals serve the collective order without being told how to behave.

This process has become so habitual that, according to Hayek, "the crucial function played by the conveying of information escapes the notice of persons" (*Fatal Conceit* 92). In this way, market competition organizes the "peaceful reconciliation of the divergent purposes" of society's many participants (*Mirage of Social Justice* 112). Using an explanation that parallels Aristotle's famous description of rhetoric as the art of discovering the available means of persuasion, Hayek contends that market competition is "first and foremost a discovery procedure" that enables us "to bring about the ideal state" (*Political Order of a Free People* 68, 66). This market process works through the mental osmosis of our sensory order in ways that are not deliberate or conscious; in fact, for Hayek, conscious deliberation is corrosive. One participates in capitalism simply by living as he or she sees fit and not by intellectually grappling with its political economic structures or their material implications.[38] Thus, the affective identification of Hayek's theory takes root within the rule of law (evolutionary habits) and weeds out legislative rule (deliberative intervention).

Protecting the economic results of liberalism, the evolutionary apex of ordered society, requires strict adherence to the rule of law.[39] Culled from tradition and habit, these rules provide a framework within which individuals act according to their own self-governing practices. People do not invent institutional rules; rather, they preserve the unwritten policies of successful exchange that guard against what Hayek labels our "fatal conceit"—the belief that humans can rationally determine future outcomes. As he says, we did not choose the rules of orderly society; on the contrary, "these constraints selected us: they enabled us to survive" (*Fatal Conceit* 14). Accordingly, policy should never be directed toward maintaining particular economic ends, but "towards securing an abstract overall order of such character that it will secure for the members the best chance of achieving their different and largely unknown particular ends" (*Mirage of Social Justice* 114). Ignorant of their motives and susceptible to socialist tendencies, individuals serve society best, says Hayek, when they follow capitalism's impersonal ordering mechanisms. For capitalism to work, individuals must concede their personal interests and their rational hubris to the impersonal forces of spontaneous order. In doing so, they will replace governmental regulation of the economy with the regulation of governing institutions by the rule of law that made such evolution possible in the first place.[40]

This means that capitalist equilibrium—the affective organization of individual energies—must be allowed to function spontaneously and not be bound to mathematical formulas. Hayek explains equilibrium as an imperfect approximation that balances over the long durée of history rather than at any given moment in time. As he says, economic equilibrium "is best conceived as the ongoing compatibility of various agents' plans" (*Pure Theory of Capital* xxvii).

Because the focus of this definition is on the coordination of individual actions over time, he emphasizes that "the continuance of a state of equilibrium in this sense is then not dependent on the objective data being consistent in an absolute sense" ("Economics and Knowledge" 41). Some economic processes, for instance, require the accumulation of wealth before they can be implemented within the marketplace. For that wealth to amass, it must be taken out of economic circulation, necessarily skewing mathematical equilibrium during that period.

Hayek bases this notion of equilibrium on Scottish Enlightenment philosophy, which maintains that the reasons for large-scale equilibrium are beyond human comprehension. Human consciousness can, however, recognize patterns of individual behavior that lead to successful economic order. In Hayek's understanding, this is what Adam Smith does when he theorizes embodied responses "in terms of the operation of feedback mechanisms by which he anticipated what we now know as cybernetics" (*Political Order of a Free People* 158). Without the help of neuroscience, Smith understood the affective foundation of modern civilization—our ability to unconsciously organize society through the mind's sensory order. More organic than mathematical, Smith's notion of economic equilibrium allows global capitalism the freedom to adapt and change along with the environment. By way of analogy, Hayek advocates for understanding equilibrium as "the course of a flowing stream, constantly adapting itself as a whole to changes in circumstances of which each participant can know only a small fraction" (159). The balance of production and consumption, like a flowing stream, ebbs and flows and yet perseveres through time. As an approximation of social and evolutionary behavior pegged to the circulation of affect, equilibrium cannot be captured, ordered, or maintained through conscious intervention. It works according to the impersonal, semi-autonomous forces of Smith's invisible hand.

Although Hayek clearly preserves the function of the invisible hand, he criticizes its transcendent implications. The attribution of anthropomorphic power leads back to the conclusion that equilibrium can be managed, which is fundamentally antagonistic to his theory. There is no external agent maintaining the capitalist order; on the contrary, capitalism self-regulates according to unconscious human negotiations. Of course, some explanation of this complex process is necessary, as the human mind requires abstractions to process what it cannot logically comprehend. Acknowledging that "custom and tradition, both non-rational adaptations to the environment, are more likely to guide group selection when supported by totem and taboo, or magical and religious beliefs," Hayek concedes a role for linguistic charms even if he disdains external causations (*Fatal Conceit* 136). Spontaneous order, a term that has become nearly as ubiquitous as Smith's invisible hand, serves this purpose: even though it is magical thinking, it explains and therefore reinforces the role of affect in organizing the political economic structure without the need for conscious manipulation.

Adorno also seeks spontaneous political economic action, but his definition of such action rests on significantly different theoretical grounds. Like Hayek, he asserts that an affect-like substance flows undetected throughout the material processes of decision making, but maintains that these processes require conscious participation from individuals to foster genuine political economic spontaneity. With his perspective threaded through Freudian instincts, Adorno is not unlike Veblen, who understood affect as biological instinct, the material environment as its constraint, and industrial labor as training workers into matter-of-fact thinkers who likely would refuse the ideological palliative of conspicuous consumption. Adorno, however, does not locate affect within the instincts. Instead, his theory of agency emerges from the circulation of a transcendental affective power through bodies that are psychologically enabled and constrained. Friction between the transcendental and the material produces an affective environment, and in the mid-twentieth century, that environment manifests as the spell of monopoly capitalism. Thus, his political economic critique focuses on the key historical changes of the era—a welfare state and mass-produced consumer goods—as well as their psychological effects on individual subjects, all of which must be consciously mediated through rational critique. To this end, Adorno contributes to Marxism with his theorization of the subject ("Reflections on Class Theory" 100; *Negative Dialectics* 111; *History and Freedom* 216). Underlying the Marxist tradition is a belief that alienation, stemming from the productive sphere, leads to a class consciousness that transforms workers into revolutionary subjects. Adorno explores how this process occurs: what, he asks, compels individuals to burst through the pervasive political economic ether and redirect history?

Adorno's investigation of the capitalist subject who, under the monopolistic spell, forgoes rational self-reflection in defense of the status quo offers a psychological twist on Marx's three affective modalities. It is not just the productive sphere of capitalism that closes down the possibilities of full species-being but the psychological weight of its totalizing dogma; it is not just rational identification that pulls individuals into capitalist practices but a group identification that displaces the egoistic individual capable of imagining the world differently; and it is not just physical exhaustion but also the ongoing psychological effort of conforming to the system that depletes individuals of the energy to resist it. In brief, Adorno suggests that monopoly capitalism psychologically drains individuals in addition to economically exploiting workers.

Adorno resists the all-encompassing political economic theories of both capitalism and communism. Capitalism reifies the transcendental world within its conception of the invisible hand, and communism reifies the material world with its valorization of the laboring subject. In both cases the "cosmic plan underlying everything which happens, must be called into question" (*Metaphysics* 121). As outlined earlier, Adorno subscribes to a theory of affect in which the transcendental ideal is in constant dialectical relationship to its material content. History proceeds through this dialectic and stalls within an unnatural perversion of its movement under the rubric of a positive directive. By transforming this fluid movement into a rigid power relation, grand narratives "conflate possibility and reality" (*History and Freedom* 68). As the source of possibility and its animating affect, the transcendental cannot be located in reality but neither can it be an external blueprint for that reality because the ideal is never fixed once and for all but evolves in dynamic relationship to the content of material existence. As Adorno says, the transcendental's "positive appearance can no more be stipulated for all future cognition than any one of the contents without which they do not exist, and with which they change" (*Negative Dialectics* 386). Sweeping political economic theories, overarching laws, and the ready-made application of theory as practice produce a closed reality from which nothing new is possible and thus disrupt the historical trajectory, which, he says, "stays alive, not despite its antagonism, but by means of it" (320).

The belief that unifying principles can organize all life experience hardens individuals within a linear, rather than dialectical, flow of affect. For Adorno, liberal capitalism offers the quintessential case of a "system from which all and everything follows" (Horkheimer and Adorno, *Dialectic of Enlightenment* 6). Completely organized—both consciously and unconsciously—"it fixes the transcendence of the unknown in relation to the known" (15) such that "nothing at all may remain outside" (16).[41] Self-responsibility, organization, the cult of efficiency, and a lack of emotion characterize the hardness of individuals under the system, who must repress the soft, recursive, and the nonconformist aspects of their personality (*Critical Models* 198–202). This is no less true under the bureaucratic onus of state communism, which he describes as "the inversion of Marxism into a static dogma deadened to its own contents" (13–14). So conceived, communism represents not the success of Marxism but its failure to theorize the political economic moment as dialectically animated and not fixed. Adorno constantly reminds readers that "Marx's reticence concerning theoretical recipes for praxis was hardly less than that concerning a positive description of classless society" (277). Moreover, he opposes frequent iterations of Marx's "Eleventh Thesis on Feuerbach"—that philosophers have only interpreted the world, while the point is to change it—with a call to interpret further the affective haze of contemporary capitalism.[42]

Adorno's vociferous critique of the culture industry, perhaps his strongest legacy, exemplifies the kind of self-reflective attitude one needs to break the affective loop of the regulated political economic world. Playing on Marx's well-known articulation of individuals transforming into characters upon entering the factory door, Adorno argues that "individuals are not merely character masks, agents of value in a supposedly separate economic sphere. Even where they think they have escaped the primacy of economics," they nevertheless "react under the compulsion of the universal" (*Negative Dialectics* 311). As discussed earlier, Marx theorized the possibility of capitalism's total subsumption (as opposed to its formal subsumption), but Adorno locates its reality in monopoly capitalism's process of integration ("Late Capitalism" 118). In the liberal era, an individual may have been able to reassert one's humanity during life outside of work; in the current stage of capitalism, however, individuals maintain their capitalist caricatures even in the most intimate parts of their lives and do so "without reservation" (117).[43] The welfare state converts people into perpetual appendages of capital (*Critical Models* 97) and the culture industry affirms this state of affairs until the underlying logic of capitalism becomes seared into their very existence as human beings (*Negative Dialectics* 354). This double absorption of politics and culture into economics so naturalizes the affective spell of capitalism that individuals no longer see value in consciously opposing its complete grip on their lives.

Because there is no outside to its sprawling system, a totalizing theory like capitalism requires collective thinking that psychologically transforms individuals into objects rather than subjects. Thus, says Adorno, capitalism extracts a psychological surplus value: "the social promise in the future for what we sacrifice in the present by performing our social roles calls for a psychological surplus value that is squeezed out of us in addition to the ordinary, economic one. The psychological surplus value is the difference between the expectation of happiness in the long term that is always being held out to us and the actual satisfaction that we generally receive" (*History and Freedom* 75). Just as we give more labor than the value that is returned in wages, so too do we put more psychic energy into sustaining the system than is returned to us as participants. Such an argument extends Marx's theory of exploitation, the extraction of surplus value in the productive sphere, into the sphere of everyday life and the movement of psychic value ("Reflections on Class Theory" 98). Adorno concludes that, in the monopoly era, "subjects of the economy are psychologically expropriated" and thus incapable of performing their role as individuals under the rubrics of liberal capitalism (Horkheimer and Adorno, *Dialectic of Enlightenment* 203).[44] Their individuality, as unconscious adaptation to the status quo, fails to produce anything outside of the iron cage of capitalism, and this is precisely because their conscious reflective capacities, their egoistic selves, have been lost to capitalism through its process of psychological appropriation.

The extension of capital throughout all life activities and the psychological exploitation of human beings requires active effort from individual subjects who, for Adorno, become less able to consciously intervene as revolutionary subjects the more they engage the capitalist system and conform to its unconscious affective spell.[45] The implementation of a total system produces the "loss of collective energies" needed for resistance because such energy goes to maintaining the system as it is, leaving none left for the construction of society as it might be (*Critical Models* 43). Instead of engaging the political and economic questions of the day, individuals turn to mass-produced entertainment, channeling their entire libidinal energies into consuming practices. As "the complement of alienated labour," consumer culture has colonized active participation for the benefit of capitalist repetition (*Minimum Moralia* 175). People, for instance, put a great deal of energy into being music fans. As Adorno sees it, "to become enthusiastic about what is forced upon you it is by no means enough to surrender yourself and toe the line passively. For people to be transformed into insects they require as much energy as might well suffice to transform them into human beings" ("Commodity Music Analyzed" 52). Individuals join the cultural craze du jour to avoid the dreaded anxiety of an existence in which one is no longer the active subject of his or her life. Doing so, consumers redirect their desire to act in the face of powerlessness from acts of willed resistance to acts of conformity.

Individuals pour their energies into maintaining capitalism in and out of the workplace, actively avoiding the realization that they are nothing more than exchangeable pieces in the chessboard of humanity, as Smith and Hayek claim. Thus, Adorno concludes in the lead article of a *Diogenes* special issue commemorating the 150th anniversary of Karl Marx's birth that "men are still the same as they were in Marx's analysis in the middle of the last century: 'appendages of machinery; no longer merely literally the workers who have to adapt themselves to the nature of the machines they serve, but in a much wider metaphorical sense, compelled as they are to adjust themselves and their very innermost feeling to the machinery of society, in which they must play their roles and to which they must shape themselves with no reservation'" ("Is Marx Obsolete?" 7). Stated differently, the funneling of affect throughout monopoly capitalism's administrative mechanisms means "the spell that the system exerts over men has become stronger" (8). But, contrary to the popular conception, Adorno's thinking is not defeatist: he contends that the affective energy used to maintain the economic status quo "bears a direct relation to the amount of potential, residing within the people, for moving in a different direction" ("Actuality of Philosophy" 976). To appropriate this energy for different political economic purposes, he argues, requires an aesthetic intervention that shocks habituated individuals out of their unconscious acquiescence in the same way a defibrillator shocks a static heart into beating once again.

The Unconscious versus the Self-Reflective

Hayek's interpretation of Adam Smith's sympathy as unconscious mimicry provides neurological evidence for what was previously only speculative and lays the groundwork for his rewriting of the invisible hand as spontaneous order. Reinforcing Smith and thus capitalism within his theory of tacit, unconscious behavior, Hayek seems to ask little of his audience—nothing more than their identification with the rules of capitalist prosperity—and offers them the possibility for much in return. Adorno's use of Marx, however, troubles his oppositional identification. Adorno refuses utopian thinking and asks individuals to engage in constant critique, using both conscious self-reflection and a spontaneous impulse that can only be found in individuals and not groups. In this way, he extends Marx's call for the *"ruthless criticism of everything existing"* without the valorization of species-being as the source of collective power (Marx, "For a Ruthless Criticism" 13). Even as these two scholars employ similar critical vocabulary (freedom, individualism, and spontaneity, for instance), their arguments are separated by the divide between Scottish Enlightenment thinking, which embraces the experiential, and German speculative thinking, which privileges the rational. This chasm is not an intellectual aporia but a concrete one whereby theorists of capital maintain hope for a thriving world with little to no conscious effort on the part of its participants and its critics beseech individuals to spend their leisure hours studying and then resisting the material embedded in such hope.

Viewed from the perspective of affect, Hayek strengthens the psychic bonds of capitalism while Adorno pulls them apart along with those of its communist alternative. Given these different affective investments, it should not be surprising that Hayek has turned into a cult figure of democracy (even though he often asserts antidemocratic positions), whereas Adorno cannot shake his reputation as a Mandarin intellectual redolent of elitism (Freedman and Lazarus). The value placed on individual human potential at the heart of Adorno's work evaporates under the searing heat of critique. His vast body of work appears to attack people as unthinking, clearing the way for Hayek's proposal, which ingeniously makes no value judgment of individual practices—critiquing only state power—and engenders ignorance (rather than thinking) as the foundational democratic value. These two reinterpretations set the path for the practical economic work of the late twentieth century and, ultimately, for the triumph of neoliberalism.

5 Milton Friedman and John Kenneth Galbraith

The Battle for Public and Political Influence

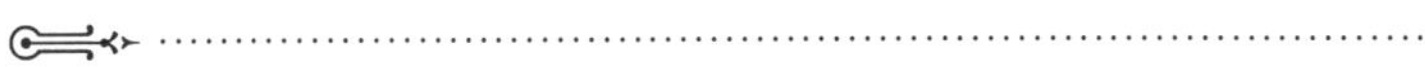

Galbraith broke important new ground in the relationship between politics and economics. He was the first celebrity economist . . . however, the pendulum is swinging to the right. First Milton Friedman at the University of Chicago, then many others.

Paul Krugman, *Peddling Prosperity*

Milton Friedman (1912–2006) died a short six months after long-time adversary and fellow "celebrity economist" John Kenneth Galbraith (1908–2006).[1] Although their economic visions differed significantly, their life stories intertwined remarkably. Friedman's parents emigrated from Eastern Europe at the close of the nineteenth century while Galbraith came to the United States from Canada to attend graduate school and never left. Friedman pursued his graduate study first at the University of Chicago and then at Columbia University, finishing coursework in 1934.[2] Galbraith earned his doctoral degree from the University of California, Berkeley, that same year and traveled across the country for a teaching position at Harvard. During the summer he took a job with the New Deal government, which he continued by commuting from Boston to Washington, D.C., each weekend. He assumed a full-time position within the Roosevelt administration in 1940 and soon was put in charge of the Office of Price Administration. Friedman also found employment with the federal government—first with the National Resources Committee and then with the National Bureau of Economic Research. This work, for each man, was foundational to his later economic writing. For Friedman, it honed his statistical skills, provided the data for his consumption analysis, and laid the groundwork for his monetary theory; for Galbraith, it offered practical evidence that government administration (wage and price controls as well as fiscal spending) had the ability to cultivate a stable economic playing field.

Separated in height by nearly one and a half feet and in ideology by the role of government intervention, the two men shared, in addition to parallel life trajectories, the core belief that economic theory should be put to the test of reality. Friedman mined statistical data from historical episodes, ones he equated with scientific experiments, to uncover economic reality. Through such analysis, he discovered that human behavior, particularly within nation-states, functions with a high degree of consistency and requires an equally consistent monetary policy to maintain market stability. Galbraith, on the other hand, located reality in his observations of contemporary political economy— a growing consumer culture, long-term planning, and the nascent transition from an industrial to a knowledge economy. These changes, he argued, reflected an entirely new corporatized marketplace. Although Friedman studied monetary events with a mathematical emphasis while Galbraith studied the corporation with an emphasis on power relations, both theorists assessed capitalism through an economic lens wiped clear of embodied affect. Consequently, contrary to earlier disputes explored in this book, the debate between Friedman and Galbraith is not about how well capitalism matches the affective capacities of human beings but about what reality best informs economic and political decision making.[3]

Indeed, both Friedman and Galbraith display a surprising disregard for the neophyte theories of affect in earlier economic models. Friedman, for instance, refers to Smith's *The Wealth of Nations* often, but rarely to *The Theory of Moral Sentiments* and never in a way that recognizes the transmission of sentiments among individuals as critical to a properly functioning economy; he acknowledges Keynes as an economist who advanced consumption theory but not as a theorist whose problematization of the circulation of affect at a global scale undergirded that theory; and while admiring Hayek's critique of socialism, he disregards his theory of the sensory order, which explains affective relations among individuals and their economic activities.[4] Following in the footsteps of these thinkers, Friedman is nonetheless constituted by the very theories he ignores. It is as though he absorbs their affective concepts—the sentiments, the dispositions, and their spontaneous order—so that he can translate them into a scientific program for macroeconomic management. In so doing, Friedman secures the free market by replacing Keynesian tax-and-spend programs with the more innocuous regulation of money.

Unlike Friedman, who transforms a philosophical (and affective) defense of capitalism into a scientific one, Galbraith simply dismisses earlier theories of capitalism along with their affective overtones. He argues, for instance, that "Smith's miscalculation was of man's capacity, perhaps with some social conditioning, for cooperation. He thought it negligible" ("The Founding Faith" 161). My reading of Smith indicates the contrary: individuals hold each other in check by sympathy, and capitalism aligns economics with this process. With no indication that he read *The Theory of Moral Sentiments*, Galbraith mistakenly condemns Smith for not espousing a larger framework for his economic theory. His criticism of Keynes—that he leaves Smith's notion of free-market exchange intact in a changed world—is similarly shortsighted. Keynes amends Smith's free market, adding macroeconomic interventions to repair the affective fissures of its global range. Although critics of capitalism appear throughout Galbraith's work, he finds them equally useless for the contemporary moment. He posits Marxism as outdated and limits the importance of Veblen, whom he read as a graduate student, to social criticism.[5] A valorization of the working body—the essence of species-being, for Marx, and the instinct to workmanship, for Veblen—lies at the heart of these critiques of capitalism; and yet it is conspicuously absent from Galbraith's reading of them.[6] Most egregious, however, is that with his emphasis on advertising and consumer culture, he fails to engage Adorno's cultural theory and its hope for spontaneous disruption stemming from both rational analysis and bodily compulsion. In short, Galbraith wrings the practical world of all its affective energies, leaving only reality and rhetoric in its place.

Friedman and Galbraith undoubtedly build economic theory along divergent paths; nevertheless, they both construct a picture of capitalism that matches the microeconomic practices of free individuals with the macroeconomic organization of interconnected nation-states. Friedman develops a macroeconomic theory consonant with a thriving free market of individual exchange. He attributes economic crises (whether depressionary or inflationary) to the Federal Reserve's monetary mismanagement and not to an internal glitch in the capitalist system.[7] This theory defines macroeconomics as monetarism and limits government regulation to its management. As long as the government maintains a slow and stable increase in the quantity of money, free-market activities will function properly and should be left undisturbed. Tackling the problem from a different angle, Galbraith tries "to develop a microeconomics consistent with the growing Keynesian trend in macro-economics" (Freedman 124). He starts with a belief in Keynesian-style government intervention and underscores the corporatization of the free market to legitimate those practices. The local marketplace attuned to individual needs, Galbraith contends, has been superseded by the modern corporation and the attendant rise of unionized labor, reconstituting microeconomic practices according to the interests of both corporate and union power. For him, this new microeconomic model authorizes the macroeconomic policies of government intervention.

Not surprisingly, alternative perspectives on affect inform these different economic pictures. Confining professional economics to the science of prediction, Friedman replaces bodily affect with a theory of rational choice supported by his famous *as if* doctrine and statistical evidence. He admits that his theory of rational choice—that individuals calculate margin utility in any given situation—does not accurately represent human behavior, arguing only that the statistical evidence makes it appear *as if* individuals act according to such rational calculations. As long as the scientific conclusions properly explain the past and predict the future, the representational accuracy of their underlying assumptions is irrelevant, says Friedman. Rather than establishing scientific legitimacy for decades of economic exploration as Friedman does, Galbraith asserts a new tradition by replacing the bodily affect implicit in Marx and Veblen's conception of human labor and in Adorno's notion of spontaneous disruption with a theory of power drained of its irrational forces. For Galbraith, power does not reside in sovereign individuals who determine market operations but in the technoculture—a vast and decentered organization of knowledge workers—that greatly influences consumer preferences and practices. This corporate control invites the countervailing power of unionization, resulting in two organizations locked in struggle without regard for the general social welfare. In this reality, one defined by power blocks and not individual relationships, the federal government offers the only means of intervention on behalf of the greater good.

Their alternative theories notwithstanding, these economists, as the epigraph to this chapter asserts, align along a shared desire to influence political decision making by means of the voting public. Selling a mass audience two versions of economic reality, they compete as what Paul Krugman calls "policy entrepreneurs" (*Peddling Prosperity* 12). In this policy marketplace, Friedman's neoliberal world, in which the individual remains the center of authority and decision making, has outsold and outlasted Galbraith's postindustrial world, in which corporations manipulate individual desire and governments rescue society with greater aesthetic and cultural attention. I suspect that Friedman's victory in this challenge may have less to do with statistical nuance and more to do with the fact that his rational-choice theory buries the affective circuitry of capitalism under the ground of a scientific landscape, whereas Galbraith builds the conspicuous circuitry of corporate power across a fairly barren world of individual relationships. More specifically, Friedman continues to work from the affective traditions of Smith, Keynes, and Hayek but does so under the guise of scientific rationality, whereas Galbraith dismisses all traces of affect in the political economic tradition as little more than magical thinking. As policy entrepreneurs marketing their theories to the same public, Friedman and Galbraith lodge nearly equivalent campaigns—regular magazine columns, best-selling books, television documentaries, and direct political advocacy. I contend that the reception of their economic positions largely reflects their different substitutes for affect: rational choice for Friedman and corporate power for Galbraith.

Affect: *As If* by Rational Choice or
the Imaginary World of Corporate Power

Friedman abandons social theory for mathematics as the undergirding frame-work of economics and thus reinvents capitalist affect as a scientific conclusion. He outlines his theory in a 1953 article, "Methodology of Positive Economics," which opposes positivism to both the art of economics (which he does not discuss) and normative economics.[8] As he explains it, normative economics exerts values and focuses on what *ought* to be the case, while positive econom-ics eschews values by simply addressing what *is* the case. Positive economics, he says, follows experiential evidence, mathematical operations, and logical coherence to the values and policies they indicate. Mirroring those in "the physical sciences," the economic positivist must find historical episodes that serve as controlled experiments (4).[9] He or she studies carefully chosen histori-cal data to abstract the essential features that explain a past event and help determine policy for future events. Of course, Friedman acknowledges that myriad complex components make up any given historical situation; thus, this method must decipher the meaningful components from the less important ones. These meaningful components, the one's that offer predictive value, do not necessarily reflect reality as we observe it. Indeed, Friedman balks at those who critique the unrealistic assumptions of his economic theory: "the relevant question to ask about the 'assumptions' of a theory is not whether they are de-scriptively 'realistic,' for they never are, but whether they are sufficiently good approximations for the purpose in hand" (15). Positive economics predicts real outcomes *as if* its abstracted features—algorithms and equations—influence financial behaviors and not because people consciously behave according to these formulas. Without an explanation for why people behave as they do, he nonetheless asserts that individual behavior produces perfect market equilib-rium *as if* individuals were rationally calculating every move.

Friedman relies on two examples to illustrate the function of this *as if* doc-trine. First, he says that a leaf positions itself "*as if* it knew the physical laws determining the amount of sunlight that would be received in various posi-tions" (19) even though leaves clearly "do not 'deliberate' or consciously 'seek,' have not been to school and learned the relevant laws of science" that inform their placement (20). Similarly, he says, a successful billiard player executes "shots *as if* he knew the complicated mathematical formulas" (21). These ex-amples, though obviously different, highlight a phenomenon Friedman takes for granted: important information takes place through unconscious and em-bodied participation in one's environment. To emphasize, he asserts that "the result achieved by purely passive adaptation to external circumstances is the same as the result that would be achieved by deliberate accommodation to them" (20). He goes on to say that if optimal outcomes emerge within the proper environment even, perhaps especially, when the processes by which those results arise are left unexplored, then "it is only a short step from these examples to the economic hypothesis that under a wide range of circumstances individual firms behave as if they were seeking to rationally maximize their expected returns" (21). Ground zero of Friedman's economic theory, rational choice assumes, but does not account for how, the tacit behavior of individuals and corporations naturally seeks to maximize economic returns.[10]

A shorthand proposition for the predictive power of economic science, rational-choice theory acts as a placeholder for unconscious affective processes. Friedman recognizes that neither individuals nor businesses "literally solve the system of simultaneous equations in terms of which the mathematical economist finds it convenient to express" his or her conclusions (22). Moreover, he offers no explanation for the actual processes by which individuals make decisions, which he relegates to the work of philosophy. Using mathematical calculations and statistical enumerations, his positive economic method brands the *as if* by rational-choice theory with a scientific ethos and pulls the classical tradition into the world of quantitative authority that had, until then, been dominated by Keynesianism. The objective predictive power of this analysis enables Friedman to reframe capitalism as an economic science rather than a moral or psychological theory. Stated differently, economic positivism substitutes the invisible-hand metaphor for another—people and firms behave *as if* by rational choice—and does so with the professional gravitas of a neutral scientific method.

Just as the invisible hand gives Smith a single overarching explanation of capitalism, rational-choice theory allows Friedman to unite diverse phenomena under the umbrella of a single scientific practice.[11] In fact, this method becomes so all encompassing that Friedman eventually positions the entire economic field under its banner of neutrality. The economic discipline, he says, uses scientific analysis of historical events to abstract causal components and predict future outcomes. It does not evaluate those components and their processes. As such, economic disputes "do not reflect differences in value judgments, but differences in positive economic analysis" ("Value Judgments" 86). In this way, rational choice establishes the noncoercive nature of capitalism—people never participate in an economic exchange unless it benefits them, and they always do so to maximize that benefit—as a mathematical certainty and not a value to be defended or a sociological capacity to be elucidated. Coming to the same conclusion as Smith and Hayek, Friedman is adamant that market economies evolve through "the spontaneous and voluntary cooperation of individual human beings and need not be imposed or constructed or legislated by philosopher-kings" (92). Free-market activities invite participation, negotiate divergent interests, and produce social coherency without any outside imposition. This self-regulating ecology can only be thrown into crisis by government intervention, and yet Friedman maintains a role for government in the production, exchange, and circulation of money. This unexpected government endorsement, too, can be explained by Friedman's appropriation of affect within scientific positivism.

Although Friedman espouses a macroeconomic role for governments just as Keynes does, two quite different rationales inform these positions. For Keynes, individuals are affectively compelled through their embodied participation with others, but that affective power weakens as it travels through national and international boundaries. Government intervention consciously fills the gaps left in the wake of affect's global circulation. According to Friedman's analysis, the Keynesian solution for governments to correct microeconomic miscommunications through direct market intervention distorts economic activities that would otherwise act *as if* by rational choice, regardless of scale. Microeconomic behaviors should always and everywhere be left to an unadulterated marketplace as evidenced by statistical data. Delimiting economics to this positivist methodology allows Friedman to capture affect within an *as if* doctrine for individual activities without accounting for the process that ensures its foundational rationality. Using this same scientific method, he is able to advocate for monetary intervention without admitting any limits, contradictions, or flaws in the affective flows of individual behavior. From Friedman's perspective, the reality of his theoretical assumptions— affect moves through individual and business activities but not governmental operations—is irrelevant to the scientific work of economics.[12] This scientific focus serves his need to simultaneously leave microeconomics free of government intervention and allow government regulation of monetary flows. Such a bivalent conclusion cannot be accomplished within an embodied social theory, and thus the integrity of Friedman's entire political economic doctrine hinges on the degree to which he scientifically appropriates the terms of debate.

Whereas Friedman colonizes the classical tradition of affect within his scientific method, Galbraith disentangles himself from the critical tradition of affect by opposing it to observed reality. Consigning affect to a form of crowd psychology that promotes mindless mimicry rather than reasoned action, he characterizes unthinking behavior as a dangerous eruption from normal relations. At the same time that he critiques the affectively motivated conformity among individuals as not grounded in reality, he establishes corporate power as a foundational reality. An increasing part of business activity, he contends, takes place within a small number of large corporations, all with the ability to override free-market constraints. Instead of being responsive to sovereign consumers as small businesses must, these corporations assert power over the individual. According to Galbraith's theory, individuals act rationally except when enchanted by the lure of speculative schemes or under overt corporate power. Unlike earlier critiques of capitalism, this theory offers no energetic replacement for these negative affective situations. The only antidote appears to be rational deliberation and the use of government resources.

Affect, for Galbraith, unequivocally emerges as the irrational underbelly of market speculation and not its rational functioning. Operating in extraordinary times, affect produces unrealistic expectations deracinated from the real world of market relations. Under its spell, the masses collectively replace reality with fantasy and thus have no basis on which to properly assess their situation. The frenzied stock market activities precipitating the 1929 crash illuminate this mass escape from reality. As he tells it, the crash was "the product of the free choice and decision of hundreds of thousands of individuals. The latter were not led to the slaughter. They were impelled to it by the seminal lunacy which has always seized people" (*Great Crash* 4). Galbraith gestures toward an affective pull or alignment among individuals but paints it in negative hues and positions it against reason: people act properly when under their own reason and improperly when under an affective spell. During speculative booms, he says, people choose "not to be persuaded of the reality of things but to find excuses for escaping into the new world of fantasy" (17). He underscores individual agency in seeking such a fantasy, but argues that once inside the fantasy, individuals are emptied of their capacity for clear thinking. Speculation, he concludes, "buys up, in a very real way, the intelligence of those involved" (*Short History* 5). Galbraith cannot embrace the unconscious world of affective persuasion—or the *as if* doctrine—because it represents, for him, the abdication of good, conscious decision making. The unconscious energies that pull one person's decision toward another's function, from his perspective, on behalf of myth rather than reality.

While affect constructs a world of make-believe during moments of high speculation, a similar haze distorts the everyday world of capitalist practices. This world functions according to the false assumption that everyone—businesses, both big and small, and people, whether rich or poor—abides by the same rules of market competition. Galbraith expresses his dismay with this make-believe in *American Capitalism,* which argues that the contemporary marketplace reflects a two-tiered system in which competition suffers at the hands of corporate power. He contends that a single free-market theory conceals the different realities with which small businesses and large corporations contend.[13] The fact that corporations have amassed enough power to supersede the rules of market competition goes unrecognized within the "economic theology" of microeconomic theory (*American Capitalism* 18). The imagined world is one of free-market competition, while the real world functions through corporate power. Galbraith claims that the free-market model of competition, although it accurately reflected the nineteenth-century world, does not hold up in the world of these large corporations. Unlike a small business, "the large corporation can have significant power over the prices it charges, over the prices it pays, even over the mind of the consumer whose wants and tastes it partly synthesizes" (7). Corporations, without overt collusion, administer production and prices according to their internal dynamics and not necessarily in relationship to consumer demand. In a rather ominous tone, he announces that "the American is controlled, livelihood and soul, by the large corporation" (116).[14] Against this danger of mass manipulation, Galbraith matter-of-factly asserts that reality can be gleaned from observing contemporary corporate power.

Corporate power, he claims, functions primarily through identification, which manifests in two forms. The first type of identification takes place between consumers and the corporate products forged by the fictional world of advertising; the second constructs employees loyal to their workplaces by means of an increasingly dispersed organization that both enables greater worker autonomy and provides a feedback mechanism whereby workers can influence the corporation. As Galbraith sees it, the decentralized corporate structure requires individuals to collaborate with a range of subgroups all attempting to achieve specific outcomes. Through this creative synergy, "the individual finds himself attracted or compelled by [the organization's] goals" (*New Industrial State* 149). Having downgraded unconscious compulsion to the world of make-believe, Galbraith cannot theorize this identification as the embodied energy circulating among and thereby animating these employees and their projects. Contrary to such an affective explanation, he conjectures that "identification is a psychological phenomenon" that "works not on the body but on the mind" (327, 330). Although this description comes close to other discussions of affect, its move away from embodiment separates his theory of power from the theories of his predecessors, leaving a cartography of accountability but few proactive possibilities other than reasoned analysis.

Not surprisingly, Galbraith theorizes how corporations—and other large organizations—use identification to compel individuals but does not offer a productive counter-power for individual agents. In *The Anatomy of Power,* for instance, he claims that contemporary power does not operate through compulsion (associated with the agricultural world) nor pecuniary incentive (as does industrial capitalism) but through identification or "conditioned power" (23). In a rough sense, he equates the power of identification with commodification. Like those who theorize the ideological work of commodities, he notes that the effectiveness of conditioned power resides in the fact that "neither those exercising [power] nor those subject to it need always be aware that it is being exerted" (24). He goes on to say that this "unnoticed—taken for granted" power works through identification with cultural products and the repetition of their importance within the media as well as educational, religious, and familial organizations (29, 30–34).[15] Rather than focusing exclusively on consumer society, Galbraith uses the politician as his crucial example. A politician, he says, is "adept at identifying himself with the conditioned will of the crowd and identifying for the crowd its own purposes" (45). This is not simply a matter of locating agreement, but of coalescing around a shared identification so that "his constituency agrees, on some matters, to accept *his* will" (45). Political power, he claims, depends on convincing the masses "to accept his solutions to their problems, his path to their goals" (46). In short, identification empowers organizations—whether political, religious, or corporate— to impose their will on individuals who nonetheless view themselves as free agentive individuals.

Using one of the prime modalities of affect (identification), Galbraith positions himself to enter an ongoing evolution in the interpretation of capitalist power; unfortunately, he does not exploit that positioning because of two critical errors. First, he seems to write under the mistaken assumption that he is the first critic of capitalism to take power relations seriously, and so he fails to build on the important cultural theory of Marx and Marxists. Second, and perhaps more disabling, he harbors an impoverished understanding of unconscious persuasion (operating through corporate power or cultural myth) that represents it negatively in relationship to conscious, real-world deliberation. Trapped within a fiction-reality binary, Galbraith misses the opportunity—one Friedman takes full advantage of—for building new capitalist identifications capable of large-scale public persuasion.

Language: Cultivating a New Worldview or Waiting for the World to Change

From the 1960s through the 1980s, Milton Friedman was the quintessential public intellectual, advocating strongly for a host of political policies consonant with his overarching economic philosophy. He frequented radio programs, wrote a triweekly column in *Newsweek* from 1966 to 1984, aired his PBS documentary to an extraordinary three million viewers, and published, with his wife, three popular economic books.[16] Friedman attributes this interventionist tendency to his experiences at the University of Chicago. As he recounts in his memoirs, "informal discussions with colleagues and friends stimulated a greater [political] interest, which was reinforced by Friedrich Hayek's powerful book *The Road to Serfdom,* by my attendance at the first meeting of the Mont Pèlerin Society in 1947, and by discussions with Hayek after he joined the university faculty in 1950" (Friedman and Friedman, *Two Lucky*

People 333).[17] Hayek, who so significantly influenced Friedman, felt strongly that one must persuade fellow economists along with the class of professional communicators who would, in turn, influence wider public opinion; he did not believe that economists should engage in direct public persuasion. Obviously, Friedman adapted the advice of this mentor as he bypassed professional communicators and addressed the public with a homegrown style that won him acolytes across the globe. This policy advocacy, however, was never far removed from his rising academic reputation.

Like Hayek, Friedman contends that an economist should be grounded in his professional field: "the task of the professional economist is surely first to persuade his fellow economists and only when something of a professional consensus has been established, to tender advice to the public at large" (*Dollars and Deficits* 4). And yet he offers an important qualification: one cannot wait until full consensus emerges because public sentiment will calcify around current opinion, creating a barrier against future counter appeals (5). In perfect alignment with this viewpoint, Friedman funnels his persuasive efforts toward cultivating a new economic worldview so as to preclude the hardening of the welfare state. He clearly insists that such overarching opinion—what Hayek characterizes as an unconscious ordering system—needs to be introduced, nurtured, and brought to fruition before concrete political change can emerge. In the marketplace, he explains, "an entrepreneur can experiment with a new innovation without first persuading the public," but "in the political process, an entrepreneur must first get elected in order to be in a position to innovate. To get elected, he must persuade the public in advance" (8). From this particular perspective, Friedman's job is to alter public opinion so that the politicians, whom he also advises, will be elected into positions whereby they can adapt the political terrain to better fit with the requirements of free-market capitalism.[18]

Asserting the same definition of opinion as Hayek, Freidman accepts that individual decisions emerge from unconscious worldviews. People work *as if* they rationally weighed evidence according to the rules of that worldview, but they do so automatically and without thinking. Therefore, one first needs to change the all-encompassing structure of opinion so that one can later persuade people to make policy changes consonant with that structure. According to Friedman, contemporary 1951 society, awash in Cold War anxiety and entering an inflationary period, provided an opportunity for a major shift in economic thinking. In proselytizing terms, his "Neo-Liberalism and its Prospects" declares that "it behooves us to make it clear to one and all what that faith is" (2).[19] Although articulated as a faith, he betrays few doubts that his political agenda—the privatization of government services, the deregulation of corporate activity, and the elimination of international trade barriers—constitutes anything but the certain blueprint for future prosperity. Neoliberalism, as he explains it, stresses "the fundamental importance of the individual" but substitutes "for the nineteenth century goal of laissez-faire as a means to this end, the goal of competitive order" (3). So defined, the neoliberal state cannot intervene in market operations; however, it does have the obligation to ensure that such operations proceed according to the rules of free exchange. Although Friedman later drops the term neoliberalism, he consistently promotes this doctrine to encourage buy-in for his lifelong political work.

As indicated in this early treatise, historical crises offer the *kairotic* opportunity for political change, but the policies driving those changes will not acquire legitimacy among the populace unless they match its taken-for-granted worldview. Within this conception of persuasion, his popular work primes the pump of popular opinion and introduces potential solutions until the economic chaos of the 1970s presents the possibility for structural change. The preface to his 1962 *Capitalism and Freedom,* his first popular book, makes this mission clear, asserting that "only a crisis—actual or perceived—produces real change. When that crisis occurs the actions that are taken depend on the ideas lying around. That, I believe, is our basic function: to develop alternatives to existing policies, to keep them alive and available until the politically impossible becomes politically inevitable" (xiv).[20] In many ways, Freidman's persistent public advocacy sustains the livelihood of his views until history enables them to become the dominant opinion. Once that happens, myriad political changes that were earlier deemed impossible become feasible. "The intellectual climate of opinion," he says, "determines the unthinking preconditions of most people and their leaders, their conditioned reflexes to one course or action of another" (285). Accordingly, Friedman consciously seeks to undermine the climate of opinion sustaining the welfare state and replace it with a new one (the neoliberal state) under the belief that individuals will eventually adopt it as their own unconscious decision-making apparatus.

The *Free to Choose* documentary and its accompanying book represent Friedman's most successful advocacy of that worldview. This project enabled the public to accommodate specific governing changes within a particular schema of the world and how it works. According to Friedman, Robert Chitester, the libertarian-leaning general manager of a PBS station in Erie, Pennsylvania, explicitly designed the documentary to spread free-market ideas and counter the purportedly collectivist doctrine of Galbraith's recent BBC program.[21] Funded entirely through private donations so as to maintain full independence, the group employed only those people who shared its political agenda. A letter from businessman–turned–TV producer Anthony Jay to Friedman describes that agenda as making "a whole new audience, hundreds of thousands—perhaps millions—of reasonably intelligent laymen, suddenly think in a new way" (*Two Lucky People* 481). Friedman was an obvious choice as host. His economic ideas aligned with the new way of thinking advocated by businessmen, but more important, he employed a well-recognized knack for persuasion. True to this reputation, Friedman immediately understood the television medium as distinct from print or radio and assigned himself the role of "a guest" in someone's home, whose job was simply to "converse" (483). He insisted on speaking extemporaneously and on complementing his lectures with dynamic group discussions. The success of the show propelled its accompanying book onto the best-seller lists, popularized his neoliberal philosophy, and opened the door to direct political maneuvering within the newly constituted Reagan administration.[22]

Clearly, Friedman was an expert speaker working from instinct rather than instruction.[23] Without theorizing rhetorical practice, he maintained a two-pronged principle. A real or imagined historical crisis must be exploited; before that can happen, one must prepare the way by cultivating a new climate of opinion through which people can instinctually embrace a ready-made program of policy changes. There is little room in this theory for rational persuasion without a complementary worldview and the correct *kairotic* moment. Only historical events predispose individuals to consider structural change, but the economist, as policy entrepreneur, needs to prepare them for that moment.

Also preparing for this opportunity was Kenneth Galbraith, who viewed unconscious opinion, like Friedman's neoliberalism, as an obstacle to rational public debate. In Galbraith's view, political persuasion must engage reality as distinct from opinion about that reality. Thus, he unveiled what he believed to be the truth of corporate power as fundamentally different from free-market ideology. From his perspective, the process by which corporations exert power is the same one by which they promote the myth of free markets—advertising. An advertisement places "a compelling image of the product in the mind of the consumer. To this [the consumer] responds more or less automatically" (*New Industrial State* 337). Although advertising simultaneously sells consumer goods and an outdated sense of market autonomy, its persuasive efforts actually undermine the free-market structure. With brand-loyal customers who respond by habit, corporations no longer adjust prices according to the rules of supply and demand; still, individuals believe they are exerting their own free choice in an open market. Corporations, according to Galbraith, use advertising to create strong identifications between individuals and specific consumer products as well as between individuals and the market economy more generally. This free-market imagination gradually becomes a "surrogate for the reality" (*Economics and the Public Purpose* 7). His persuasive goal is to distinguish between reality and its surrogate so that individuals might better understand and eventually combat corporate power.

However, like Friedman, Galbraith contends that the stronghold of identification does not loosen through logical argumentation alone. Inundated with consumer products, advertisements, and a plethora of competing information, the contemporary individual develops a coping strategy for negotiating the world: he or she disregards the vast majority of information (*New Industrial State* 336). As a consequence of this lack of engagement, which to Galbraith is a rational decision in the face of an oversaturated discursive field, individuals operate according to their psychologically constructed and often taken-for-granted motivations. Returning to his thesis on corporate power, Galbraith proposes that these motivations are crafted through corporate mythology. The anachronistic free-market doctrine, he suggests, works on the consumer mind and "serves the evangelizing instinct" as does a "rite" or a "ritual" (*Affluent Society* 10). Its repetition calls the free market into being and maintains its applicability as a structuring apparatus for understanding the world. Just as Friedman seeks to replace the welfare state with the neoliberal state, Galbraith seeks to replace belief in free-market fiction with cognizance of the reality of corporate power, but because he refuses to offer another organizing myth, his desired transition becomes impossible without the slow-baking process of historical change.

Staging the debate according to true and false worldviews, Galbraith concedes that economic change must wait until historical events run too far afield from the surrogate reality built up around the idea of market freedom. Buoyed by a consumer identification that insulates it from sound argument, market ideology will only be susceptible to "the march of events" (11). Moreover, only those historical events that impose substantive costs on people will challenge conventional wisdom and open the door to perceiving reality. As Galbraith puts it, "pain or even modest discomfort is better for persuasion than more abstract argument" (*Economics and the Public Purpose* 223). The persuasive capacity of a historical event stems from its ability to provoke individuals with a particularly troubling reality that conflicts with their operating fantasy. Thus, further economic initiatives, he says, are "unlikely to be authorized in the future except in the aftermath of disaster" (*Affluent Society* 154). When that happens, there must be a ready doctrine that "will have only crystallized in words what the events have made clear" (12). For Galbraith, as for Friedman, disruptive events persuade best. Unlike Friedman, however, he offers no plan to change public opinion in advance of those events. Thus, the publicly minded economist must wait for history to catch up to his or her analysis of real-world problems.

There is no place in this model for subverting one conventional wisdom (a belief held so deeply that it becomes immune to reason) with another, and so Galbraith lodges his intervention at a surface level, stressing both reality versus mythology and clarity versus confusion. This strategy, although generally applicable, boils down to a host of rhetorical platitudes. As Galbraith says, "the real test of a writer is whether he remains with a difficult subject until he has thought through not only the problem but also its exposition" ("Language of Economics" 33).[24] Such exposition combines reasoned analysis with lively prose that clarifies the analysis to others. This requires time. Indeed, Galbraith claims that the hours logged during his own writing process enable him to offer practical advice: a writer must "go to his or her typewriter every morning and stay there regardless of the seeming results" ("Writing, Typing, and Economics" 2).[25] He further counsels that the initial attempt at writing often produces "a very primitive thing" because "first drafts are deeply flawed by the need to combine composition with thought. Each later draft is less demanding in this regard. Hence the writing can be better" (2). With revision, a writer can construct not only clear causal claims but do so within a language that brings them to life for the reader. Such writing, he counsels, must never be "devoid of humor" and should not rely too much on equations and models ("Language of Economics" 29). The reality of many economic processes, like the persuasive power of identification, cannot be quantified and is "not easily adapted to the simplifications of mathematics and symbolic logic" (*New Industrial State* 153). In short, careful writing should be neither mechanical nor abstract but should illuminate reality in an effort to displace mythology.

Although good economic writing takes this form for the general public, it requires a different skill set when addressing fellow economists. According to Galbraith, the requirement that one must "master difficult models, including ones for which mathematical competence is required, is a highly useful screening device" ("Language of Economics" 41). Nonetheless, this gatekeeping strategy, as well as a hierarchy of prestige that positions practical economics, such as his own, on the lowest rung of the academic ladder, prevents many economists from offering public advice in clear prose style. In a revealing footnote to this discussion of disciplinary conventions, Galbraith claims that relying on mathematics leads "to the atrophy of judgment and intuition which are indispensable for real solutions and, on occasion, leads also to the habit of mind which simply excludes the mathematically inconvenient factors from consideration" (41). Aside from condemning the willful avoidance of evidence, he bemoans a lack of independent economic thinking. He never explains what that means, but the combination of judgment and intuition suggests a notion of spontaneity in the sense put forth by Adorno—reasoned thinking that emerges through bodily compulsion.[26] In this way, Galbraith hints at a positive affective moment in economic thinking that opposes the negative affect of corporate power. However, he offers no elaboration of this point, much less a method for producing such thinking, indicating that the intellectual heavy lifting should be left to the few who are privileged enough to possess the capacity for economic intuition and the time to develop it into sound prose. Indeed, the affectively inspired individual missing from Galbraith's persuasive theory is also absent from both his and Friedman's economic theories as they focus on their respective versions of reality.

Political Economy: Intervention in the Quantity of Money or the Quality of Life

For Friedman, the psychosocial world of affect functions beyond the realm of logical prediction and is, therefore, not the proper object of investigation for economic science. Instead, his economic theory focuses on a number of quantifiable characteristics that replace affective functions. To be specific, the ability to open markets and individuals for capitalist activities depends on the quantity of money and not the circulation of affect; identification with capitalist practices requires mathematical analysis and statistical regressions rather than affective alliances and embodied mimicry; and the increase or decrease of market energies (the supply-and-demand curve) does not operate automatically through the transmission of affective energies but through structural changes, creating a delay or lag that can be built into policy initiatives.[27] Even as his methodology zeros in on quantifiable objects, the residue of capitalism's affective tradition nevertheless follows Friedman's economic theory as it appropriates Keynesianism on behalf of Chicago School neoliberalism.[28]

Friedman pulls macroeconomics into the Chicago School's free-market theory by claiming an implicit and unbroken tradition for dealing with the aggregate economy that does not involve government intervention. *Studies in the Quantity Theory of Money,* a 1956 collection of articles by Friedman and his students, articulates monetary theory as a macroeconomic tradition discarded by Keynesians but kept alive within the Chicago School. In his lead article, "The Quantity Theory of Money—A Restatement," Friedman characterizes this Chicago School tradition as an overall economic vision; it is not, he says, "a rigid system, an unchangeable orthodoxy, but a way of looking at things" (3). As he explains it, this general approach emphasizes both the microeconomics of price theory and the macroeconomic theory of monetarism. According to Friedman's historical account, this economic linkage emerged in tandem with economics itself, but it was Irving Fischer who provided the first modern equation for the taken-for-granted relationship between the quantity of money and prices. Fischer's formula, MV=PT, asserts that the amount of money in circulation equals the average price of goods being exchanged. His equation, however, does not tell us which one of its factors—the amount of money or the average price—functions causally on the others.[29] According to Friedman's narrative, Keynes attempts a solution to this question of causality but is unsuccessful because he mischaracterizes monetary demand as a psychological "will-o'-the-wisp, shifting erratically and unpredictably with every rumor and expectation" and incorrectly claims that monetary supply produces inconsistent results (16). Ultimately, monetarism, for Keynes, presents an economic dead end, and thus he abandons it in favor of fiscal policy. Friedman's return to monetary theory attempts to correct Keynesianism by asserting that monetary demand is, in fact, highly stable.

To make this argument, Friedman converts Fisher's equation into a function of the demand for money and shifts the data set from nominal income to real income. As he sees it, money is not simply a medium of exchange; it is also "one way of holding wealth" with its own demand function: people desire a given amount of money just as they desire a specific house or a particular portfolio of stocks (4). Like everything else, the demand for money rests "on the maximization of utility function defined in terms of 'real' magnitudes" (10). Decisions about how much savings one needs calculate according to the amount of goods and services money can acquire. By focusing on real values, monetary demand emerges as a constant, but in a "more sophisticated form"— real values do not simply equate to dollar values but to what those dollars, in general and on average, can purchase (21). If the data is adjusted for this relationship between a dollar amount and the average "basket of goods" it can acquire, then the aggregate of national savings in relationship to the overall quantity of money in circulation stabilizes.[30] Using this economic framework, Friedman's theory begins to reorient macroeconomics toward the regulation of the quantity of money and away from the regulation of market activities.

Published the following year, *A Theory of Consumption Function* continues this economic agenda by engaging Keynesianism in its home field of consumption studies. The theoretical linchpin that authorizes Keynesian fiscal intervention is the assumption that as income increases, a proportionally larger share of it goes into savings. These additional savings represent, for Keynes, money that is not reinvested in the economy. Consequently, as a society's wealth increases, it becomes susceptible to a lack of investment that cannot be stimulated through monetary policy. Even with low interest rates and an increased supply of money, individuals may not choose to invest, believing that if interest rates go up, their money will be locked into less remunerative obligations. Friedman admits that empirical data confirms Keynes's consumption function: savings do appear to increase with income, and thus capitalist societies run the risk of reoccurring crises. The Keynesian function, however, relies on annual income, which, from Friedman's perspective, amounts to a flawed data set: the economy regulates according to real rather than nominal values. As a rule, he argues, people do not consume based on an income at a given time (temporary or nominal income) but on income conceived over a lifetime—what he calls permanent or real income (*Theory of the Consumption Function* 28). For instance, when an individual buys a house or starts a retirement account, he or she is doing so with an eye toward lifelong income, assets, and debts and not the dollar amount of one's annual salary for that year.

With different terms of analysis, Friedman constructs a consumption function that contradicts the Keynesian assertion that increased wealth leads to increased savings and stalls economic productivity. According to this new consumption function, "the ratio of savings to income is independent of the size of permanent income but dependent on interest rates; relative importance of property versus nonproperty wealth"; and on "tastes and preference for consumption versus additional wealth" (26).[31] To emphasize, there is no correlation between individual savings and annual income. In the aggregate, savings depend on the quantity of money in circulation; in the individual case, it depends on a rational choice derived from the cost-benefit calculation of various assets as well as personal preference.

Friedman completes this tour-de-force revision of macroeconomics in his "The Counter-Revolution in Monetary Theory." This 1970 lecture explicitly positions monetarism as a Chicago School tradition that supplants four decades of Keynesianism with a reinvigorated macroeconomic worldview. In the process of economic evolution, Friedman says, a counterrevolution "produces a situation that has some similarity to the initial one but is also strongly influenced by the intervening revolution. That is certainly true of monetarism, which has benefited much from Keynes's work" (65).[32] In accordance with this view, Friedman's counterrevolution reasserts free-market capitalism, but it does so by replacing laissez-faire activities with the Keynesian belief that the government must ensure economic stability. Of course, Friedman does not accept the Keynesian tenet that stability requires state involvement in the marketplace. On the contrary, he maintains that such stability can be achieved through proper monetary policy while leaving the microeconomic field untouched. In the spirit of Hayek, Friedman offers an explanation that successfully shifts blame for economic crises from capitalism to its mismanagement by the federal government: economic problems emerge from erratic Federal Reserve decisions and not from unwieldy affective contagions. By first reasserting the importance of monetary theory and then dismantling the Keynesian critique, Friedman reframes macroeconomics from fiscal intervention (tax-and-spend initiatives) to Federal Reserve policies that replace the uncertainty of affect with the certainty of rational choice theory.

From the perspective of monetarism, economic instability results exclusively from government intervention. As Friedman puts it, the desire to hold money acts as a mathematical constant—people in any given country maintain a stable equilibrium between savings and the overall quantity of money.

Consequently, if the quantity of money increases, money holders will want to spend it. As people increase their spending, others will take this as a sign to expand production and increase employment. Eventually, this will send prices up, and the real amount of savings will recalibrate to the original equilibrium point but with inflated nominal values.[33] From this viewpoint, inconsistent Federal Reserve policies—which contracted the monetary supply to exacerbate the Great Depression and expanded the monetary supply in the 1970s to fuel inflation—disrupt supply-and-demand signals and prevent rational market operations. Freidman claims that government-imposed wage and price controls further "distort the price structure" (*Money Mischief* 226). What is needed is an unbroken circuit through which price signals may properly communicate supply-and-demand needs.[34] This cannot be left to chance (laissez-faire capitalism) but must be cultivated through proper government activities (neoliberal capitalism). If, for instance, the Federal Reserve expands the quantity of money at a consistent rate—Friedman advises 3–5 percent annually—then the market and those individuals operating within it will not mistake an increase in the quantity of money as an increased desire for a particular product ("Role of Monetary Policy" 16). Instead, they will build modest monetary expansion into their rational expectations. In this way, Friedman's monetary theory provides a scientifically compelling macroeconomic complement to the affectively driven microeconomic theory of free markets.

Unlike Friedman, Galbraith places the onus of postwar problems on corporations rather than on government. His theory rests not on abstracted statistical quantification but on observations about contemporary life. His major contributions, elaborated in books targeted for mass audiences, span two decades and include his so-called trilogy: *The Affluent Society* (1958), which suggests that the wealthy private sphere has impoverished the public sphere; *The New Industrial State* (1967), which discusses the shift in power away from the individual capitalist toward the more diffuse "technostructure" of knowledge workers; and *Economics and the Public Purpose* (1973), which contends that increased consumptive patterns require management and that this disproportionately falls on women, whom he labels the new "crypto-servant class." These books cover a wide range of material, but they do so while focusing on Galbraith's main theme: the classic free market has been replaced with a market dominated by the modern corporation, which exercises enormous power on individuals as well as on the larger society.[35] In this new world of corporate power, those dedicated to less income inequality, greater environmental health, and a more robust public sphere must intervene through the available political apparatuses. Because Galbraith has replaced affect with power and shed the traditional critics of capitalism, he is left with only one means—political power—by which to negotiate the consequences of capitalist production. The mantra of a government-fashioned quality of life that improves upon the one produced through corporate power becomes the unmistakable conclusion of his economic theory.

Coming to economics from a popular and normative perspective, as opposed to Friedman's disciplinary and positivist one, Galbraith paints an entirely different economic picture. As he sees it, Hayek's *Road to Serfdom* fueled a free-market revival that was emboldened by "an energetic group of evangelists and scholars" at the University of Chicago who helped circulate its doctrine (*Affluent Society* xi–xiv). As a consequence of these efforts, "the case for public spending became the case against freedom" (xvii). The *Affluent Society* represents Galbraith's conscious effort to counter this prohibition against government intervention. It argues that capitalism no longer functions according to the impersonal market forces described by Hayek and his Chicago School brethren. Instead, large corporations have amassed a great deal of power, enabling them to reverse the direction of influence from consumers who vote for products with their dollars to corporations that persuade individuals to embrace their preselected products.[36] He asserts, for instance, that the growing advertising industries "cannot be reconciled with the notion of independently determined desires, for their central function is to create desires—to bring into being wants that previously did not exist" (129). Given this revised sequence wherein corporations directly influence the lives of individuals, the argument against government intervention as impeding free-market agents appears, from Galbraith's perspective, quite thin.[37] The extent of corporate power not only justifies but in fact demands that the state work toward "the development of countervailing power" (133). In particular, he suggests that the federal government fund programs for the wellbeing of a public sphere that has not kept pace with the expanding productive sphere.

This argument considerably dampens the unquestioned enthusiasm of post–World War II production. As he sees it, the effort to increase production within an unlimited horizon produces an irrational belief that any increase in the gross national product reflects national wellbeing regardless of the specific products produced, their social value, or their environmental consequences (110). Galbraith contends that production "is not a goal which we pursue either comprehensively or even very thoughtfully" (112). The historically specific problem of affluent society is that it produces goods ad nauseam, cultivates new desires for those products through advertising, and then scrambles to provide the financial means by which consumers acquire those extra goods. Within this narrow focus, contemporary society fails to take account of the larger structures that provide the foundation for private life. Affluent society, he says, welcomes credit for "automobiles, vacuum cleaners, television sets, and wall-to-wall carpeting" but condemns debt for "schools, hospitals, libraries, museums, police and street-cleaning" (154). Obviously, this is not simply a descriptive assessment but a prescriptive one as well: Galbraith calls on government spending to construct a better quality of life than the one produced through the corporatized marketplace. He does not dispute that corporate capitalism has increased the material wellbeing of the average person, but he does question whether this plethora of material products creates a richer educational, cultural, and physical environment for the community at large. More specifically, he questions the belief that if left to its own devices, capitalist power will produce a world in which everyone prospers.

The New Industrial Society, Galbraith's next major book, highlights the extent of this corporate power by articulating the vast gulf between the corporate structure and the free-market model. Contemporary production, he says, has become increasingly complex. Spanning time and crossing distances, the production process encounters more uncertainty and risk than ever and thus requires planning to negotiate a labyrinth of potential dangers. This planning takes place throughout what he calls the technostructure of "organized intelligence" (*New Industrial Society* 60).[38] The modern corporation relies on technostructure as "an apparatus for group decision-making—for pooling and testing the information provided by numerous individuals to reach decisions that are beyond the knowledge of any one" (81). Corporate responsibility no longer lies with the individual entrepreneur nor with the stockholders, but is distributed across numerous professional knowledge workers. As power disappears into this nearly unmappable technostructure, it moves, he claims, beyond "the reach of social control" (110). Accountability is difficult to determine because "distinctions between those who make decisions and those who carry them out, and between employer and employee, are obscured by the technicians, scientists, market analysts, computer programmers, industrial stylists and other specialists" (276). This model efficiently assembles divergent expertise at the same time that it protects the corporation against outside pressure and thus structurally bolsters Galbraith's assertion that corporate power, operating above the citizenry, drives society.

The complex structure of the new industrial corporation allows it to control, rather than respond to, a host of external stimuli. Most obviously, it manages demand through the persuasive powers of advertising that creates "a loyal or automatic corps of customers" through "brand recognition" (214). Of course, technostructure spreads its messages through "ready access to communications media—press, television, radio" (313). But its true power emerges from a blitzkrieg of influence: one part of the organization bombards consumers with advertising across all media outlets, including highway billboards; another group develops financial tools to sell products on layaway; others negotiate long-term contracts that keep wages down; and still others lobby Congress to ensure favorable legislation. In this reality, he says, the modern corporation is "inextricably associated" with state planning (26). The quintessential example of this relationship can be found in the one area of government spending that Friedman, Hayek, and other Chicago economists endorse—defense contracts. The defense budget keeps afloat such obvious companies as Lockheed Martin as well as less obvious ones such as Goodrich and emerges from the designs of a dispersed technostructure rather than backroom deals between specific individuals (241). Weapons manufacturers and tire companies represent just two of the many businesses that are so deeply entwined within the national economic fabric that Galbraith deems them too big to fail. Because the interlacing character of corporate power cannot easily be located and brought to bear in the court of public opinion, he endorses the government as a counterpower capable of filling in the social gaps and cultural fissures left in the wake of this nearly ubiquitous corporate power.

Whereas *The New Industrial State* describes the tectonic changes in the productive sphere of corporate power, *Economics and the Public Purpose* explores the changes it has wrought in the consumptive sphere. In particular, Galbraith focuses on the fact that increased consumer products and services necessitate additional time and labor. Consumer society requires a generally unrecognized form of labor to deal with its vast array of goods: "the distribution of time between the various tasks associated with the household, children's education and entertainment, clothing, social life and other forms of consumption becomes an increasingly complex and demanding affair" (*Economics and the Public Purpose* 32). This management, he argues, falls on women as a consequence of what he labels the convenient social virtue. In his assessment, such consumer-driven labor "hitchhikes on [a woman's] sense of duty and her capacity for affection" (36) and, in so doing, persuades her that its remuneration exists as a "social virtue" and not as a monetary reward (77). Although not calculated in any economic matrices, the labor women put into organizing the household, its individuals, and their products and services literally enables the expanding productive sphere.[39] Galbraith calls on women to eschew this responsibility in order to construct a healthier private and public sphere in which their work is economically rewarded and their affective responsibilities are more evenly dispersed across society. The overarching goal here, as throughout his entire economic schema, is to recognize the myriad social changes that corporations forge and then to authorize governments to act as counteragents in the conscious construction of a better quality of life than the one enabled under the corporate marketplace. This realist approach to economic power falls flat in the face of Freidman's affectively derived economic science, which allows corporate capitalism to enlist government aid rather than conform to government regulation, underscoring the importance of affect in public debates about the capitalist political economy.

Affect, the Public Sphere, and the Future of Anticapitalist Persuasion

Friedman and Galbraith steered the economic conversation in a more public direction than the theorists discussed previously.[40] No doubt, this new public veneer of economic investigation reflects its historical moment. Friedman and Galbraith were professionally trained economists with intellectual identities that emerged in the Cold War years—a time dedicated to scientific investigation on behalf of capitalist agendas worldwide. As others have argued, the Cold War years moored the university to the government's domestic and international political economic efforts as never before, particularly within social science fields such as economics.[41] It is difficult to image how these two thinkers, housed in prestigious universities, could have escaped the pressures of this unique moment in the professionalization of economics. Yet, as recognizable figures who regularly published books and magazine articles and appeared on radio and television, they were more than a sign of their times. Friedman and Galbraith were celebrities as well as political insiders who believed that economic theory held the key to not only political economic questions but social and cultural concerns as well. In addition to advising politicians worldwide, Friedman advocated for national educational reform, Galbraith protested the Vietnam War, and they both addressed racial and gender equity. Crucially, as the breadth of issues assessed through an economic lens radically increased, the range of acceptable economic solutions significantly contracted.[42]

The dispute between Friedman and Galbraith represents the conversion of an ongoing economic discussion about capitalism's strengths and weakness into a much more pointed concern for how best to foster capitalism by hedging off its occasional economic hiccups. This signals a dramatic shift in the political economic conversation. Only a generation earlier, Veblen—located in the same Chicago School that became synonymous with Friedman's neoliberal doctrine—engaged Marxist theory as legitimate economic doctrine, publishing essays and book reviews in the in-house *Journal of Political Economy*, which later crusaded against Keynesianism as ill informed and dangerously anticapitalist. In this new era, reputable economists no longer critique the exploitation of workers (as Marx did); they no longer chastise owners for not understanding the production process of their own businesses (as Veblen did); and they no longer assert capitalism as a dehumanizing and anti-intellectual force (as Adorno did). Instead, they work to extend free-market practices into every nook and cranny of society and to position able capitalist subjects within these spaces. Milton Friedman undoubtedly emerged as the preeminent spokesperson of this carefully confined economic field.

At least some of Friedman's success stems from his ability to legitimate economics within a scientific worldview at the same time that he allowed the affective discourses of his predecessors—illustrated in their discussions of the invisible hand, the animal spirits, and the spontaneous order—to inform his positive method and its *as-if*-by-rational-choice doctrine. Attuned to this notion of affect, his advocacy work sought to instill an entirely new neoliberal faith. Galbraith, on the other hand, abandoned the affective theories of earlier critics of capitalism, relying solely on rational, disembodied, and supposedly more realistic persuasive tactics. He offered affectively bereft policies that failed to secure themselves within the prevailing worldview. From this perspective, it is entirely feasible that the public embraced Friedman because of his superior, though perhaps unconscious, mobilization of the affective aptitudes of individuals and groups.

For those not entirely captivated by the affective hold of capitalism, who feel instead that its political economic structures limit the possibilities of what Marx calls our species-being, Veblen names our instincts, and Adorno conceives of as our potential for spontaneous action, there is much to learn from Friedman, Hayek, Keynes, and Smith. We must take seriously precisely what Galbraith did not—the need to create a political economic vision of the world that balances the importance of rational analysis with nonrational human capacities. Such thinkers could, taking a cue from Freidman, initiate a counterrevolution against neoliberalism, chipping away slowly at its foundational faith and replacing it with another.[43] There is much practical rhetorical work to be done in this vein and much to be gained from it, but it does require a full-fledged vision of the world that Adorno and his fellow theoretical traveler Walter Benjamin cautions us to avoid.[44] If we heed their warning and do not wish to mirror capitalist apologists in their impressive coup d'état of human value on behalf of a predetermined economic doctrine, what else might be gleaned from these two and a half centuries of political economic debate? For me, the answer to that question—one that this book's investigation has inspired—points to a source whose theory of biopolitics lies at the margins throughout this study. Whether he intended this or not, Michel Foucault's late lectures on biopolitics as a regulating mode of power coupled with his lectures on *parrhesia* as a critical mode of resistance indicate an important rhetorical entry point for the critique of capitalism.

Conclusion

*Rhetoric, Biopolitics, and the Capacity
for Anticapitalist Agencies*

We cannot miss the rhetorical short-circuit on which the entire argument rests: no
longer does the theory interpret reality, but reality determines a theory that in turn
is destined to corroborate it. The response is announced even before the analysis is
begun: human beings cannot be other than what they have always been. Brought back
to its natural, innermost part, politics remains in the grip of biology without being able
to reply.

Roberto Esposito, *Bios*

People are continuously molded from above because they must be molded if the overall economic pattern is to be maintained, and the amount of energy that goes into this
process bears a direct relation to the amount of potential, residing within the people,
for moving in a different direction.

Theodor Adorno et al., *The Authoritarian Personality*

John Kenneth Galbraith's popular economics takes the wind out of the sails of anticapitalist criticism in large part because it characterizes unaccountable economic behavior as irrational, mythical, and spellbound. Dismissal of the affective behaviors that invisibly guide economic decision making leaves anticapitalist discourse bound to a false binary between the rational and the irrational. Procapitalist discourse escapes this bind because, for it, the market serves as the affective force corralling human behavior before and alongside rational decision making. Consequently, those who advocate on behalf of capitalism maintain a rhetorical edge through an all-encompassing theory that relies on the complex interactivity among physiological affects, social, political, and economic organizations, and the material and symbolic fields. This model, however, does not allow for conscious renegotiation of the realities produced from its interwoven biological, environmental, and discursive threads. The human being, it implies, is subject to (rather than author of) the market's governing rationality. Market theory's superior affective sensibility of various unconscious modes of communication immunizes it against criticism at the same time that it prevents substantive change: alternative practices go against a human nature that, although it evolves, cannot be other than it is. As Roberto Esposito describes it in the first epigraph to this chapter, capitalist political economy emerges through a "rhetorical short-circuit" that produces variations on an intractable mold.

Decades before Esposito theorized this biopolitical phenomenon, Theodor Adorno and his coauthors came to similar conclusions in *The Authoritarian Personality*. A collaboration between Berkeley psychologists and Frankfurt School theorists, this study locates agency within the biologically and culturally formed nature of an individual personality, which it defines as a potential "readiness" or "disposition to behave in certain ways" (7). It maintains that the capitalist political economic terrain links biological drives and impulses to market desires so fully that agentive powers manifest along a prescribed range of responses. As Adorno and his coauthors explain it, belief systems work through unconscious, bodily structures that delimit the meaning of future experiences (617). Biological drives route data along preformulated pathways, organizing new information according to predisposed belief systems, and there exists no easy way to counter the personality's conservative tendencies. Mandating different material encounters fails "to influence people who are largely characterized by the inability to have experiences" (973), and continual self-reflection impedes the "warmth and spontaneity" necessary to full participation in life's dynamic unfoldings (975). Yet, as they maintain in the second epigraph, this work of subjectification actively enlists individuals in the process of personality formation; thus, individuals possess the possibility for differently mobilizing those energies. This hopeful declaration notwithstanding, the authors remain silent on how individuals break free from current orienting structure to organize human energy along pathways different from the well-trodden capitalist ones.[1]

Although many contemporary theorists offer biopolitics as a site for reconstituting the relationship between life experience and political economic structures, they often fall into the same conundrum: they know life potential can be mobilized otherwise and still refuse to engage the question of how to activate that alternative capacity (Hardt and Negri; Esposito; Lazzarato). For instance, Esposito sees capitalism as a mobilization of human energy within the biopolitics of neoliberalism and argues that those who oppose it must counter with a biopower that stems from *communitas,* or an unstructured democracy of equals. He argues for a shift in the relationship between human-cultivated *bios* and political economic structures so that life potential frees itself from the biopolitics of capitalism and constitutes its own life power.[2] Fighting affect with affect, these theorists incorporate the somatic into the political economic. However, like the anticapitalist thinkers discussed in this book, they presume a collective potentiality lying dormant deep within individuals that only needs to be awakened for it to exert its full force. Because these theorists conceive human agency as an ontological capacity always ready at hand, there is no need to create this life-engendering power. Moreover, because this power functions autonomously, they provide no instructions for activating it. Picking up on this line of thinking, I contend that capitalism relies on a set of imagined values and relationships (ideology) just as much as it relies on a constructed set of bodily responses, intuitions, and instincts (affect). Therefore, anticapitalist discourse must learn to reconstitute people's conscious understandings as well as their natural instincts. In doing so, we will learn to activate different potentialities.

Michel Foucault's late lectures are foundational to this goal as he outlines embodied practices for building such agency rather than simply presuming its a priori existence. For Foucault, biopolitics—the imposed regulation of populations that are "free to choose" from among the capitalist smorgasbord of life patterns—organizes contemporary subjectivity within the needs of an evolving capitalist political economy. After exploring this contemporary power formation, he begins what he refers to as a "Greco-Latin trip" (*Courage of Truth* 2). In his last three annual lecture series, he mines the classical world for its cultivation of critical subjectivity, one capable of not only speaking truth to power but also of conceiving new possibilities in that speaking. This sojourn into the ancient world positions the physical body at the center of a complex matrix of knowledge, rhetoric, and social change aimed at producing spontaneous opposition. Offering a material constellation that operates through automated and unconscious communication, this production parallels market governmentality without abandoning rationality and its discursive terrain. From this perspective, these lectures inject a living dose of ontology into a capitalism critique that has suffered from an inferior affective sensibility. This conclusion uses Foucault to make two complementary claims. First, it argues that the biopolitics of neoliberalism function as a governing rationality to constitute individuals as spontaneous subjects of capitalist nature, dissolving their rationality into their instinctual desires. Second, it contends that Foucault's exploration of ancient *ethopoetic* practices provides insight into the construction of bodily dispositions that break with the biocultural circuits of capital. Such bodily training produces individuals capable of *parrhesiastic* speech acts that, in turn, have the power to reinvent the political economic sphere. Before turning to Foucault, however, I briefly outline the theoretical uptake of his late lectures on neoliberalism and biopolitics to better position my own intervention.

Neoliberalism, Biopolitics, and the Agentive Subject of Anticapitalist Discourse

Foucault's conceptualization of biopolitics emerges hand in hand with modern state capitalism. Indeed, his first mention of biopolitics maintains that "for capitalist society it is the biopolitical that is important before everything else" (qtd. in Esposito 27). From this 1974 comment onward, Foucault tracks modern power through biopolitical techniques. In this way, says Esposito, Foucault marks out a different thread of agency: he "uncovers in *bios* the concrete power from which [nature and history] originate and toward which they are directed" (29).[3] He asserts that modern life is the result of the interanimation of biological and cultural forces and defines biopolitics as the governing authority that regulates those forces. Governmentality, the term Foucault uses to describe the circulation of power among political structures and freely chosen individual behaviors, regulates this web of quasi-independent and yet networked relations.[4] Wendy Brown stresses four critical features of governmentality: first, it organizes individual and mass energies; second, it operates through multiple sites; third, it moves "through a range of invisible and non-accountable social powers"; and finally, it functions outside official political spaces (*Regulating Aversion* 81). In other words, modern power derives its exceptional strength from the fact that it operates unconsciously, in a variety of ways, and in spheres not traditionally associated with politics.[5] With governmentality, the binary opposition between state sovereignty and the citizen of rights disappears under the fog of multiple, indeterminate, and invisible power formations.

Those critical of Foucault's governmental phase, not surprisingly, tend to pose a shared concern, though variously manifested: he analyzes a terrain bereft of individual agency. For instance, although Esposito credits him with identifying *bios* as the source of power that moves throughout society, he bemoans the neglect of an affirmative biopower.[6] He claims that this lacuna emerges from Foucault's failure to theorize the notion of life: "despite describing the term analytically in its historical-institutional, economic, social and productive nervature, life remains, nevertheless, little problematized" (44). Several political theorists have taken issue with Foucauldian biopolitics on similar grounds. Notable among them are Wendy Brown and Jodi Dean, both of whom see the left as virtually paralyzed by neoliberal capitalism and hold this Foucauldian shift partially responsible for the situation.

In her much-anticipated book-length discussion of neoliberalism, *Undoing the Demos,* Brown adamantly opposes the invisible governmentality of contemporary capitalism, arguing that it eviscerates state politics, rational critique, and collective will. In her account, "neoliberalism transposes democratic political principles of justice into an economic idiom, transforms the state it-self into a manager of the nation on the model of a firm . . . and hollows out much of the substance of democratic citizenship" (35). Although Foucault de-scribes this process with prescience, he lacks, she says, human beings capable of responding to the situation. "There are subjects," Brown asserts, "but not *citizens* in Foucault's genealogies and theories of government, governmental-ity, and biopolitics" (74). Posing *homo politicus* as the antidote to *homo œco-nomicus*, Brown defines the politically constituted human as a rational subject who consciously opposes his or her self-interested instincts with the collective good and criticizes Foucault for abandoning this agent in his single-minded fo-cus on the political economic subject of capitalism.[7] Neoliberalism, she admits, "departs from the domain of agency and instead governs the subject through an external moral injunction—through demands emanating from an invisible elsewhere" (133). Unlike Foucault, she responds to this invisibility with a visi-ble agenda: the critic must map power relations, promote democratic agents, and foster a collective political body that speaks and acts on behalf of its own sovereignty.

Attributing the loss of anticapitalist agency to the economization of politi-cal discourse, Brown asserts democracy (public deliberation among rational agents) as the solution to neoliberalism. For her, political liberalism holds its own against economic liberalism except in the contemporary stage in which the economic and political spheres merge. In earlier market phases, she main-tains, political opposition "operated in a different lexical and semiotic register from capital," and that provided a platform through which "to limit capital-ist productions of value and market distributions" (208). In the contempo-rary moment, however, both neoliberal economics and excessive patriotism displace this active citizenship onto external authorities—the market or the state—which individuals passively follow. Freedom, in her view, stems from individuals who actively construct a different set of values. Consequently, she advocates political staples such as the sovereign subject, critical analysis, and collective action, arguing for the importance of humanities education to the reconstruction of a vibrant political space.[8]

Framing politics as a conscious choice to assert individual agency in the face of psychic state and market dependencies, these solutions do not ade-quately address the problem of embodied affect.[9] Brown reads classical politi-cal and economic liberalism through her habituation within political science scholarship, rational deliberation, and political engagement. This disposition reorients information within a liberal political framework significantly un-dermined by its inattention to nonconscious decision making. For instance, to defend the political sphere as the space of active individual and collective sov-ereignty, she elsewhere argues that "whereas classical liberalism articulated a distinction, and at times even a tension, among the criteria for individual moral, associational, and economic actions (hence the striking difference in tone, subject matter, and even prescriptions between Adam Smith's *The Wealth of Nations* and his *Theory of Moral Sentiments*), neoliberalism normatively constructs and interpellates individuals" (*Edgework* 42). The classical political subject, in this view, is capable of decoupling itself from economic interpellation, presumably through the humanities training she advocates. Such a reading, turns a blind eye toward sympathy as an affective process that undergirds Smith's theorization of the social, the political, and the economic. But, once we understand *The Theory of Moral Sentiments* as affectively aligned with *The Wealth of Nations,* the grounds for asserting the political sphere as a viable opposition to neoliberalism disappear. In this view, one Foucault gestures toward, liberalism itself, and not just its neoliberal variation, constitutes the problem of modern power as it supplants state authority with the processes of capitalist circulation.

More attuned to the thoroughgoing subjectification of neoliberalism, Jodi Dean views Brown's political agent as out of step with the communicative landscape of contemporary capitalism. From Dean's perspective, democratic values have been so thoroughly colonized by the political economic and discursive machinery of capitalism that humanistic values cannot straightforwardly assert their independence. Conservative appropriation of democratic terminology produces a kind of leftist mutism: "because our enemy has adopted our language, our ideals, we lack the ability to say what we want" (18). Arguments on behalf of humanist values—democratic cooperation, multicultural understanding, and economic sustainability, for instance—are equally deployed on behalf of and against capitalism. In such a situation, it is difficult to distinguish the way that anticapitalist arguments use democratic discourse from the ways that capitalist advocates do, and thus training in rhetorical deliberation loses its critical edge.

The predominance of digital communication further undermines an oppositional politics based solely on discourse. Contemporary capitalism encourages individuals to engage in discussion from the hermetic space of their homes, cars, and offices, instantly satisfying one's desire to participate in collective decision making. This digitalized deliberation circulates content, but it does not sufficiently elicit action; indeed, Dean believes that citizens funnel their energies into blogs, Facebook pages, and online petitions as a fetishistic substitute for political power. Assuming the powerful force of their technologically disseminated words, people feel themselves to be politically engaged; yet, economic problems—unemployment, unaffordable housing, and the skyrocketing costs of social services—remain structurally insulated from the torrent of outrage proliferated throughout cyberspace. This engagement not only assuages the guilt of inaction; it also produces a pleasure that satiates one's biological urge toward transgression.[10] Frequent and nearly immediate feedback bolsters one's sense of contribution, increasing the time one spends with technology and decreasing other potential activities.[11] For Dean, this loop is threaded through unconscious rather than conscious choice: biological drives to defy normative boundaries direct us toward online outlets that fulfill our needs. As she characterizes it, digital communication "enjoins subjects to develop our creative potential and cultivate our individuality" (*Democracy and Other Neoliberal Fantasies* 66). People, in this account, do not abdicate their citizenship roles. On the contrary, they actively and often fervently engage online discourse; however, this affectively rich terrain frequently lacks politically meaningful consequences.[12]

To emancipate leftist politics from the repetitive circuits of cultural, political, and economic neoliberalism, Dean focuses on the constitution of differently desiring bodies and not simply the production of different ideas. Political economic change, she contends, requires bodies that are affectively mobilized in different ways. For Dean, both capitalism and its opposition advocate a more just and ideal future. She, therefore, anchors the difference between these two agendas not in their values but in their modes of subjectification. Capitalism, she says, "interpellates bodies as individuals," while "communist desire can only be collective" (*Communist Horizon* 191). Anticapitalist politics requires "the deliberate and practical subordination of self in and to a collective communist will. This subordination requires discipline, work, and organization. It is a process carried out over time and through collective struggle. Indeed, it is active collective struggle that changes and reshapes desire from its individual (and for Lukács, bourgeois and reified) form into a common, collective one" (197). Collective struggle takes place in groups with bodies precariously gathered face-to-face in material spaces rather than in virtual terrains. In addition to making arguments, such collective action changes those bodies from ones governed by capitalist individualism to ones governed by a collective will. Emphasizing the importance of reconstituting bodily desire, Dean implicitly argues for what other theorists, following Foucault, call biopolitics.[13]

For such theorists, Foucault's discussion of biopolitics not only interrogates neoliberalism, it also positions the governmentality of life as a necessary component of anticapitalist politics. Its challenge is less ideological and structural than ontological: the production of subjects disposed toward alternative methods for navigating life events.[14] According to Terry Flew, for instance, Foucault's biopolitical lectures inquire into whether "the political left was as capable of such innovations in governmental practices and institutional frameworks" as were advocates of capitalism (35). Similarly, Michael Behrent suggests that Foucault's lectures on biopolitics identify the "constitutive shortcoming" of socialism in its failure to produce a mechanism that orients the freely determined actions of human populations (564). The left's emphasis on state power (welfare politics) and individual rights (democratic citizenship) falls short because it works within capitalist governmentality. Alternative political economic theories must construct their own biopolitics rather than borrow from or resist the existing model. Implicit in Foucault's lectures is a provocation to develop an anticapitalist governing structure—one that operates through unconscious, bodily modes of communication.

Foucault locates the persuasive power of modern political economy in the market's invisible vitality, or what I have been calling its circulation of affective energy. Breaking with tradition, he does not censure market thinking; instead, he consents to Smith's explanation of the market as an ordering mechanism that exceeds full human understanding. Accepting the invisible hand as a real power, Foucault characterizes it as a governmentality "that produces specific forms of life extending across circuits of production and consumption, affecting the individuation of milieus and, at the limits, the quality of the 'life of the spirit'—that is, subjectivity" (Terranova 249). This is not a state of nature in a transhistorical, static sense but a process of naturing nature, in the Spinozian sense. Social cooperation among human beings circulates life energy that orients and automates everyday activities, aligning bodies and their ambient environments with an evolving capitalist order. Because of previous bodily habituation (both as individuals and as a species) everyday activities unfold automatically. The process produces subjectivity—embodied human beings disposed toward particular actions and ideas—and it is this subjectivity that we have taken for granted as either an a priori fact of species-being or an a posteriori result of dangerous power structures. Foucault, however, challenges theorists to engage this formation of subjectivity through ongoing life practices.[15] Agency, he teaches us, exists as a continuous ontological becoming that must be crafted in the flesh.

Such Foucauldian subjectivity has a double formation but not one located within a binary grid of intelligibility.[16] Subjectivity arises from the matrices of power/knowledge—the subject constituted by power relationships, institutions, and discourse—as well as through ecological processes that orient and tune bodily materiality, pulling the pre-rhetorical within the purview of rhetoric. Those who oppose capitalism too often assert the market as an ideological shorthand for capitalist subjectification that must be opposed by different knowledges and alternative institutional practices. This position, though not untrue, fails to deal with the constitution of individuals capable of creating a different world rather than simply opposing one. In contrast, Foucault's work on biopolitics explains the importance of somatic processes to the maintenance of sociopolitical cooperation within the capitalist market, calling its critics to invent an alternative governmentality—what he calls a transactional reality. His final lectures add to this by exploring care of the self as the means by which individuals become critical subjects. These two sets of lectures can be seen as complementary: first, Foucault interrogates the affective milieu of capitalism; and second, he explores bodily constitution as the site for inventing an affective terrain suitable to anticapitalist politics.

Market Subjectivity: Biopolitics and the Capitalist Milieu

Foucault's first extended discussion of biopolitics appears in his March 17, 1976, public lecture at the Collège de France, inaugurating a multiyear exploration.[17] As he characterizes it, the modern state relies on institutional apparatuses of disciplinary power that cultivate useful bodies as well as state apparatuses that regulate heterogeneous populations of free individuals through biopolitical power.[18] Whereas disciplinary power works directly on bodies to mandate correct behavior, biopolitical power applies to "man-as-living-being" or "man-as-species" and uses statistical measurements to determine its operations (*Society Must Be Defended* 242–43). These statistics provide evidence for the biopolitical interventions that Foucault names "security mechanisms" (246). Thus, a host of numerical indices emerges with the modern state to monitor a population and calculate its best course of action. Health statistics, for example, indicate moments when a population's productivity risks dipping too low. Driven toward wealth making, nation-states began tracking illness because it "sapped the population's strength, shortened the working week, wasted energy, and cost money" (244). With these numbers at its disposal, the state can weigh the cost in lost production against the cost of treating illness to determine the threshold beyond which intervention becomes economically sound. In this and myriad other ways, the modern state surveys the populations to avoid interruption in the productive forces of capitalist society. On this point Foucault does not equivocate. Biopolitics, he declares, "was without question an indispensable element in the development of capitalism: the latter could not be possible without the controlled insertion of bodies into the machinery of production and the adjustment of the phenomena of population to economic processes" (*History of Sexuality* 140–41).

Although it emerged with capitalism, biopolitics, he says, has also been appropriated by socialist states. Such states employ biopolitical regulation differently, but, at a fundamental level, they have not "reexamined its basis or its modes of working" (*Society Must Be Defended* 261). Lying at the center of modern governmentality, the algorithmic regulation of uncertain and freely chosen but predictable biopolitical behaviors becomes the crucial site for both maintaining and revising the political economic organization of society. Implicitly entering a debate he explicitly eschews, Foucault contends that "what socialism lacks is not so much a theory of the state as a governmental reason, the definition of what a governmental rationality would be in socialism" (*Birth of Biopolitics* 91). This, Foucault continues, must be created on its own terms and not through adherence to any preconceived philosophy, whether about authentic species-being, commodity fetish, or rational deliberation (94). At stake in modern state formation, regardless of its political economic fidelities, is the overarching governing structure that manages productive populations of free individuals who nonetheless have pattered behaviors, predictable orientations, and regimented attunements.

Given its central importance to modern state power, it is little wonder that biopolitics becomes the focus of Foucault's public lectures for two successive years. Beginning with *Security, Territory, Population,* he argues that biopolitical power intervenes into the capitalist milieu so as to entice, rather than command, desiring bodies. Two important realities emerge alongside this governance: *civil society* as the milieu of free circulation and the *population* as the aggregate of freely choosing subjects. Foucault defines the modern milieu, what he later calls civil society, as the open space-time environment "in which circulation is carried out" (*Security, Territory, Population* 21). That circulation includes the movement of capitalist products, as well as the flow of human beings and the transmission of their social bonds. He stresses that the milieu and the population within it, although constructed, become the naturalized environmental and biological conductor of modern power. The milieu "functions as a nature in relation to a population that, while being woven from social and political relations, also functions as a species" (22). Targeting statistical variance, biopolitics maintains a close watch on this milieu and makes adjustments when necessary to optimize the population's freely chosen behaviors: it operates in the space of civil society and through desiring bodies but does not attempt to eliminate choice or normalize individual desire.[19] Biopolitics accounts for a population's activity and adjusts the field in which it operates to build the social edifice through which its desires properly circulate.

In this way the population emerges as both a political subject—one that follows its differentiated desires—and an object of political intervention.[20] Individually, this "new political personage" may act as it wishes; collectively, however, it must be corralled within acceptable ranges (67). "From one direction," Foucault argues, "population is the human species, and from another, it is what will be called the public" (75). As a public, the population has "opinions, ways of doing things, forms of behavior, customs, fears, prejudices, and requirements; it is what one gets a hold on through education, campaigns, and convictions" (75). This desiring subject maneuvers through the open milieu of the capitalist city-space and requires constant monitoring so that, viewed as a productive species, it "will work properly, in the right place, and on the right objects" (69). As a species, the population has birth rates, disease statistics, spending and savings habits, as well as life expectancies. The state manages these statistical occurrences through security apparatuses to produce an environment through which political economic stability emerges on its own and according to its own nature. Simultaneously a public with particular opinions and a species with anticipated average behaviors, the population acquires enormous importance. As Foucault sees it, the modern state has two entangled modes of power: the conscious manipulation of opinions that work on public bodies through the disciplinary power of institutions and the mobilization of desire through indirect biopolitical interventions into the milieu of civil society.

Biopolitics simultaneously presumes a desiring body and manipulates the terrain of that desire so that different choices fit together into a coherent whole. It does this through interventions that alter the milieu in such a way that an undesirable phenomenon is "corrected, compensated for, checked, and finally nullified" (40). The behavior is not eliminated, but matched by alternatives and thereby maintained within a numerically safe range. This new conception of government—one that has market subjectivity at its core—requires the "management of populations on the basis of the naturalness of their desires, and of the spontaneous production of the collective interest by desire" (73). No historical teleology, no world spirit, no primary antagonism underscores this natural spontaneity; on the contrary, it emerges from the concrete confluence of differently desiring bodies circulating in a free milieu. The population has a public facet wherein individuals exchange things and ideas that carry ideological messages (whether oblique or overt) and this ideologically grounded disciplinary power intersects with and becomes embedded in another form of power that tracks, calculates, and orients those bodies on behalf of the market regardless of ideological messaging.[21]

Biopolitical power works on the milieu to guide, incentivize, and enable the vast population and its freely chosen actions. The population, Foucault summarizes, is "the subject of needs and aspirations, but also the object of government manipulation," and thus it "is both aware of what it wants and unaware of what is being done to it" (105). In other words, biopolitical power sets the scene wherein free agents follow their self-determined goals. These agents know they are following ideologically crafted desires, but they do not fully recognize the way in which those desires are productively mobilized by the constantly adapted milieu through which they move. Because the modern state produces individuals free to pursue their own preferences, that state must take account of the population at all times—not to eliminate or directly intervene in those desires, but to regulate them through the constant reconstruction of the field in which they operate. The state observes, measures, and modifies in response to piecemeal population data, maintaining a biopolitical governance that remains ignorant of the political economic totality and exercises its power invisibly. Foucault spent the next year exploring this fundamental proposition, one emphasized by free-market economists from Smith to the present.

Birth of Biopolitics, which compiles the subsequent year's lectures, identifies the invisible hand of the market as the heart that circulates power throughout the interstitial veins of modern governmentality. More than a mere principle, the market turns sentient bodies into capitalist populations and social spaces into capitalist milieus. Foucault specifically locates the birth of biopolitical governance in the market's ability to produce the self-interested subjects of capitalism as individuals who follow their natural desires. As he says, by the mid-eighteenth century, "the market appeared as something that obeyed and had to obey 'natural', that is to say, spontaneous mechanisms" (31). The market has no choice but to fluctuate with supply and demand, responding to economic subjects who act in accordance with nature.[22] These individuals are free to act according to natural, instinctive, affective motivations because the state regulates and manages the entire population through "the principle of calculation" (65). As Foucault discussed the previous year, the modern state constantly intervenes in the open environment of individual and material activities to compel particular behaviors that then feed into spontaneous individual actions. The market, therefore, creates individuals who instinctually correspond to the needs of an evolving capitalist political economy through "the interplay of freedom and security" (65). In short, the political economic processes that sprout from the ground of civil society do not exist without governing apparatuses that evolve alongside an equally evolving human society and its calculated nature.

As a sequel to his genealogy of state power, Foucault's analysis of the capitalist market attributes agency to invisible ordering processes with the caveat that this power derives from the structural relations defining civil society and the embodied practices of those in its open environment. Biopolitics and its security measures enable capitalist political economic interests to acquire the felt quality of instinct: capitalism does not have a preexisting essence or ontology but creates one. Foucault underscores that capitalist principles like competition have a history: "competition is an essence. Competition is an *eidos.* Competition is a principle of formalization" (120). Capitalism, as a set of biologically intuited behaviors, "will only appear and produce its effects under certain conditions which have to be carefully and artificially constructed" (120). The essence of the market—what Smith famously labeled the invisible hand, Keynes characterized as the animal spirits, Hayek explained as the spontaneous cooperation among tacitly communicating subjects, and Friedman memorialized as rational choice—is, for Foucault, a manufactured ontology.[23] Because the capitalist milieu determines a market structure and enables certain affective circulations that habituate into automatic responses, it is able to invisibly manage its subjects through biopolitical interventions that modulate and direct the free flow of affect, and it does so with an always evolving and incomplete agenda.

According to Foucault, the twinning of invisibility and incompleteness as the hallmarks of biopolitical governmentality finds its clearest representation in Smith's invisible-hand metaphor. Smith establishes the market as the all-encompassing, gravity-like force that authorizes individuals to act in their own interests without regard to the interests of society at large. The capitalist marketplace, "founded on the unknowability of the totality of the process," forms the foundations for a civil society that works through similarly unknowable and invisible affective bonds. As Foucault explains it, "civil society is the concrete ensemble within which these ideal points, economic men, must be placed so that they can be appropriately managed" (297). So conceived, civil society is not a check on state power, as is traditionally conceived, but an invention whereby modern state power maintains authority over free subjects. Foucault turns to Adam Ferguson's treatise on civil society to describe the self-regulating relationships of the open milieu. In his reading of Ferguson, "what links individuals to each other in civil society is instinct, sentiment, and sympathy, it is the impulses of benevolence individuals feel for each other, but is also the loathing of others, repugnance for the misfortune of individuals" (301). Foucault concludes that "civil society serves as the medium of the economic bond" and sympathy serves as the connectivity that renders predictable its innumerable individual components (302). Although civil society and economic interests work together, there exists an underlying tension between them: civil society encourages local cooperation, whereas capitalist interests compel global competition. Smith's *The Wealth of Nations* resolves this tension through the invisible hand that nudges merchants toward safer and more familiar local investment, illustrating how the sympathetic impulse naturally checks capitalist greed.

Foucault ends his yearlong inquiry, however, by suggesting that this potential mismatch between the communitarian subjects of civil society and the interested subjects of economics has come of age in the neoliberal era. Sophisticated communication and transportation technologies have made global competition less risky, calibrating our natural, bodily instincts to the global marketplace. Yet, in this political economic moment, the structure of global competition does not adequately meet the needs of local populations, and so alternatives become imperative. Foucault locates the crucial site for anticapitalist intervention in those sympathetically driven actors of civil society and not the external, transcendental hand. In a revelatory comment, he asserts that civil society, rather than the free market, "secretes a power" that could be equated with "the motor of history" (305). Civil society, the space in which affect freely circulates, determines the instinctual actions of human subjects and marks biopolitical governmentality as the proper object for political economic opposition. Consequently, he implies that the missing link in the armature of oppositional politics is the ability to mobilize the power of human affect differently by addressing the dynamic relationship between intuitively-driven subjects freely operating in an open milieu and the persuasive quality of the milieu itself.

More than a simple fantasy made up of key discursive elements—the invisible hand, the animal spirits, spontaneous action, and rational choice—that can be ideologically interrogated and disabled, the market structures civil society as the capitalist milieu and cultivates its political subjects as naturally self-interested economic agents. If we want to reinvent civil society according to community-based interests, then we need to mobilize affect according to different governing circuits, ones aligned with collective rather than individual interests that, over time and through spontaneous circulation, produce different aggregate expectations. Foucault's final public lectures provide the theoretical groundwork for such a project. Focused on *ethopoetic* behavior and *parrhesiastic* speech, the last three annual lectures investigate the cultivation of a critical subjectivity with the capacity for reflexive truth-telling. In so doing, they also inspire the construction of individual instincts capable of an anticapitalist agency, a desire implicit in his biopolitical explorations.

Oppositional Subjectivity: *Ethopoesis* and the *Parrhesiastic* Life

The move from contemporary collective governance to Greco-Roman practices of individual governance marks an abrupt historical shift, and yet it remains focused on the same question that drives Foucault's biopolitical lectures: what is the relationship among power, subjectivity, and discourse? Whereas biopolitics reflects the indirect manipulation of predictable instinct-driven bodies, care of the self consciously realigns one's automated bodily responses so as to oppose institutional injustice through the eruption of *parrhesia* or courageous truth-telling. In *Hermeneutics of the Subject,* Foucault positions *epimeleia heautou,* or care of the self, as foundational to enlightenment. Taking oneself as an object of study and work, care of the self involves the "search, practice, and experience through which the subject carries out the necessary transformations on himself in order to have access to truth" (15). In this period, the famous imperative to know oneself—*gnothi seauton*—could not be carried out without an attendant transformation of subjectivity. This differs from the modern period in which knowledge production takes place without these embodied practices; one can indict others as corrupt from a platform forged through one's own corruption. As presidential candidate Donald Trump aptly acknowledged, he could shoot someone on highly trafficked Fifth Avenue and not lose a single vote. Although an outrageous assertion to many political commentators, it cuts to the quick of the break "between access to truth" (25) and "the requirement of the subject's transformation of himself and his being" (26).[24] Critical of this tendency, Foucault turns to the ancient Greco-Roman world because of its emphasis on the complex and malleable relationships among subject formation, bodily instinct, and truth. Whereas modern governmentality stems from invisible and uninterrogated desires, the subject of Foucault's final public lectures undergoes continuous embodied and mental exercises designed to create free individuals—ones capable of assessing, mobilizing, and reorienting the fleshly impulses of their experience in the world.[25]

Care of the self recognizes that individuals are enslaved to their preestablished passions, which must become the objects of analysis. This philosophical tradition engages an individual's "irrational impulse(s)" (98). Unlike the Platonic or Christian ascetic traditions, these bodily signals are not meant to be eliminated; ever present, they are experiences to be examined and directed. Impulses are irrational because they are ontologically prior to rational thought and not because they lack logic. Care of the self aims to cultivate a subject capable of interrupting the automatic relationship between stimulus and response in order to engage the world differently. Foucault asserts that these embodied practices craft the desiring self into an individual "capable of orienting the will, of appearing as the will's free, absolute, and permanent object and end" (133). Much like Adorno's negative dialectics, this work founds itself on refusal, never "allowing ourselves to be induced to make involuntary movement at the behest of or through the instigation of an external impulse" (207). So conceived, care of the self converts a subject enslaved to an inherited set of desires into a subject whose automatic bodily instincts align with his conscious beliefs through a practice Foucault calls "self-subjectivation" (214).

A lifelong vocation of deliberate subject formation, care of the self includes artificial challenges designed to reinvent one's instincts. Individuals learn to attune themselves to their bodily impulses and train themselves for different instincts. The desired control over bodily responses requires the ability to remain deeply focused amid the hustle and bustle of life's distractions, to endure unexpected emotional hardships, and to live a materially ascetic lifestyle. In partnership with a committed teacher, a student undergoes constant self-assessment and learns "techniques for concentrating thought" (418). He or she adopts bodily habits such as "sleeping on a pallet, wearing coarse clothes, eating little, and drinking water" (429). Moreover, this student engages in regular tasks aimed at bodily fortitude: walking through the busy marketplace without acknowledging its sights, sounds, and smells; sitting at a table filled with elaborate foods and only consuming a simple meal of water and bread; playing affectionately with one's child while reciting the truth that this beloved individual will die. In the aggregate, these practices are meant to cultivate a subject capable of self-governance.

Exercises in concentration, restraint, and physical endurance are the mechanisms by which individuals produce a subjectivity capable of engaging a situation beyond its imposed definitions and responses. One must practice turning away from expected, desired, automated responses until this ability to act contrary to expectations becomes perpetually "available and can be resorted to whenever the opportunity arises" (231).[26] In Foucault's reading, these *ethopoetic* activities transform the individual "into a free subject" (241) and cultivate the "boldness and courage, which enables him to stand firm not only against the many beliefs that others wish to impose on him, but also against life's dangers" (240). The process of self-subjectivation enables one to replace imposed instincts with self-constituted instincts. Viewed in tandem with his biopolitical lectures, one can see that cultural norms and daily practices discipline individuals into compliant subjects of their historical milieu, and care of the self makes conscious use of this process so that alternative actions will manifest "as if spontaneously" (323). Alternatives must be immediately available when needed. As Foucault says, "we must have it, so to speak, in our sinews. We must have it in such a way that we can actualize it immediately and without delay" (326). Foucault's self-subjectivation acknowledges the persuasive quality of instinctual drives and stresses the ability to harness, assess, and retrain those unconscious bodily drives. Care of the self reorients habits so that one's instincts are not enslaved to the normative sociopolitical and cultural matrices, but are self-fashioned according to a critical examination of the world.

Even the student's intellectual training is pegged to embodied conduct. For instance, a student listens to a teacher in absolute silence "without intervening, objecting, [or] giving his opinion" (341), all while holding one's body "as immobile as possible" (343). A student who interrupts relies too quickly on imposed instincts, and a moving body lacks concentration. Alternatively, a student who listens, reads, writes, and speaks within the constraints of the practice absorbs knowledge and allows a different instinct "to become a kind of habit for the body" (359). Ultimately, this physical and intellectual engagement with one's passions endows students with a "particular kind of rhetoric, or nonrhetorical rhetoric" that Foucault calls *parrhesia* (368).[27] For Foucault, an affect-like quality adheres to *parrhesia* insofar as the speaker's truth erupts spontaneously in the form of critique. Whereas traditional rhetoric works through identification, this practice intends to "throw the individual off balance" and "to force him to adopt a different mode of life by pushing and pulling him" (154). The *parrhesia* he endorses unfolds in the sphere of everyday life as opportunities arise.[28] Before discussing this radical variation of *parrhesia*, what Michael Hardt underscores as the militant life, Foucault traces its historical evolution in the following year's lectures.[29]

Foucault's lectures in *Government of Self and Others* discuss *parrhesia* as a benchmark for self-subjectivation: in becoming a *parrhesiastes*, one has achieved a form of autonomy from historical and cultural knowledge production. Extending his commentary from the previous year, he explains that the *parrhesiastes* engages in constant self-critique or what he calls an investigation into the "ontology of ourselves, of our present reality" (21).[30] Rather than assessing the truth content of a person's speech, Greco-Roman society assessed the orator's ethos, asking whether the speaker is someone whose embodied practices enable him or her first to determine and second to pronounce truth (Foucault, *Fearless Speech* 15). Of course, *parrhesia* has generic features. It generally occurs within an agonistic structure in which one speaks "the truth as quickly, loudly, and clearly as possible," and this "opens up a space of risk for the person who tells the truth" (*Government of Self* 54, 56). The speaker destabilizes his or her audience, creating an "an irruptive event" that becomes the condition for the possibility of change (63). Yet, as a discursive practice, *parrhesia* can emerge in ersatz form. One can claim to speak frankly for suasive effect; one can hedge against risk; one can speak for personal gain. Even if these cases presume to use *parrhesia*, the speaker in each is not a *parrhesiastes*. Tethered to embodied subject formation, the speech act derives its legitimacy from its ontological quality and not from its discursive structure—*parrhesia*, for Foucault, depends on a "mode of being" rather than a rhetorical form. Because these individuals engage in a lifelong training of their affective makeup, they become people whose bodily instincts compel them to stand up to oppression. By choosing this lifestyle, the subject conditions his or her being so that *parrhesia* bursts forth at particular moments without much (or any) internal deliberation or conscious will.

Foucault highlights this spontaneity in his extended discussion of Euripides's tragedy *Ion*. He stresses, for instance, a moment during which Creusa, the female protagonist, driven by sheer frustration, unexpectedly decries the god Apollo. Ion, the adult son of Apollo and Creusa, has been falsely identified as the son of her husband, Xuthus. Creusa spontaneously erupts with a scathing indictment of the god who raped her. She tells the truth about her child, at great personal risk, because she cannot bear further humiliation and not because of a carefully crafted strategy. Foucault says that this form of *parrhesia* emerges "through the clash of passions" (135). Driven by feelings of betrayal by social laws that compelled her to abandon her own child (conceived outside wedlock), but now require that she take in her husband's illegitimate child, she speaks a dangerous truth. Cognizant of the potential censure from Apollo, from her husband, and from the Athenian community, Creusa simply cannot constrain herself, and so she speaks the truth. Unlike a skilled rhetor, she does not choose this moment nor this audience. In fact, the absence of such conscious choices distinguishes *parrhesia* from a typical rhetorical situation. Of course, this instinctual truth-telling is not the only form of *parrhesia*.

If Creusa underscores the impassioned spontaneity of *parrhesia,* Ion represents the conscious will of its democratic modality. Once he discovers his maternal tie to Athens, Ion wishes to return to the city as a citizen with full political rights to speech so that he can ascend the ranks of power. According to Foucault, Euripedes uses Ion to found Athens on the twin pillars of democracy and *parrhesiastic* speech. This founding narrative, however, creates the possibility for both deserved and undeserved criticism, or good and bad *parrhesia*. It allows "the one who used an uneducated *parrēsia*, a *parrēsia* not indexed to the logos of reason and truth" to nonetheless ascend the political ranks by telling others what they want to hear (167). Discursive strategies aimed at moving particular audiences through flattery, bad *parrhesia* fuels "the deterioration of the relations between *parrēsia* and democracy" (173). To be clear, the problem Foucault identifies is not inherent in rhetorical practices (a good *parrhesiastes* uses rhetoric as well) but located in democratic structures: *isegoria*—the right to speak granted by the state—calls for *parrhesia* and yet does not require care of the self. This opens a door for the bad *parrhesiastes,* one who presumes to speak the truth without simultaneously submitting to a lifestyle that trains one in the intellectual discernment of truth and the courage to assert it under threat of blowback. Institutionalized democracy encourages free speaking, but does not demand that those speakers undergo the embodied practices of self-subjectivation; therefore, it both enables and threatens the power of truth-telling (184). From Foucault's perspective, *parrhesiastic* truth-telling requires adherence to a particular lifestyle designed to cultivate the kind of person who, like Creusa, spontaneously confronts injustice.

Although Foucault's analysis privileges the philosophical life over the political one, it does not valorize *logos* at the expense of *pathos*. Philosophical *parrhesia* self-consciously engages, embodies, and directs passions against the prevailing customs to establish differentiation, whereas political *parrhesia* (or rhetoric) strategically deploys speech according to commonplace norms so as to foster identification. Within sanctioned democratic spaces, a *parrhesiastes* may speak what he or she believes to be true but does so through historically and culturally cultivated instincts. A philosophical *parrhesiastes* differs because he or she speaks the truth in a way that interrupts and redirects those automatic responses. Foucault argues that a bad *parrhesiastes* understands unconscious desire and uses it to "guide the mass in the same direction as it desires it to go" (212). Good *parrhesia*, on the other hand, emerges only when taken-for-granted desires are themselves interrogated.[31] Such questioning requires a set of activities that bring philosophy into one's everyday existence to produce an antagonistic habituation with received knowledge so as to arrive at a critical perspective. The philosophical *parrhesiastes* constitutes oneself through *tribe*—a relationship of "friction" with both commonsense and erudite beliefs (251). A perpetual student, the true *parrhesiastes* struggles with conventional knowledge to arrive at different truths. Part of that struggle takes place through "the secret oil of the soul," or that element that spontaneously triggers actions apart from one's designed will (248). This training, fundamental to care of the self, recalibrates affective, bodily habituation so that will and flesh work together in the pursuit of new truths.

Too much emphasis on the impossible differentiation between authentic truth and rhetorical flourish risks missing the significance Foucault places on the *ethopoetic* rescripting of spontaneity alongside and in accordance with conscious decision making. The philosophical *parrhesia* Foucault valorizes cannot be understood by opposing it to rhetoric, though he often highlights this differentiation. Philosophy and rhetoric "are not just two techniques or two ways of speaking" (309); on the contrary, the differentiation at stake rests on "the mode of being peculiar to this or that discourse" (310). Foucault endorses a mode of being in which intellectual activity includes exercises designed to interrogate embodied instincts. This self-constructed modality endows the subject with the "capacity for free action" (310). More than the freedom to follow unexamined desires, *parrhesia* "owes its *dunamis* to the fact that it *springs* from the very being which speaks through it" (327). It demands an embodied instinct that is self-cultivated vis-à-vis constant testing and refinement. Critical thinking, at least for Foucault, requires coupling self-subjectivation activities with intellectual exercises so that the individual becomes a subject who is courageous enough to speak truth to power, bringing politics to bear on one's everyday life.

Up to this point, Foucault has problematized what he calls political *parrhesia* (founded in democratic city-states) and promoted philosophical *parrhesia* (illustrated within the Socratic-Platonic tradition). In the former, one speaks on behalf of the city-state but does so in a formal democratic structure that requires speakers to accept and valorize cultural commonplaces.[32] Because of this reliance on identification, it becomes structurally impossible to make "a full and positive use of *parrhesia* in democratic institutions" (40). Alternatively, the Socratic-Platonic tradition utilizes a physiological disidentification with community-based instincts to enable a different truth to emerge. This philosophical practice, however, corrals individual instinct within transcendental truths, delimiting its potential in a different way. Consequently, neither official democratic structures nor traditional philosophical training allow for "ethical differentiation" or radical change (64). Because political *parrhesia* grounds itself in identification, flattery, and persuasion while philosophical *parrhesia* premises itself on aligning individual *bios* with predetermined truths, these two modes of *parrhesia* produce variations on normalized practices but do not produce a different world. Consequently, in Foucault's reading, the golden age of *parrhesia* occurs in a third modality: the scandalous conduct of the Cynics. This form of *parrhesia* asserts that transformed subjects can create spaces for change through an unpredictable and antagonistic form of critique.

Foucault's final lectures, published as *The Courage of Truth*, explore this third variation of *parrhesia*, distinguishing it both from the work of political advocacy and the cultivation of subjects capable of leading a community according to idealized prescriptions. This lecture series begins and ends with the question of revolution. There is, for Foucault, a strong tie between the revolutionary life and the *parrhesiastic* one that can be located in a shared critical discourse. As he sees it, "revolutionary discourse plays the role of parrhesiastic discourse when it takes the form of a critique of existing society" (30). Such discourse, which he elsewhere characterizes as the rules defining what is and is not permissible, emerges from individuals self-cultivated in critical opposition to dominant cultural sentiments and not from individuals subjectified through state or party apparatuses.[33] Eschewing doctrine, these revolutionaries commit themselves to a lifestyle that "bears witness, breaks, and has to break with the conventions, habits, and values of society" (184).[34] The revolutionary fractures the production and reproduction of power relations through a lifestyle in which one's impulses align with his or her intellectual will in a spontaneous and aggressive critique of dominant society. So conceived, revolutionary discourse foregoes economic and social policies in favor of disruptive moments from which alternative practices might emerge.

These lectures highlight *parrhesia* as a specific formulation of the triangulation among subjectivity, knowledge, and power. The *parrhesiastes* develops subjectivity through care of the self, examines received truths, and does so from a position antagonistic to the privileged power formations.[35] One is not born a truth teller nor does one discover truth from a predetermined positionality; on the contrary, one becomes a truth teller through a life dedicated to capacitating oneself with the ability to parse out the truth and then proclaim that truth. This mode of *parrhesia* does not advocate a particular course of action but directs itself "towards *bios* as existence," or what Foucault calls "the aesthetics of existence" (161).[36] Its goal is to produce people compelled to confront injustice even at the risk of retribution, requiring a practice of everyday life that constantly adjusts one's knowledge, behavior, and instincts.[37]

This lifestyle focuses on praxis, and yet it "does not entitle [the *parrhesiastes*] to remain uneducated" (199). Rather than abandon the production of knowledge, it demands an enlarged education in which *bios* becomes "an *oeuvre* to be fashioned in all its possible perfection" (163).[38] Life becomes the object of study, and the body becomes an instrument to be tuned in atonal relationship to the ambient rhythms of normative culture. Truth tellers do not segregate themselves from others as experts but engage the world as its sociopolitical and economic critics. They do this at any moment and in any site that grabs their attention. What appears unpredictable, however, results from rigorous self-fashioning. Disciplined training enables the *parrhesiastes* to act as the spontaneous opposition to injustice even in the face of danger—challenging hypocrisies, complacencies, and normative practices so as to open up possibilities for change.

These individuals, exemplified best by the Cynics, perform this political function for all of humanity rather than on behalf of a particular community or for personal benefit. As Foucault sees it, the Cynics constitute *bios* as truth-telling by enacting a "form of existence as living scandal of the truth" (180). They take to the streets to discover and tell a truth that is not confined to one's individual life but must also exist "in their social life, their public and political life" (224). Such a life is "a sort of carnivalesque continuity," extending the Socratic/Platonic philosophy into the Roman empire (228).[39] Like Socrates, the Cynic provokes "people to condemn, reject, despise, and insult the very manifestation of what they accept" (230). Indeed, this critique attacks "the very way in which one lives" (234). Anyone, at any moment, may become the subject of the Cynic's derision. Working on the *bios* and in the everyday world, this practice resembles the Socratic/Platonic tradition in its aim to reconstitute subjectivities and yet differs from this tradition in that it is also intended to produce radically new sociopolitical structures and not simply better leaders.

Not only do Cynics engage in care of the self—the daily administration and recalibration of one's beliefs, instincts, and behaviors—they also have the further task of reinventing the sociopolitical norms of the community. Foucault explores the possibility of this social change by comparing Plato's philosopher king with the Cynic king. In *The Republic,* he says, Plato argues for arduous personal and intellectual training so that a leader can achieve "that ideal point where the philosopher will really be able to exercise a monarchy over others" (274).[40] The Cynics offer an alternative model. They assert themselves as kings—as leaders who need no political apparatus to exercise their authority. Contrary to the political king who requires pedigree (proper filial lines and educational training) to achieve political status and additional apparatuses (armies and counselors) to maintain authority, the Cynic audaciously asserts himself as king with no material resources or justification. Moreover, the Cynic is not identified with a particular city or nation, but establishes himself as king "for the whole of humanity" (280). This Cynic king battles the human vices that foster problematic institutions and customs. For a Cynic, politics "is not just a question of war and peace, of duties, taxes, and revenues in a city, but of happiness and misfortune, the freedom and slavery of the whole of humanity" (303). Such a life is not a choice, but a responsibility, a mission, a duty: alter one's fleshly impulses so that one is instinctually driven to confront injustice throughout the entire human experience.

Blending embodied spontaneity and conscious decision making, this *parrhesiastic* mode offers a reinvigorated notion of agency. The agency that founds the Cynic lifestyle is not a simple decision one makes like any other but a decision that is simultaneously made for and by the individual. For that decision to be made accurately, however, there must be affective as well as intellectual training. Or, as Foucault notes in his manuscript but does not say in his lecture, there must be "care of the self via its ethopoetic role" (338). The one who asserts him or herself as social critic, poking holes in standard practices so as to produce *kairotic* openings for change, must first be a self-critic willing to partake in the lifelong pursuit of self-subjectivation. Geared toward the production of alternative bodily instincts, such training has the potential not only to develop an anticapitalist agency, but also to produce a biopolitics suitable to an alternative political economic agenda.

Rhetoric, Affect, and an Anticapitalist Agency

Biopolitics, as the regulation of free citizens within capitalist democracies, provides a space for unknowability, uncertainty, and invention and yet delimits that space through the production and circulation of affective desires tethered to the political economic needs of capitalism. Anticapitalist discourse has not learned to disentangle these ties and produce equally free and dynamic alternative affective energies. Certainly, the anticapitalist theorists explored in this book—Marx, Veblen, Adorno, and Galbraith—critiqued the problematic ontological foundations in the prevalent market theory of their day. Indeed, many of them envisioned different ontologies—Marx's species-being, Veblen's instinct for workmanship, and Adorno's collusion of spontaneous action and rational reflection—but they did not articulate a program for the production of such embodied responses. They did not instruct us how to cultivate an artful life in antagonistic relationship to both capitalist knowledge and capitalist instincts. It is here that Foucault's lectures on ancient *parrhesiastic* practices has much to teach us about critical political economic discourse and the production of oppositional rhetoric more generally.

Rhetorical work aimed at countering dominant ideologies and the structures they enable must begin to take the production of affectively disposed bodies more seriously. We must engage in what Foucault calls a critical "ontology of ourselves" (*Government of Self* 21; "What Is Enlightenment?" 50). Without neglecting the important intellectual labor requisite to critical thinking, our scholarly efforts must extend into embodied practices. Critical rhetoricians must perform ideological analyses as James Aune, Dana Cloud, and others argue; but, we must also retrain our affective experiences to disrupt the circulation of nonconscious choices aligned with the very terrain we critique in our intellectual studies. The latter project requires that we pay attention to and assess the persuasive work of our bodily instincts so as to invent an alternative affective milieu in which to assert newly cultivated agencies, ones simultaneously empowered by our conscious and unconscious choices. Although critical affect studies have punctured the intellectual impasse of rhetorical and political economic theory, these studies often stop short of promoting alternative ontologies.[41] In part, this stems from a lack of clarity—and sometimes conflation—among affect, bodily sensation, and emotion.

Many interventions into the persuasive role of affect advocate conscious self-reflection on our emotional ties rather than the production of different bodily instincts. For instance, Dana Cloud and Kathleen Eaton Feyh offered "emotional fidelity" as a concept to note the practice whereby individuals "distinguish between ersatz identification and faithful collectivity" (313). Acknowledging the capacity for affect and emotion to sweep individuals into collective projects, they suggest that those tides can match one's material realities and rational beliefs just as they can forge false alignments. Therefore, they seek "a critical approach to emotion in rhetorical action" that requires participants to inquire into the strong pull of collective identification (314). This important intervention asks that we rationally reflect on both our material and emotional experiences in the world. However, because it does not acknowledge affect as a semiautonomous ontology motivating our bodily instincts, it fails to offer a method for reconstituting one's instincts beyond conscious self-reflection.

Like many others, Cloud and Feyh abbreviate the three concentric circles of affect—physiological energy, sensation, and emotion—into two levels. They define affect as "embodied desires and intensities" and emotion as "the product of organizing affect and bringing it, albeit incompletely, into social intelligibility" (301). In not differentiating the physical materiality of affect from sensation, they impede our ability to rewrite that affective material. From the perspective of this book, affect serves as a shorthand for an entire range of matter—the chemical and biological circulation of physical material—that cues our bodily experiences. Bodies respond to that matter—heart rates alter, glands secrete pheromones, temperatures change, muscles contract, skin viscosity tightens—and our conscious minds give meaning to it all. These are three distinct stages that need to be parsed out and engaged, a task not lost on neoliberal economists.

Behavioral economists since Gary Becker have explored these dual processes to explain rational decision making as automated decision making. As they tell the story, environmental stimuli prime the body, and bodily stimuli prime instinctual thinking.[42] For them, the stages of affect, sensation, and emotion reveal two moments of contact and thus two possibilities for intervention. First, there exists an ontological intervention that engages how bodily responses are triggered by material context and the unconscious intake of multiple, simultaneous signals; and, second, there is a rational/emotional response that can be critically assessed according to our standpoints. The first moment cannot be absorbed into the second as they are both materially and temporally distinct. Modeling themselves on capitalist advocates, critics of capitalism must learn to tackle these two processes by adding affective production to ideological interrogation.

Although misplaced within the ideological tradition, affect studies can contribute to the tradition of invention, allowing the rhetorical subject to be conceived as an object of its own becoming. Foucault's final lectures on *parrhesia* help us imagine the affective work required for the production of rhetorical subjects. He offers us a concrete, embodied glimpse into individuals who interrogate and self-consciously craft bodies through their response to external stimuli. From such practices emerge the possibility of critical thinking tethered to affective acumen. We cannot, I believe, presume the success of emotional fidelity without this embodied practice. Not only will this critical ontology of our selves revive anticapitalist discourse, but it also stands to propel a number of other oppositional movements that have been stymied by a biopolitical governmentality at odds with its critique. From this perspective, the importance of activist politics, from Occupy Wall Street to Black Lives Matter to the #Me Too Movement, lies less in their policy making and more in their subject making. Active participation in disruptive moments produce different bodies, different subjectivities, and different affective terrains. Such movement politics cultivate the possibility for an entirely different biopolitical governance, one that is neither innate nor simply a response to neoliberalism. Movement politics produces the possibility of a fundamentally altered world, one in which oppositional critiques become the spontaneous choice of diverse publics. As individuals cultivate different intuitive responses to their environments, they revise the affect circulating through and orienting the world and its inhabitant. Consequently, there is an accumulating process that, at some tipping point, alters sociopolitical and cultural thresholds for economic injustices. Once altered, the unconscious attunements among individuals and their milieu open up the rhetorical field to a range of as yet unexplored possibilities. If Smith's invisible hand of the market describes the productive attunement to capitalism's circulating affects, then oppositional subjectivities—ones designed specifically to interrupt and confront those visceral bodily cues—hold the key to a different pattern of affective governance.

Notes

Introduction

1. The tradition of autonomous Marxism can be traced to worker movements that grew out of Italy in the late 1960s. The founding essay for this movement is often linked to Mario Tronti's "Strategy of Refusal," originally published in 1966. See also Michael Hardt and Antonio Negri's *Empire* for a perspective on the social factory that aligns it with what they call "affective labor."

2. This three-part structure is employed by cognitive psychologist Silvan Tomkins. As a practicing clinician, he added the notions of mood (the collective result of various affective threads) and mood disorder (the way that those results can be reorganized). A brief summary of this embodied and cognitive engagement with affect can be found in the prologue to his *Affect, Imagery, Consciousness.*

3. See, for instance, the special issue of *Rhetoric Society Quarterly,* edited by Jordynn Jack, on neurorhetorics. Her introduction to the issue, "What are Neurorhetorics?," offers a good overview, as does her edited collection, *Neurorhetorics.* For a more recent mapping of this literature, see Elizabeth Beam et al., "Mapping the Semantic Structure of Cognitive Neuroscience." Lakoff's reframing theory offers the most direct deployment of cognitive psychology for practical ends. See his "Neural Social Science."

4. Marx was banished from Germany, Paris, and Belgium before arriving in England. As an independent writer, he was often penniless. He was evicted from his first apartment, regularly pawned his few possessions, suffered illnesses for which he could not afford medicine, and buried three children. An excellent biography is Francis Wheen's *Karl Marx: A Life;* see also Mary Gabriel's *Love and Capital,* a more recent account that focuses on his relationship to his wife, Jenny.

5. As Paul Samuelson explains, Marx had significant philosophical training, but his political economic studies betray his own autodidacticism. As he puts it, "Although Marx was a learned man, he shows all the signs of a self-taught amateur: overelaboration of trivial points, errors in logic and inference, and a megalomaniac's belief in the superiority of his own innovations" ("Marxian Economics as Economics" 616). Samuelson locates Marx's contribution in his philosophical orientation to economic thinking.

6. See Althusser's "On the Young Marx."

7. According to Althusser, when Marx suggests that the Hegelian dialectic rests on its head and needs to be turned right-side up again, he prompts a reframing rather than a methodological reversal. Marx's critique, he says, poses "not the problem of the inversion of the 'sense' of the dialectic, but that of the *transformation of its structures*" ("Contradiction and Overdetermination" 93).

8. Althusser's position is that the epistemological break means that we cannot read *Capital* as "the development of a youthful intuition" found in his earlier work ("The '1844 Manuscripts' of Karl Marx" 156).

9. *The German Ideology* explains how Hegelian thinking, even in its reformed versions, dominates intellectual inquiry in his homeland; the writings in *Economic and Philosophic Manuscripts* reveal the ideological basis of bourgeois political economy; and "On the Jewish Question" demonstrates the limitation of political emancipation.

10. See Aune, "Cultures of Discourse: Marxism and Rhetorical Theory."

Chapter 1: Affect as Capitalist Being

1. This additional materialism is informed by and expands on Ronald Greene's "Another Materialist Rhetoric."

2. Althusser illustrates this position by exploring the reception of what he esteems as "Marx's greatest work" among two different groups: the working class and the intellectuals (71). According to him, the working class understands *Capital* easily "because it speaks in scientific terms of the everyday reality with which they are concerned," whereas intellectuals falter in their comprehension of the text because "they are subject to the ruling ideology (the ideology of the ruling class) which intervenes directly in their 'scientific' practice, falsifying their objects, their theories and their methods" (73).

3. See Diana Coole and Samantha Frost's *New Materialisms* for an excellent survey of these different branches.

4. See my "Rhetorical Circulation in Late Capitalism," as well as "Affect and Belonging in Late Capitalism." For a critique of this argument, see Jamie Merchant's "Immanence, Governmentality, Critique."

5. This was, of course, Ronald Walter Greene's important insight in "Rhetoric and Capitalism: Rhetorical Agency as Communicative Labor."

6. Shannon Walters's *Rhetorical Touch* revises these proofs as well as other foundation concepts in her theorization of rhetorical communication among differently abled bodies.

7. The passions feature prominently in discussion of Renaissance rhetoric. See, for instance, Wayne Rebhorn's *The Emperor of Men's Minds,* as well as the collections *Reading the Early Modern Passions,* edited by Gail Kern Paster, Katherine Rowe, and Mary Floyd-Wilson, and *Politics and the Passions, 1500-1850,* edited by Victoria Kahn, Neil Saccamano, and Daniela Coli.

8. This embodied notion of rhetoric can be found in images of Hercules Gallicus, the god of eloquence, who is often linked to his audience by a chain emanating from his speaking mouth to their listening ears. In this representation something literally emerges from the body of the speaker and enters the bodies of the listeners. For a detailed discussion, see Rebhorn.

9. See, for instance, "The Rise of Capital" in Giovanni Arrighi's *The Long Twentieth Century;* "The Secret of Primitive Accumulation" in Marx's *Capital;* and Peter Burke's "The Spread of Italian Humanism."

10. For discussion of nonrational rhetoric, see *Philosophy and Rhetoric* 47.4 (2014), a special issue titled "Extrahuman Rhetoric: Addressing the Animal, the Object, the Dead, and the Divine." Also, see *Thinking with Bruno Latour in Rhetoric and Composition,* edited by Paul Lynch and Nathaniel Rivers.

11. For a discussion of big rhetoric, see Dilip Gaonkar's "The Idea of Rhetoric in the Rhetoric of Science," Herbert Simons's "Rhetorical Hermeneutics and the Project of Globalization," and Edward Schiappa's "Second Thoughts on the Critique of Big Rhetoric." See Nathan Stormer's "Rhetoric's Diverse Materiality" for a perspective that diversifies rhetoric's character as it extends its scope.

12. Burke's use of the term "consubstantial" invokes the Catholic use of the term to explain the being of God within a tripartite structure as well as the communion ritual wherein God is understood to exist materially within the bread that worshippers consume. In this tradition, the material being connecting separate bodies is literal.

13. The chapter of Davis's that deals with Burkean identification was originally published as "Identification: Burke and Freud on Who You Are" in *Rhetoric Society Quarterly* 38.2 (2008): 123–47. Thomas Rickert explores similar aspects of Burke, but through Heidegger and not Freud, in chapter 5 of his *Ambient Rhetoric*. Rickert sees more equivocation and possibility in Burke's understanding of language and intuition.

14. See Chris Mays, Nathaniel Rivers, and Kellie Sharp-Hopkins's *Kenneth Burke + The Posthuman* for a range of such readings.

15. Lawrence Grossberg connects this political style to the new conservatism, arguing that it has colonized values-based arguments in American debate. Such colonization, he says, results from the affective shift in people's mattering maps. See, especially, "Ideology and Affective Epidemics" in *We Gotta Get Out of this Place.*

16. For a more extended treatment of this theory, see George Kennedy's *Comparative Rhetoric.*

17. Many theorists believe that affect is a material thing. Deleuze and Guattari see it as an energy, as does Brian Massumi. Hardt and Negri understand it primarily through human interaction, but do include mediated forms of contact. Hardt explains that affective production is "associated with human contact, with the actual presence of another, but that contact can be either actual or virtual. In the production of affects in the entertainment industry, for example, the human contact, the presence of others, is principally virtual, but not for that reason any less real" ("Affective Labor," 96). Teresa Brennan explains that affect is a physiological thing that enters the blood stream through sensuous interactions much like a pheromone. Patricia Clough also sees it as an energy that unites humans and nonhumans.

18. For many, affect studies picks up from the limitations of ideology, but does not replace ideological analysis as they operate on different levels and reveal different modes of control (Deleuze and Guattari; Massumi; Grossberg).

19. Michel Foucault discusses the biopolitical as the decentralized power that works primarily through statistics such as birth and death rates, literacy rates, probabilities of terrorist threats, interest rates, and other numerical indices. As long as these numbers fluctuate within specific intervals, society is healthy. Once the numbers deviate beyond safe levels, however, society is insecure. For Foucault, this form of power emerges hand-in-hand with neoliberalism. See *Security, Territory, Population* and *The Birth of Biopolitics.* Gilles Deleuze argues that the contemporary proliferation of biopower constitutes what he calls a control society, a concept intended to parallel Foucault's notion of disciplinary society. See "Postscript on the Societies of Control" in *Negotiations.*

20. Because of this concrete and ephemeral quality, Marx says commodities are both sensuous things and "suprasensible or social" things (*Captial* 165).

21. Clough and her coauthors theorize affect "as a property of matter generally, disregarding distinctions between the organic and the non-organic, the open and the closed, the biological and the physical, even the simple and the complex" (Clough et al. 67).

22. Rodney Herring and Mark Garrett Longaker have a different take on the relationship between use value and exchange value, which they attribute to not only John Locke but also William Petty. For them, economic arguments that derive from the labor theory of value are "quasi-arguments" that rely primarily on hope and are ultimately extinguished by mathematical reason. See "Wishful, Rational, and Political Thinking."

23. For an excellent discussion of the circulation of affect, see chapter 2 of Ahmed's *The Cultural Politics of Emotion* and an even more developed treatment in "Affective Economies."

24. Bill Brown's *Critical Inquiry* article was at the forefront of thing theory. Jane Bennett extends this thinking by theorizing things through "an energetic substantiality" that gives them their vitality and their power ("Force of Things" 350). Exploring such power within networks of associations, actor network theory, associated with the work of Bruno Latour, maps agency through a range of human and nonhuman objects. Graham Harman, who uses Heidegger's notion of the tool, has developed a theory of things under the title of object-oriented ontology. See also Peter-Paul Verbeek's work on the persuasive function of things.

25. For a discussion of this posthumanist notion of agency within rhetoric, see Christian Lundberg and Joshua Gunn's essay "Ouija Board, Are There Any Communications?" as well as chapter 4 of Diane Davis's *Inessential Solidarity*. For a more tentative argument, see Carolyn Miller's "What Can Automation Tell Us about Agency?"

26. An extended description of Marxist dialectics can be found in Friedrich Engel's *Anti-Dühring*. For contemporary explanations of these dialectical processes, see Bertell Ollman's *Dances with Dialectics* and David Harvey's "Dialectics" in *Justice, Nature, and the Geography of Difference*, 46–68.

27. In *Rhetoric and Marxism,* Aune argues the opposite point: "classical Marxism tends to see the need for revolution as self-evident, without considering that people might need to be persuaded to that belief" (14).

28. Cloud's "Therapy, Silence, and War" theorizes affect as a rhetorical strategy that inhibits public deliberation. Her book *Control and Consolation in American Culture* similarly argues that psychological approaches individualize and domesticate national political issues, preventing more thoroughgoing critiques. I do not disagree with these analyses, which approach affect as emotion from a psychological perspective and not from a physiological one that is more aligned with a materialist critique, but they miss important persuasive opportunities by not engaging affect as a physiological function.

29. Many activists, for instance, explain that they simply had to participate in the Occupy Movement. They were somehow compelled to act even though they often did not have a clear rationale for that decision. See, for instance, Kelly Happe's "*Parrhēsia*, Biopolitics, and Occupy."

30. Others have attempted to theorize this process. For instance, Louis Althusser calls it "overdetermination" and Raymond Williams names it a "structure of feeling." See "Contradiction and Overdetermination" and "The Analysis of Culture," in *The Long Revolution* respectively.

31. I agree with the posthumanist claim that there is no longer a clearly distinct boundary between subject and object, as evidenced by the work on mirror neurons, for instance. I believe, however, that such insights call us to complicate our notions of the

dialectic between the subject and the object and not simply collapse the two together. As Rickert asserts, ambient rhetoric "simultaneously includes and exceeds the 'subject,'" and yet he suggests that theorists resist "collapsing distinct realms into an abstract unity" (123). Ambient rhetoric offers a theory in which the two are enmeshed in a world connected through being, whereas I offer a theory in which the two are materially connected through affect. For Rickert, ambient rhetoric is a "metaphor" (122). For me, affect is a literal connecting.

32. These affective modalities are based on Gilles Deleuze and Félix Guattari, who explain that affect vibrates, increasing or lowering the intensity of energies, and it clinches us together or withdraws us from each other. Teresa Brennan furthers describes this affective movement as capable of unlocking our fixations or sealing our hearts around particular positions. See Deleuze and Guattari's "Percept Affect and Concept," and Brennan's *Transmission of Affect*.

Chapter 2: Adam Smith and Karl Marx

1. See Philip Mirowski's *More Heat Than Light* for a detailed history of how economics imported key metaphors and methodologies from physics.

2. This supposed gap between the "moral Smith" and the "economic Smith"—as well as the reputed dominance of the latter over the former—has been countered in other scholarship. Jerry Muller, for instance, argues that Smith "showed that it was possible to direct the passions through the marketplace in a way that would lead to 'universal opulence' and help make life more decent for all" (60). In Muller's view, Smith sees economic self-interest as originating in our "reactions to the sentiments and opinions of others" (94). What unites *The Wealth of Nations* and *The Theory of Moral Sentiments* is the study of sympathy in individual and institutional terms. As Roger Frantz reads Smith, individual sympathy and the invisible hand "were two parts of the same phenomenon" (11).

3. For Marx the commodity fetish represents the fact that laboring bodies become interchangeable things while commodities become "citizens of the world" (*Capital* 128). In *The Sublime Object of Ideology*, Slavoj Žižek discusses how this notion of commodity fetish produced the ideological symptom or the belief in a hidden truth buried within texts.

4. The universalization of such truths helps account for the general impoverishment of invention and deliberation in Enlightenment rhetoric as well the increase in historical and literary narration of universal good taste. See James L. Golden and Edward P. J. Corbett's *The Rhetoric of Blair, Campbell, and Whately*.

5. Many theorists have latched onto this concept of alienation as a theory that explains why capitalist workers do not identify with the products of their labor, live in relative isolation from others, and feel displaced from their authentic selves as well as from nature. See also Bertell Ollman, Dorothee Soelle, Kōstas Axelos, Kai Erikson, and Michael Maidan. For comparative accounts of the role of alienation in Adam Smith and Karl Marx, see Dionysios Drosos and E. G. West.

6. See Albert O. Hirschman's *The Passions and the Interests* for an intellectual history of the evolution of avarice from greed to self-interest and from a passion to rational regulating mechanism.

7. Affect theory is fundamentally intertwined with the body and its sensory capacities. For this reason nearly all theorists of the Enlightenment, during which empiricism—the notion that all knowledge comes to the mind via the senses and that the scientific method includes observation and experimentation—prevailed, have a nascent theory of

affect. Indeed, the melding of the mind and the body or reason and passion result in such phrases from Hume as "passion of interest" or "interested affection." See Victoria Kahn, Neil Saccamano, and Daniela Coli's edited collection, *Politics and the Passions,* for an account of the intellectual lineage of the Enlightenment's conception of affect.

8. Smith makes the first of his three uses of "invisible hand" in this text. He argues that while less advanced and less reasonable populations require the invisible hand of God to explain anomalous natural events, advanced societies call on science and philosophy to explain the ordinary course of life (25). He also uses the analogy in *The Theory of Moral Sentiments* and in *The Wealth of Nations.* Each time Smith employs this metaphor, he references a different, though related, external force that naturally regulates material life.

9. This scenario results from mirror neurons—neurons that respond in the same way to external stimuli regardless of whether one receives a blow or watches another receive the blow. See Evelyne Kohler et al., "Hearing Sounds, Understanding Actions."

10. Teresa Brennan says, similarly, that affects may "hover in the air" (x). Thomas Rickert calls for attention to an ambient rhetoric, which he defines as "the active role that the material and informational environment takes in human development, dwelling, and culture" (3).

11. Rickert addresses the role of sound throughout his analysis and music more particularly in chapter 4 of *Ambient Rhetoric.*

12. Smith uses the terms nature, providence, and God somewhat indiscriminately to discuss this external force. There is much debate about whether or not he intended this power to be God, a secular version of God, or to have no relationship to religious power. Richard Whately, one of the early popularizers of Smith, took his invisible-hand argument as proof of the existence of God. As Salim Rashid explains it, Whately "argued that the coherence achieved by free competition was a proof of the existence of God" (219). Other interpreters place the argument in relation to Hume's notions of sympathy. Fonna Forman-Barzilai, for instance, sees "the hand" as the end result of Humean sympathy or the social practice "through which morality is intersubjectively produced in shared physical spaces" (190). Forman-Barzilai claims more strongly that "Smith's impartial spectator is merely an artifact of human experience" (208). Similarly, Eric Schliesser views Smith's argument as following from his distinction (made in *The Theory of Moral Sentiment*) between natural and moral sentiments: natural sentiments come to us as part of our human nature and constrain moral sentiments, which develop through social interaction and social institutions (15). This second type of sentiment is conveyed between bodies and is understood by Smith as being "rapid, mostly uncontrolled, and strangely emotional rather than cognitive" (Zak 54).

13. Even though Marx arrived at the University of Berlin in 1837, six years after Hegel's death, the philosophical *zeitgeist* was still teeming with Hegelian thought. In *The Phenomenology of Mind,* Hegel described alienation as the process whereby one human being fails to see his relationship to another human being. Ludwig Feuerbach, in his *Essence of Christianity,* seized upon this idea to argue that religious and political institutions serve this alienating function through their externalization of agency. Influenced by these young Hegelians, Marx went one step further and suggested that our material relations alienate us from each other, from ourselves, from our labor, and from our nature.

14. This conception of double life resonates with Frantz Fanon's conception of a double consciousness. Although Marx limited his concept to the split between our private selves and our public citizenship while Fanon specifically addressed the divided consciousness of a colonized subject, both theories stem from the psychological divide created through institutionalization of identity. See Fanon's *Black Skin, White Masks.*

15. This theory of sensory capacity links consciousness, perspective, and the senses. As chapter 4 will show, Friedrich Hayek in *The Sensory Order* develops a more sophisticated version of these linkages in his neurological discussion of the senses. Much contemporary science lies at the crossroads of such studies as well. For a popular discussion of unusual cases of neurosensory differences impacting individual consciousness, see Oliver Sack's *An Anthropologist on Mars; The Mind's Eye;* and *Seeing Voices.*

16. As Kenneth Burke puts it, Marx exemplifies the "study of capitalistic rhetoric" par excellence (*Rhetoric of Motives* 24). For him, Marx interprets rhetoric, whereas someone like Adam Smith theorizes rhetoric and instructs others in how to produce it.

17. According to the editor's preface, this extensive text, comprising more than 700 pages, was written during the same period of exile as the *Economic and Philosophic Manuscripts.* Because Marx could not find a publisher, it was packed away for, as he says, "the gnawing criticism of the mice," leaving only pieces of the original work (1).

18. Antonio Gramsci defines these professionals as traditional intellectuals opposed to the organic intellectuals who emerge through concrete struggle. Althusser makes a similar point of distinction between those intellectuals who reproduce the dominant ideology and those who challenge it. See Gramsci's *Selections from the Prison Notebooks* and Althusser's "Ideology and Ideological State Apparatuses."

19. Andreas Kalyvas and Ira Katznelson's "The Rhetoric of the Market" makes a persuasive case for the interrelationship of sympathy, speech, and the marketplace in the work of Adam Smith.

20. Ronald Walter Greene posits the court's decision to fuse money and speech under the rubric of free speech, what he calls "money/speech," as a particular articulation between money and advocacy that can manifest in different forms from the political to the everyday ("Rhetorical Capital" 329). Other authors note that Smith's economic construction allows money to substitute for speech, producing significant consequences for his sympathetic structure of social relations. See Charles Bazerman's "Money Talks: Adam Smith's Rhetorical Project" and Mary Poovey's *A History of the Modern Fact.*

21. Although Adam Smith advocated free trade, he was not uniformly against government regulation. He favored usury laws and supported the Navigation Acts, for instance.

22. The importation of market values with market language has been a much-explored area, especially since the late 1990s. See, for instance, James Arnt Aune's *Selling the Free Market,* Kuttner's *Everything for Sale,* Carter Locke's *Market Matters,* and Evan Watkins's *Everyday Exchanges.*

23. Marx turns this notion around, arguing that commodities are citizens of the world (*Capital* 155).

24. Picking up on this quote, Marx compares capitalism to a lottery. In both cases, all participants believe they have a chance to strike it rich even though only a small minority does so (*Economic and Philosophic Manuscripts* 91).

25. Gavin Kennedy's "Adam Smith and the Role of the Invisible Hand Metaphor" offers a close reading of this metaphor as Smith uses it in *The Theory of Moral Sentiments* as

well as in *The Wealth of Nations.* He does so in relationship to Smith's discussion of the use of metaphor in his *Lectures on Rhetoric and Belles Lettres.*

26. "Capitalism" is a term Marx does not use; he uses "capital" and "capitalist." Smith does not use any of these terms, instead referencing "industry" and "merchants."

27. Recall from the *Economic and Philosophic Manuscripts* that nature is the external body of man such that his species-being realizes itself when it consciously works to create its own life within nature. Nature belongs to humans, and although an external force, it is not alien or necessarily antagonistic.

28. Many theorists have noticed the plethora of supernatural phenomenon in Marx. For an extended discussion, see Jacques Derrida's *Specters of Marx.* For an analysis of the monstrous, see Antonio Negri's "Art and Culture in the Age of Empire and the Time of the Multitudes" as well as "The Political Monster." For an exploration of Marx's vampire metaphors, see Andrew Smith's "Reading Wealth in Nigeria" and Richard Godfrey's "Sucking, Bleeding, Breaking." See Jason Morrissette's "Marxferatu" for an interesting pedagogical take on this imagery.

29. This is the foundational assumption of Georg Lukács's notion of reification. For Lukács, there are a host of relationships, struggles, and exploitations that go into commodity production but are erased from the final product and its consumption. See "Reification and the Consciousness of the Proletariat." See, also, Cloud's review of Lukács in the *Quarterly Journal of Speech.*

30. Dead value and living value are terms that Marx borrows from Smith's *The Wealth of Nations.*

31. For a critical discussion on the relationship between capitalist exploitation, critique, and pleasure, see Žižek's "Class Struggle or Postmodernism? Yes, Please!" and *The Plague of Fantasies,* as well as Jodi Dean's *Democracy and Other Neoliberal Fantasies* and "Enjoying Neoliberalism."

Chapter 3: John Maynard Keynes and Thorstein Veblen

1. Although many view the great debate of the early twentieth century as between Keynes and Friedrich Hayek, that discussion, which primarily took place between 1931 and 1932 and centered around Hayek's poor reception of Keynes's *Treatise on Money,* was, according to Keynes, a failure of goodwill (*Collected Writings* 243–65). From Keynes's perspective, Hayek refuses to entertain the central ideas in his *Treatise* before giving them a fair hearing. Perhaps the same could be said of Keynes's reception of Hayek, whom he claimed not to understand. This lack of engagement may provide an interesting case study in affect between and within the two economists, but it does not fit the scope of my current analysis, which is to study those arguments in favor of capitalism alongside those against it. When one keeps that charge in mind, Keynes, whose greatest desire was "to save the free market economy by showing how to correct its main defects," compares more fruitfully to Veblen, who viewed capitalism as a defect corrupting the human instinct of workmanship (Robinson 140).

2. In Veblen's time "the academic woods were full of instincts," but C. E. Ayers asserts that "it is now quite conclusively established that no such complex of behavior patterns are in any literal sense 'inborn'" (28, 29). He claims instead that such traits are cultural (30). Robert Lekachman's introduction to *The Theory of the Leisure Class* makes the same point, saying Veblen's use of "instinct psychology" to discuss class behavior is "not at this time very convincing" (xi). This point of view is not currently so clear-cut; indeed,

many theorists of affect reference William James, both his theory of instincts and his classic essay "What is an Emotion?" Moreover, chapter 3 of Brennan's *The Transmission of Affect* assesses how these early-twentieth-century theories, often dismissed as racist and classist, influence her understanding of affect as a physiological entity that moves among people.

3. For an excellent overview of Keynes, see Robert Skidelsky's three-volume biography. Also of note is Roderick O'Donnell's *Keynes: Philosophy, Economics, and Politics.*

4. For a good discussion of Veblen's personal and intellectual life, see chapter 1 of Douglas Dowd's *Thorstein Veblen.* Also see Joseph Dorfman's *Thorstein Veblen and His America,* which is generally accepted as the definitive book on Veblen.

5. For two interesting takes on the relationship between Keynesianism and Veblen's economics, see Adil H. Mouhammed and L. Randall Wray, both of whom see significant overlap.

6. Although Keynes is well known for his discussion of animal spirits, Karl Marx used this phrase earlier. Marx, however, cited the animal spirits as a positive affective mobilization. In his discussion of factory labor, he argued that "mere social contact begets in most industries an emulation and a stimulation of the animal spirits that heighten the efficiency of each individual workman" (*Capital* 229).

7. See, for instance, George A. Akerlof and Robert J. Shiller's contemporary take on Keynes's animal spirits. They identify five innate proclivities and argue that these irrational spirits can account for the economic crisis of 2008. Other theorists have seen Keynes's psychological explanation as an indication of Freud's influence; his discussions, however, do not bear the marks of a Freudian critique. See J. E. King for a critique of the Freudian argument.

8. Most reviews comment on his dramatization of the world leaders. For instance, Veblen's review of the book, which is generally positive, takes Keynes to task for his "ungracious characterization of the President" (469). Rod O'Donnell's "Keynes as a Writer: Three Case Studies" provides an overview of critics who found his writing to be exemplary as well as those who viewed it as convoluted. See also Alessandra Marzola's "Rhetoric and Imagination in the Economic and Political Writings of J. M. Keynes."

9. The propagators of laissez-faire ideology, says Keynes, are not professional economists but popular textbooks, political speeches, and everyday discourse (*End of Laissez-Faire* 24–28).

10. Many theorists uphold *The Instinct of Workmanship* as Veblen's greatest work (Ayers 25; Diggins 63). Most explain its theory dialectally as "the antithesis between workmanship and 'exploit'" (Ayers 26) or the continuous interplay between "the 'instinct of workmanship' and the instinct of 'predatory exploit'" (Penner 156). See also Ayers's student Donald A. Walker for a similar account. Interestingly, such scholarship takes predatory nature to be an innate human characteristic, but for Veblen this instinct derives from the corruption of innate instincts.

11. To be clear, this is a somewhat coincidental alignment. Veblen never read Marx's early work on species-being and ideology. The *Economic and Philosophic Manuscripts of 1844* and *The German Ideology* were first published in 1932, three years after Veblen's death. The precise relationship between Marx and Veblen is unsettled among scholars. Michael Spindler, for instance, contends that Veblen superseded Marx and that their relationship is overstated. Devin Penner argues that Veblen's theory does not withstand the critical test of Marxism, and Douglas Dowd views Veblen's contribution to Marxism

as developing a theory of the ideological superstructure ("Depths below Depths"). See Forest Hill for a further comparison of these two thinkers.

12. According to Murray Murphey, contamination results in historically outdated practices, emulative behavior, and animism, while institutions normalize and maintain these contaminations. In this way, Veblen's notion of historically inherited practices mirrors Raymond William's conception of residual culture as he defines it in *Marxism and Literature* as well as his notion of a structure of feeling articulated in *The Long Revolution*.

13. As Dowd explains it, "Veblen used the term 'instinct' to cover much of what is loosely called 'human nature'" and argued that instincts were "contaminated" by institutional habits and other instincts, both of which altered the original predispositions (*Thorstein Veblen* 28).

14. *The Instinct of Workmanship* also argues that business practices produce a contaminated form of thinking. As Veblen sees it, the "frequent recourse to statistical argument" that purports to "determine the course of efficient transition from a putative cause to a putative effect" is often false thinking (261). Statistical thinking, a rationalization derived from the transformation of workmanship into a predatory instinct, offers a form of efficiency that is "not a fact of observation, but of imputation" (261). This argument about the role of statistical thinking, though undeveloped, overlaps in significant ways with Michel Foucault's argument about the function of statistics in regulating biopower. See his *Security, Territory, Population*.

15. Keynes certainly read and appreciated Smith's economic work but did not read his lectures on rhetoric, which only became available in 1963. And although he cites Aristotle's *Rhetoric* on the definition of probability and references Richard Whately (a prominent nineteenth-century political economist and rhetorical theorist) on the combination of premises in argument, Keynes makes no explicit reference to the study of probability as the art of rhetoric. Instead, he discusses it as a branch of logic—a near analogue to Aristotle's positioning of rhetoric as the counterpart to dialectic. In this way, *A Treatise on Probability* previews the new rhetoric's attempt to deal with logical decision making within the contingencies of time, place, and individual perspective. See, for instance, Chaïm Perelman and Luce Olbrechts-Tyteca's *The New Rhetoric*. See also Celeste Condit's response, "Chaïm Perelman's Prolegomenon to a New Rhetoric."

16. Keynes repeatedly introduces his books as impartial and imperfect contributions to an ongoing deliberation that will be picked up and extended by others. See, for instance, the prefaces to *A Treatise on Probability, A Treatise on Money,* and *The General Theory of Employment, Interest, and Money.* According to O'Donnell, this was because Keynes believed that "scientific advance came, not from a few supreme minds, but from the cooperation of many minds" ("Keynes's Principles of Writing" 406). Economic writers, who are often forcefully gripped by ideas, need to allow that force to be amended by others. This requires, Keynes says, intelligence, cooperation, and goodwill. It requires what he calls a "meeting of the minds" (*Collected Writings* 469–71). Argument works not simply by logical coherence, but by sympathy. It requires two minds to meet through ideas, language, and persuasion. A recipient must be open to the message delivered by the speaker or writer. Not only is that affective component uncertain, but it is also unmanageable. Keynes felt this as he spoke to the public, doubting "whether I can hope to bring what is in my mind into fully effective touch with the mind of the reader" (*Essays in Persuasion* 136). The urgency underlying his beliefs (in this case, the need for government spending) pushed him on, even though there was no certain outcome.

17. Rousseau's concept of the general will is located in the French *Declaration of the Rights of Man and the Citizen,* which states that the law expresses the general will or the consent of all citizens. This notion of universal rights and punishments has been critiqued by such prominent thinkers as Hegel, Karl Popper, and Isaiah Berlin for its lack of reasoned grounding. Indeed, the notion of the general will is not all that different from the concept of "the multitude" made famous by Michael Hardt and Antonio Negri (*Empire; Multitude; Commonwealth),* which receives similar critiques.

18. For Keynes, rational argumentation often gets usurped by the media, especially political discourse and official journalism, both of which tend to spoon-feed the public dogmatic simplifications (*Essays in Persuasion* 48–50). This argument, which is rather nascent here, garners strength as communication technology develops. It is especially strong in the work of the Frankfurt School, a slice of which will be examined in the next chapter. For a particular version of this argument, see Jürgen Habermas's *Structural Transformation of the Public Sphere* and his critics in Craig Calhoun's *Habermas and the Public Sphere.*

19. In their insightful essay, William Waller and Linda R. Robertson suggest that an accurate assessment of Veblen requires that economics be approached "as argumentation, including debate about fundamental premises" rather than just the application of transhistorical premises (1032). This requires understanding Veblen as engaging in a process of inquiry about how "warranted knowledge is acquired and refined" (1043). Without this perspective on argumentation, they say, Veblen appears as a pundit rather than a serious economist.

20. Veblen's rhetorical contributions have been much discussed. In fact, an excerpt from *The Theory of the Leisure Class* was printed in the commentaries section of a 1953 issue of the *Quarterly Journal of Speech* under the title "Conspicuous Consumption of Language" (306). Moreover, Kenneth Burke says that from the perspective of identification, Veblen should be "considered a theorist of rhetoric" (*Rhetoric of Motives* 24). But he later complains that Veblen is more skilled in the use of rhetoric than its study, saying, "Veblen's psychology is not so much dramatistic, as dramatized" (125). Burke suggests that Veblen used a writing style that paralleled the arguments he was making. If he was trying to discuss the outdated or wasteful use of a particular practice, he would describe it in damning terms and with such erudite language that his style reinforced his argument, an insight that Daniel Aaron also notes. This tendency, say William Waller and Linda R. Robertson, helps explain why Veblen's *The Theory of the Leisure Class* has had such a large audience at the same time that it has had so little effect on economics. They argue that Veblen "does not write as an economist ought to. He is therefore conceived as a satirist rather than an economist" (1030). For other discussions of Veblen and rhetoric, see Daniel Aaron and Gary Alan Fine.

21. In an interesting application of Veblen, Paul Frijters and Andrew Leigh argue that the increasing mobility of the U.S. population has shifted conspicuous display from leisure, which often requires long-term and engaged relationships with others for these activities to be noticed, to commodities.

22. This is not so much an extension as a rationalization of Marx's theory of false consciousness. Veblen criticizes Marxist theory for being an abstract materialism rather than one grounded in actual material practices. Marx's social progress, he says, "moves on the plane of human desire and passion, not on the (literally) material plane of mechanical and physiological stress" ("Socialist Economics of Karl Marx" 415).

23. Like many critical assessments of Adam Smith that suggest a radical break between his early *Theory of Moral Sentiments* and his later *The Wealth of Nations*, scholars dispute the so-called continuity problem of whether Keynes subscribes to the rational human motivation of his early work or to the irrational ones they impute to his later work. Brad Bateman proposes this break between Keynes's early and late work, but several scholars, most notably Roderick O'Donnell, see a clear connection between Keynes's *A Treatise on Probability* and his *General Theory*.

24. The preface to the *General Theory* explains that the book represents a "natural evolution in a line of thought" from *A Treatise on Money* (5). Milton Friedman disagrees and repeatedly cites *The General Theory* as a break from Keynes's earlier work. In a longer trajectory, there seems to be a similar evolution in thinking from his *Treatise on Probability*. For a range of perspectives on the relationship between this work on probability and his *General Theory*, see Jochen Runde and Sohei Mizuhara's *The Philosophy of Keynes's Economics: Probability, Uncertainty, and Convention*.

25. Marx similarly comments on this false analogy, saying that "political economists are fond of Robinson Crusoe stories" (*Capital* 169).

26. Keynes says that because "the expectation of the future influences the present" and the future is unknown, we must always act in the space of uncertainty (62). Brian Massumi's "Fear (The Spectrum Said)" relates this grip of the future within the present to affect, arguing that political mobilization of fear about the future after the September 11 terrorist attacks worked affectively to change policy in the present.

27. Michael Kaplan argues that this function of the economy erases the distinction between language and the market, especially for high-profile individuals such as the U.S. Federal Reserve chairman. He says that such speech is "iconically identical to the economic 'reality' to which it appears to refer" and coins this relation "iconomics" (479). It is also, however, related to the affective function of the market that Karin Knorr Cetina and Urs Bruegger theorize.

28. Keynes asserts that socialism is "little better than a dusty survival of a plan to meet the problems of fifty years ago, based on a misunderstanding of what someone said a hundred years ago" (*End of Laissez-Faire* 45), and he says of communist Russia that its "Bible," presumably Marx's *Capital*, is "an obsolete economic textbook which I know to be not only scientifically erroneous but without interest or application for the modern world" ("Short View of Russia" 99).

29. Veblen and Keynes, because of their focus on overproduction and on the problems of national struggle for imperialist positioning, foreshadow many of the arguments discussed by theorists of monopoly capitalism. For instance, Veblen argues that overproduction in this era needs to be absorbed by conspicuous consumption: "the need of conspicuous waste, therefore, stands ready to absorb any increase in the community's industrial efficiency or output of goods, after the most elementary physical wants have been provided" (*Theory of the Leisure Class* 110). Paul Baran and Paul Sweezy suggest that Veblen was "the first economist to recognize and analyze many aspects of monopoly capital" (132). Although they acknowledge the contributions of Keynes to the problem of overproduction, they view his work as circumscribed within "the tradition of orthodox business cycle theory" (55).

30. See chapter 5 of John Locke's *Of Civil Government* for a full discussion of the natural-right doctrine.

31. While this argument seems to prefigure Louis Althusser's concept of ideological state apparatuses, Veblen, in keeping with the brute materiality of his theory, sees this form of reasoned persuasion as only mildly influential.

Chapter 4: Friedrich Hayek and Theodor Adorno

1. After a brief period working with Ludwig Mises on business-cycle research, Hayek moved to England. He took a visiting lectureship at the London School of Economics, which turned into a permanent position that kept him in England until after World War II. In 1950 he joined the Committee on Social Thought at the University of Chicago, where he stayed until moving to Freiburg in 1962. Following roughly the same path, Adorno began his career in the Philosophy Department at the University of Frankfurt, where he worked for several years before relocating to England. Adorno's first move, as a student at Oxford University from 1934 through 1938, was less stimulating than he would have liked, and so he welcomed the opportunity to move to the United States when Max Horkheimer helped him secure a position with the Princeton Radio Research project led by Paul Lazarsfeld. After being let go from that project, Adorno followed Horkheimer to Los Angeles. He returned to Frankfurt after the war and became the director of the Institute for Social Research in 1959. Interestingly, Rolf Wiggershaus explains that Adorno's enrollment at Oxford was aided by his father's friendship with John Maynard Keynes (158). For biographical information on Adorno, see Martin Jay's *The Dialectical Imagination* as well as his *Adorno,* Rolf Wiggershaus's *The Frankfurt School,* and Susan Buck-Morss's *The Origin of Negative Dialectics.* For biographical information on Hayek, see Alan Ebenstein's *Hayek's Journey,* Stephen Kresge and Lief Wenar's *Hayek on Hayek,* and Bruce Cadwell's *Hayek's Challenge.*

2. See Albert Hirschman's *The Rhetoric of Reaction* and Jim Aune's *Selling the Free Market* for discussion of the rhetorical nature of this perversity thesis.

3. As Foucault explains it, the Frankfurt School pits social rationality against capitalist irrationality, whereas the Freiburg School positions economic rationality as the antidote for capitalism's social irrationality (*Birth of Biopolitics* 106). For an interesting interview with Foucault on the Frankfurt School, see his "Adorno, Horkheimer, and Marcuse: Who Is a 'Negator of History'?"

4. For discussions of Hayek's spontaneous order, see chapter 6 of Bernard Harcourt's *The Illusion of Free Markets,* Müfit Sabooglu's "Hayek and Spontaneous Orders," and Paul Lewis's "Emergent Properties in the Work of Friedrich Hayek."

5. According to Rolf Wiggershaus, the Frankfurt School's discovery of the young Marx, especially his *Economic and Philosophic Manuscripts of 1844,* "confirmed for them that criticizing capitalist society was a matter of reflection on the true nature of humanity"; but he also says that for Adorno "the young Marx was not a decisive influence" (5). Nigel Gibson agrees with this statement, saying, "Adorno sees little in Marx's early writings" (290n23). Susan Buck-Morss, however, leaves the role of early Marx as an open question (32).

6. There exists a growing body of research exploring Hayek's *The Sensory Order.* See, for instance, William Butos's *The Social Science of Hayek's 'The Sensory Order'* and Leslie Marsh's *Hayek in Mind.* See also Thomas McQuade and William Butos's "The Sensory Order and Other Adaptive Classifying Systems," Adam Gifford's "The Knowledge Problem, Determinism, and *The Sensory Order,*" Steven Horwitz's "From *The Sensory Order* to the

Liberal Order: Hayek's Non-rationalist Liberalism," and Bruce Cadwell's "Some Reflections on F. A. Hayek's *The Sensory Order.*"

7. Both scholars, in fact, approach politics through the backdoor. Hayek founded the Mont Pèlerin society for the pursuit of liberal economics and inspired the founding of the Institute of Economic Affairs, which began in London but spawned similar organizations in countries worldwide (Blundell, "Introduction: Hayek, Fisher," 33). Against such organized collectivism, Adorno confined his political activities to academic lectures, radio appearances, popular periodicals, and occasional television appearances. Although Adorno "vacillated between sympathy for the student protest movement and aversion to it," he steadfastly refused to participate in the activism of the late 1960s (Wiggershaus 621).

8. For an excellent discussion of the role of Freud in Adorno's Marxism, see Deborah Cook's "The Sundered Totality." She argues that Adorno uses Freud to retain the individual as a placeholder for "the ideas of autonomy and spontaneity—the emancipatory goals of Adorno's theory" (192).

9. Adorno does not characterize this method as negative dialectics, but the philosophy articulated in "the inaugural lecture demonstrates the remarkable consistency of his thinking over time" (Buck-Morss xii). For instance, Adorno is adamant in the lecture that there is no "secret world which is to be opened up through an analysis of appearances" ("Actuality of Philosophy" 126). Here, as in his later method, he eschews a positive assertion of truth in favor of persistent critique.

10. Adorno borrows the term constellation from Walter Benjamin, whose work significantly impacted his own, to describe structural relationships forged by such critique. In fact, Adorno hoped to publish his inaugural lecture and dedicate it to Benjamin, but its poor reception among faculty as well as his colleagues at the Institute for Social Research prevented the realization of this plan (Wiggershaus 94). For Benjamin's discussion of constellation, see his "Theses on the Philosophy of History"; and for his analysis of mass culture, which serves as a foil for much of Adorno's cultural criticism, see "The Work of Art in the Age of Mechanical Reproduction."

11. Hayek explicitly states here, and implies elsewhere, that his theory of the mind parallels his theory of spontaneous economic order. In *The Political Order of a Free People,* he notes this parallel, arguing that "the spirit of enterprise will emerge by the only method which can produce it. Competition is as much a method for breeding certain types of mind as anything else" (76). See also *The Fatal Conceit,* in which he says that "structural changes in the human body have occurred because they helped men to take fuller advantage of opportunities provided by cultural developments" in the economic sphere; he argues these changes take place in "the abstract structure we call mind [which] is transmitted genetically and embodied in the physical structure of our central nervous system" (17).

12. In other words, Hayek supersedes Smith's premise of sympathetic alignment without following the rational, scientific route forged by Keynes. In *The Counter-Revolution of Science* Hayek blames science and the incursion of mathematics into economics for distancing individuals from the rule-driven spontaneous orders of our dispositions. He argues that "science breaks up and replaces the system of classification which our sense qualities represent" (19). He goes on to say that economists, unlike scientists, do not study the physical world, which can be observed and measured with precision, but study "the mind of man" (23). The knowledge it produces acquires "the dispersed, incomplete, and inconsistent form in which it appears in many individual minds," and these findings

are not tested by "whether these laws of nature are true in any objective sense but solely whether they are believed and acted upon by the people" (30). For a short history of economic theory, see Hayek's "The Transmission of the Ideals of Economic Thinking."

13. Hayek's faith in such order rests on the premise he attributes to Bernard Mandeville: "we do not know why we do what we do, and that the consequences of our decisions are often very different from what we imagine them to be" ("Dr. Bernard Mandeville" 250). The version of this sentiment he most frequently cites comes from Adam Ferguson, who, in *An Essay on the History of Civil Society*, argues that "nations stumble upon establishments, which are indeed the result of human action but not the result of human design" (187). Ferguson belongs to the same category of Scottish Enlightenment thinkers as Adam Smith and David Hume. Although Mandeville was not well received among these theorists, he was among the first, says Hayek, to maintain that individuals cannot rationally organize society.

14. This lengthy discussion of the instincts is reminiscent of Veblen, who also subscribes to a theory of social evolution. It is worth noting that Hayek attended at least one lecture by Thorstein Veblen during his 1923–24 stay in New York City (Kresge and Wenar 7). Veblen insists on the foundational value of innate instincts, suggesting that social institutions have corrupted them, whereas Hayek argues that innate instincts are the outstanding remnants of uncivilized human beings that need to be held in check by the rules of spontaneous order. For Hayek, bodily instincts represent our animal heritage and are fifty thousand generations old, whereas intuited rules are only a few hundred years old. As he says, "one of the main functions of the rules learned later was to restrain the innate or natural instincts" (*Political Order of a Free People* 160). See Charles Leathers's "Veblen and Hayek on Instincts and Evolution" for a more detailed comparison of these two thinkers.

15. Hayek distinguishes dispositions from class-based ideologies, as they were often conceived at the time, because they evolve and shift with experience rather than being tied to materiality in a one-to-one relationship. Class-based arguments, which aim "at explaining why people as a result of particular material circumstances hold particular views," are, says Hayek, "fundamentally misconceived" (192–93). For him, such knowledge "aims at precisely that kind of specific explanation of mental phenomena from physical facts which we have tried to show to be impossible" (193).

16. The principle of the individual mind as functioning in ways that we cannot fully understand underscores Hayek's embrace of human ignorance. In *The Mirage of Social Justice*, he says that economic "rules are a device for coping with our constitutional ignorance" (8); in "The Theory of Complex Phenomena," he asserts that we must "take our ignorance seriously" (39); in *The Constitution of Liberty*, he outlines a "philosophy of freedom" that ultimately rests on "man's fundamental ignorance" (73). *Economy and Society* dedicated a 2012 special issue to ignorance as a founding economic tenet. Of particular interest is William Davies and Linsey McGoey's "Rationalities of Ignorance."

17. The corollary to this argument is that the unsuccessful are less evolved. Hayek, for instance, says that "alienated or estranged" individuals are "the non-domesticated or un-civilized" people who merely "want to impose upon [civilization] their instinctive, 'natural' conceptions derived from tribal society" (*Mirage of Social Justice* 147). He sees Marx, communism, and planned capitalism to be the imposition of new morals to fit old instincts. As he says, "the whole of socialism is a result of that revival of primordial instincts" (*Political Order* 169). Such instincts confuse information communication with

the labor theory of value: "what prevented [Marx] from appreciating the signal-function of prices through which people are informed what they ought to do was, of course, his labor theory of value. His vain search for a physical cause of value made him regard prices as determined by labor costs" (170). Hayek is equally suspicious of our human instincts—which, he says, "were not made for the kinds of surroundings, and for the numbers," characteristic of contemporary society—and of rational or scientific methods (*Fatal Conceit* 11). Neither of these motivational forces works as well as the rule of law.

18. In this discussion of facial tracking, Hayek overlaps with Silvan Tomkins's studies of affect; see, for instance, *Affect, Imagery, Consciousness*. As Hayek continues, he asserts that our everyday expressions exist as "more than merely metaphors" because they emerge from repeated experiences ("Rules, Perception, and Intelligibility," 52). In this suggestion, he prefigures the linguistic work of George Lakoff and Mark Johnson, whose collaborations with cognitive psychology intersect significantly with affect studies. See, for instance, *Philosophy in the Flesh: The Embodied Mind and Its Challenge to Western Thought*.

19. Although the invisible-hand metaphor is a staple of our contemporary lexicon, this was not so in the mid-twentieth century. In fact, its popularity can be partially attributed to Hayek who recuperates the invisible hand from those who "still pour uncomprehending ridicule on Adam Smith's expression" (*Rules and Order* 37). Hayek positions Smith as "the first to perceive that we have stumbled upon methods of ordering human economic cooperation that exceeded the limits of our knowledge and perception" (*Fatal Conceit* 14). For a discussion of Hayek's use of the invisible-hand metaphor, see Eugene Heath's "Rules, Function, and the Invisible Hand: An Interpretation of Hayek's Social Theory."

20. As Adorno makes clear, "Freud does not challenge the accuracy of [Gustave] Le-Bon's well-known characterization of masses as being largely de-individualized, irrational, easily influenced, prone to violent action and of an altogether regressive nature" (*Critical Models* 125). Adorno locates Freud's contribution as explaining the psychological forces responsible for this shift from individual to group identity. Freud does this in *Group Psychology and the Analysis of the Ego* (1921), *The Future of an Illusion* (1927), and *Civilization and Its Discontents* (1930), which all build on his work in *Totem and Taboo* (1913) to discuss group identification, specifically religious and nationalist identifications, as large-scale psychological instantiations of what he earlier perceived to be filially-bound structures. As Adorno sees it, Freud "tracked down conscious actions materialistically to their unconscious instinctual basis, but at the same time concurred with the bourgeois concept of instinct which is itself a product of precisely the rationalization that he dismantled" (*Minimum Moralia* 60). The problem, for Adorno, is that Freud "takes over the antithesis of social and egoistic, statically, without testing it" (60). See Adorno's interview with Elias Canetti, "Crowds and Power," for further discussion of instinct and group psychology.

21. Freud speculates about communism in both its concrete instantiations and its theoretical modes throughout his later work. He suggests, for instance, that "a real change in the relations of human beings to possessions would be more help in [quelling social unrest] than any ethical commands" (*Civilization and Its Discontents* 90). Yet he states that socialist doctrines suffer from a "misconception of human nature" (90). Socialists tend to think of human beings as creative and altruistic, while capitalists tend to think of human beings as destructive and self-interested. These musings notwithstanding, Freud concludes that he has "neither the special knowledge nor the capacity to decide on [communism's] practicality" (*Future of an Illusion* 11).

22. Max Horkheimer's early study *Authority and the Family* (1936) argued that the German family lost authority under totalitarian rule. Horkheimer and Adorno pursued this thesis in their collaboration with the Berkeley Public Opinion project that culminated in the multiauthored *The Authoritarian Personality* (1950). This immense research project, jointly conducted by the Institute of Social Research and the Berkeley Public Opinion Study Group headed by Nevitt Sanford, Daniel Levinson, and Else Frenkel-Brunswik, was funded by the American Jewish Committee's Department of Scientific Research. The group analyzed more than eighteen hundred interviews to determine several contemporary personality types. Overwhelmingly, these personality types, Adorno argues, reflect weak egos that make individuals unable to regulate their impulses (240). The personality types, he says, are at the root of the social turmoil unhinging democratic states: without healthy personalities, citizens cannot correctly gauge the social and material problems facing them and are open to fascist manipulation.

23. Hayek feared the manipulation of neurocircuitry as a significant danger in the fight against communism. Recall that, according to his theory, the brain responds to stimuli with a succession of neurological firings; each detail and its implications trigger different neurological points that the brain organizes into patterns. These firings do not happen simultaneously or in a continuous flow but as "a succession of shocks following each other at very short intervals" (*Sensory Order*, 56). Each impulse initiates its own series of associations so that there are clusters of intersecting patterns or "bundles of connections" (67). Repetition of similar events strengthens these patterns, whereas an alteration in predicted events weakens the patterns, making the brain vulnerable to manipulation. He claims in the *Constitution of Liberty*, for instance, that "the greatest dangers to freedom are likely to come from the development of psychological techniques which may soon give us far greater power than we ever had to shape men's minds deliberately" (503).

24. In many ways, this is the precise argument Marx lodges against the young Hegelians, who "are merely combating the phrases of this world" with other phrases and ignoring its real material existence (Marx and Engels, *German Ideology* 41).

25. This argument runs contrary to the Giorgio Agamben's assertion that economic and rhetorical organizations align and have their origins in the ancient Greek world. Specifically, Agamben traces Foucault's attempt to locate biopower within the liberal marketplace to its roots in the Ciceronian rhetorical canon of *taxis* or arrangement. See "The Mystery of the Economy" in his *The Kingdom and the Glory*.

26. This essay is by no means anomalous. The explicit goal of *The Mirage of Social Justice* is to police against the use of the term "social justice." As Hayek says, he wishes to make writers "thoroughly ashamed ever again to employ the term 'social justice'" (97). It is not merely a small irritation. Such "an empty phrase," he says, "has become a powerful incantation which serves to support deep-seated emotions that are threatening to destroy the Great Society" (133). It is worth noting, according to Hayek, that this desire for collective-minded thinking reflects an atavistic trait from tribal society (134–35). Social justice, that is, fits within a local model that does not scale up to the global, or even national, orders. Language was "formed during long past epochs in which our minds interpreted very differently what our senses conveyed," and thus "the meaning of individual words lead us astray" as outdated "connotations cling to many basic words" (*Fatal Conceit* 107).

27. According to Hayek, Richard Whately suggested catallactics as a term to describe market order. This was picked up by Ludwig Mises, among others, before being endorsed

by Hayek (*Fatal Conceit* 111–12). See Whately's *Introductory Lectures on Political Economy*, where he adds to Adam Smith's description of national wealth with his name for the method whereby such wealth is acquired: "the name I should have preferred as the most descriptive, and on the whole least objectionable, is that of catallactics" (6). See also Mises's *Human Action*.

28. It is likely for this reason that Hayek invited several high-profile journalists to the inaugural conference of the Mont Pèlerin Society "not in order that the meeting should be reported, but because they have the best opportunity to spread the ideas to which we are devoted" ("Opening Address" 153). If these individuals came to understand the liberal political and economic order of catallaxy as distinct from economic order, Hayek maintained, it would shape how they report on other ideas and thus reframe the public sentiment.

29. Written during Hayek's time with the London School of Economics, *The Road to Serfdom* was first published for an English audience in 1944. It was picked up within a year by the University of Chicago, and in 1945 Hayek boarded a ship from England to New York, where he was scheduled to deliver a five-week lecture tour to promote the American publication. While en route, *Reader's Digest* published an abbreviated version of the book to such acclaim that Hayek encountered three thousand audience members at the first public lecture (19). There was also a concise eighteen-page graphic form published by *Look* magazine and reprinted by General Motors. For an analysis of this text as an action-oriented narrative, see Jukka Törrönen's "On the Road to Serfdom?"

30. This linkage between totalitarianism and democracy as well as communism and capitalism begins, not surprisingly, with discursive miscegenation: liberal freedom, which opposes coercion, bleeds into socialist freedom, which opposes poverty (77). Such terminological slippage opens the floodgates of rational economic planning, equating the values of democracy and the values of socialism. This is all accomplished by public debate in which people "use the old words but change their meaning" (174).

31. According to Edwin Feulner, many business people have read this essay as "a challenge to build up our own class of intellectuals made up of those who loved liberty. We trained, hired, networked, and supported academics, policy analysts, journalists, radio talk show hosts, and even political leaders who would shape public opinion and influence the politics of tomorrow" (94). John Blundell encapsulates Hayek's influence through an aphorism: "be utopian and believe in the power of ideas" (98). Similarly, he interprets Hayek as instructing the business class that "intellectuals decide what we hear, in what form we hear it and from what angle it is to be presented. They decide who will be heard and who will not be heard" ("Introduction: Hayek and the Second-Hand Dealers" 100).

32. Adorno appears to align himself with Keynes on this issue. "I do not think it is usually realized," he says, "how much the notions of so-called everyday life—what I call 'bleating', the ideas passed uncritically from mouth to mouth, or presented as self-evident in leading or not-so-leading articles in newspapers—how much almost all these notions are cultural assets which have sunk down from the upper stratum, to use the language of sociological literature" (*Minimum Moralia* 77).

33. This theory accounts for the particular difficulty of Adorno's style, which embraces parataxis rather than traditional argumentative organization. According to Robert Hullot-Kentor's introduction to Adorno's *Aesthetic Theory,* a "paratactical text demands that every sentence undertake to be the topic sentence and that the book be composed of

long, complex phrases, each of which seems under the obligation to present the book as a whole" (xvi). Adorno's style is not designed to make a coherent argument as much as it is meant to serve "as a catapult for new insights" (xvi). In *Marxism and Form,* Jameson explains Adorno's belief that "the serious writer is obliged to reawaken the reader's numbed sense of the concrete through the administration of linguistic shocks" (20–21). Consequently, Adorno avoids clarity, believing that it attempts "to hurry the reader past his own received ideas" and that only complicated prose forces the reader "to think real thoughts" (24). As Susan Buck-Morss says, Adorno composed texts like music with sentences that follow "a sequence of dialectical reversals and inversions" and themes that "break apart and turn in on themselves in a continuing spiral of variations" (101). See also Gillian Rose's *The Melancholy Science,* which argues that Adorno's key contribution to Marxism is this style. Adorno explains these stylistic decisions in *Notes to Literature* (91–97, 185–99).

34. Adorno studied music as an experience and not as a semiotic text. Music, he says, "resembles" language but is not "identical" with it ("Music and Language: A Fragment"; "Music, Language, and Composition"). The major distinction is that language references an external signifier, whereas musical concepts exist in themselves "and not in a signified outside them" ("Music and Language" 2). In this way, music functions experientially and not intentionally. For a collection of Adorno's analyses on the musical experience of radio, see *Current of Music.* Thomas Rickert discusses this form of ambient music, a term coined by Brian Eno, at length. Although he cites Adorno's critique of music listening as a hobby rather than a serious experience, Rickert misses an opportunity to connect Adorno's analysis of music to his discussion of spatial environment. For instance, Adorno's notion of "hear-stripe"—the technological interference of radio broadcasting on the listening experience—exemplifies Rickert's exploration of how sound "takes on aspects of the spatial environment in which it was produced and recorded" (108).

35. Adorno describes Brecht's political theater as a "muddle [of] aesthetic semblance and reality" (*Critical Models* 275), whereas Beckett offers a theatrical structure that submits the cultural "curse to interrogation" (45). See *Aesthetics and Politics* by Adorno and others for Adorno's correspondence with Benjamin and critique of Lukács.

36. The more detailed explanation of this argument is found in *The Pure Theory of Capital,* which offers a precise account of the accumulation of wealth and the production of long-term durable goods viewed through the lens of time. As Hayek explains it, the push toward private investment produced only those goods that can be constructed in a short time period and thus prevents the accumulation of larger surplus necessary to produce more expensive, long-term goods. What he emphasizes here is that capital goods are not completely versatile: different products require more and less economic resources and more and less time. Thus, there is no such thing as equilibrium at any moment but only a conception of "equilibrium through time," which works through the "ongoing compatibility of various agents' plans" (xvii). This book, which failed to receive the welcoming reception of his earlier lectures, was according to Hayek primarily meant to illustrate the limits of the Keynesian model (Kresge and Wenar 142).

37. This famous debate is explored in detail in Nicholas Wapshott's *Keynes Hayek.*

38. This accords with Hayek's belief that the spontaneous alignment between individuals and capitalism can be taken off course by popular, and often logically persuasive, socialist arguments. Market competition is so vulnerable to the power of discussion that "unlimited democracy will destroy it" (*Political Order of a Free People* 77).

39. For Hayek, truth comes from consensus, which is why the government should be regulated by the rule of law or the few premises that are universally shared. As he says in *The Road to Serfdom,* "it is the price of democracy that the possibilities of conscious control are restricted to the fields where true agreement exists" (109). This runs contrary to Adorno, who values disagreement. He concurs with his coauthor, Max Horkheimer, who "find[s] it repellent for people to believe that if only everyone could agree, something essential would have been achieved. In reality, the whole of nature should tremble at the thought. The truth is, on the contrary, that all will be well only as long as they keep one another in check" (*Towards A New Manifesto* 46). His notion of politics comports with that of Jacques Rancière, who defines it as making disagreement visible, and this rubs up against Burke's famous definition of rhetoric as the understanding of misunderstanding. In this sense, Horkheimer and Adorno seek to politicize rhetoric—to highlight disagreement where there existed the appearance of agreement. Hayek, on the other hand, avoids rhetoric because of his deep discomfort with disagreement.

40. The emphasis that Hayek gives to the impersonal nature of market forces overlaps significantly with the description of affect as an impersonal passion. See, for instance, Denise Riley's *Impersonal Passion.*

41. Like Hayek, Adorno says that monopoly capitalism as well as state communism leads to fascism ("Reflections on Class Theory" 96). For Adorno, it is the exchange relationship, capitalism's fundamental principle, that becomes "an instrument of rational administration by the wholly enlightened as they steer society toward barbarism" (Horkheimer and Adorno, *Dialectic of Enlightenment* 20). Adorno differs from Hayek in locating the source of fascism in the exchange principle (where difference collapses into sameness) and not in the administrative apparatus. This principle, he asserts, is no less barbaric outside of government administration.

42. In defense of further theorization, Adorno argues against "simply invoke[ing] the thesis against Feuerbach. Dialectics also includes the relation between action and contemplation" (*Prisms* 29). Although Adorno opposed the eleventh thesis, he does not think that Marx advocates a quick movement from theory to practice, citing, for example, Marx's "Critique of the Gotha Program."

43. Adorno's extension of Marxism beyond the productive and political spheres and into everyday practices foreshadows the autonomist Marxist tradition that studies the "social factory." In this way, Jameson is likely correct when he says that "Adorno's Marxism, which was no great help in the previous periods may turn out to be just what we need today" (*Late Marxism* 5).

44. Adorno argues, for instance, that unlike the liberal era, "today's operation of the economic apparatus demands that the masses be directed without any intervention from individuation" (Horkheimer and Adorno, *Dialectic of Enlightenment* 204). He goes on to say that in the current state of capitalism "the notion which justified the whole system, that of man as a person, a bearer of reason, is destroyed" (204). In short, monopoly capitalism "has put an end to the episode of liberalism" ("Reflections on Class Theory" 100). He bemoans this loss, saying that "whatever was once good and decent in bourgeois values, independence, and perseverance, forethought, circumspectivity has been corrupted utterly" (*Minimum Moralia* 34). Clearly, Adorno holds bourgeois individualism in high regard, likely influencing his one-time student Jürgen Habermas, who idealizes the bourgeois public sphere in *The Structural Transformation of the Public Sphere.* While much is made of the break between Habermas and the Frankfurt School, Habermas characterizes

his mentor in unequivocal terms as a great thinker: "Adorno was a genius; I say that without reservation. . . . He had a presence of mind, a spontaneity of thought, a power of formulation that I never have seen before or since" ("A Generation Apart" 122).

45. Through their integration into capitalism, the masses become "the objects and not the subjects of the social process that as subjects they nevertheless sustain" ("Late Capitalism" 117). Class antagonism, although it continues to exist, becomes difficult to detect for two reasons: first, the owning class has shed its like interests, which were bound up in overthrowing feudalism in favor of competition; and second, the workers are able to identify with the owners through the commodity culture ("Reflections on Class Theory" 99). The material and psychological stakes are simply higher in the late twentieth century than they were in 1848, when Marx and Engels wrote the *Communist Manifesto,* and so Adorno concludes that "the proletariat does have more to lose than its chains" (103).

Chapter 5: Milton Friedman and John Kenneth Galbraith

1. Krugman is not the only economist to note the parallelism between Friedman and Galbraith. Critics often frame their reviews as a competition between Galbraith and Friedman: Cherrier argues that *Capitalism and Freedom* was a direct "reaction to the success of Kenneth Galbraith's *The Affluent Society*" (358); Gordon's overview of *Free to Choose* says that it was it was more popularly received than even Galbraith's books (301); and Wasserstein's assessment of Galbraith's *Money* positions it as a critique of Friedman's monetary theory (182–83). Others highlight their symmetry, suggesting that they both thought "it was important for economics to be directly applicable to social problems" (Hammond 44). Stapleford underscores that their interest in policy making, though divergent in method, equally tied economics to politics (24); Widmaier argues that they both abandoned the economic field to address the public directly (438); and Lanny Ebenstein asserts that Friedman and Galbraith were "outcasts from much of the academic economic mainstream for much of their careers" (158). Furthermore, from a biographical perspective, Freedman comments that "it is possible to contrast Friedman's experience with that of John Kenneth Galbraith" by comparing their formative years (203n3).

2. Friedman entered Columbia University in 1933 and studied there for one academic year, primarily focusing on statistics under the mentorship of Harold Hotelling. The following year, he returned to Chicago as a research assistant to Henry Shultz. He then worked as a statistician for the federal government from 1935 to 1945, gathering data on professional salaries for his dissertation. Even though this work was finished in 1940 and turned into a book coauthored with Simon Kuznets and published by the National Bureau of Economic Research, its controversial findings—that professional organizations contribute to inflated wages—delayed the conferral of his doctoral degree until 1946. See Lanny Ebenstein's *Milton Friedman: A Biography,* as well as the two useful overviews of Friedman by Eamonn Butler, director of the Adam Smith Institute. For a biography on Galbraith, see Richard Parker's *John Kenneth Galbraith;* an excellent survey of his work and life can be found in *The Galbraith Reader* and in Charles Hession's *John Galbraith and His Critics.*

3. Not only does the affect conversation recede into the background, so does a serious critique of capitalism: there is no anticapitalist theory espoused in this debate. This pull to the political right has many likely causes, not the least of which is the professionalization of economics as a discrete scientific discipline separate from the more broadly

ranging work of political economy. Even though Galbraith did not oppose capitalism, his embrace of Keynesian economics earned him an anti-capitalist reputation. According to Galbraith, Keynes's call for government intervention "made him as inimical a figure as Marx" (*Economics and the Art of Controversy* 50). To the extent that Galbraith was understood as a Keynesian, he too was a de facto Marxist. Indeed, Friedman purportedly harbored suspicions that Galbraith was secretly a communist (Freedman 209). In this metonymic link, Keynes and Galbraith become surrogates for a critique of capitalism even though they both adamantly establish their economic visions squarely within capitalism. See Galbraith's "How Keynes Came to America" on his role in the growth of American Keynesianism, a process that, he proudly declares, "brought Marxism in the advanced countries to a total halt" (44).

4. Paul Turpin's *The Moral Rhetoric of Political Economy* argues that both Adam Smith and Milton Friedman emphasize economic exchange over communicative exchange, resulting in a particular version of justice. Rather than cite both Smith and Friedman as turning a blind eye to noneconomic exchanges, I locate Smith's communicative role in his implicit theory of affect and suggest that Friedman unconsciously appropriates it.

5. Instead of building on Veblen's economic theory of absentee ownership, Galbraith calls it "a blind alley" that does not offer a sufficiently complex picture of corporate management ("Who Was Thorstein Veblen?" 219). Ironically, he says that Veblen was more of a sociologist than an economist—the precise assertion so often lodged against him. For instance, Milton Friedman characterizes Galbraith's work as "not so much economics as it is sociology" (qtd. in Frank 1). Barry Smart positions Galbraith as an institutional economist whose analyses "warrant sociological consideration" ("An Economic Turn" 54). Olson says he is "the Thorstein Veblen of our time" (87), a point noted elsewhere by Smart ("Economics, Politics *and* Sociology" 339) and picked up on by William Waller (13).

6. Galbraith ignores these important contributions to affect by regularly placing the life of the mind above any kind of embodied life. In fact, he often discusses his distaste for the kind of physical labor that characterized his childhood on an Ontario farm. As he says in *A Life in Our Times,* farm labor gave him an "enduring knowledge of its unpleasantness" and thus he sought instead a career that used his intellectual capacities (3). Also, in a 1966 interview with Anthony Lewis, he claims that "the desire to escape sustained manual effort can be put down as one of the fundamental human qualities" (5). Clearly, there is no privileged place for the laboring body within Galbraith's theory.

7. Friedman makes this case in his landmark study, coauthored with Anna Schwartz, *A Monetary History of the United States, 1867–1960.* Although this book surveys several illustrative moments in monetary history, the most important of these is its reassessment of the Great Depression as less an ebb in the business cycle and more a response to the federal government's reduction of the money supply. This chapter was excerpted and republished by itself as *The Great Contraction.* For Friedman, studying this monetary data produced "the experience of coming on a fact that suddenly illuminated an issue in a flash" (*Monetary History* 4). With this information, he understood that capitalism did not fail; instead, the government failed capitalism by not providing the stable monetary conditions for it to thrive.

8. Intriguingly, Paul Samuelson divides political economy—as opposed to economics—into art and science, asserting that the art is foundational to the science. He then positions Galbraith within this art form. In a commemorative piece, he says, "political economy is an art as well as a science. Kenneth Galbraith has always been a creative artist in

formulating theories of the social world. His fabrications constitute the stuff of economic science" ("Galbraith as Artist and Scientist" 128). He goes on to argue that professional economists have erred by not taking Galbraith's work more seriously.

9. Friedman further asserts economics as a scientific pursuit in his Nobel Lecture, titled "Inflation and Unemployment." His introduction addresses "the appropriateness of treating economics as parallel to physics, chemistry, and medicine" (1). He emphasizes that all these pursuits follow the same scientific method except that some study historical episodes and others controlled experiments. From his perspective, these differences are slight because "experience often offers evidence that is the equivalent of controlled experiment" (2). Economics, he concludes, is a scientific pursuit and not a value judgment. This emphasis on scientism was important to the success of the Chicago School, say Van Horn and Mirowski. They argue that Friedman and his colleagues "came to realize it was a deadly error to set one's political commitments as pitted against science in the era of the Atomic Bomb. Their embrace of statistics and their evocations of the mystique of science thus became one of the major neoliberal calling cards of the Chicago School" (163). Friedman similarly links the Chicago School with this scientific sensibility. He so highly esteems the University of Chicago department, he says, because it viewed "economics as a serious scientific project, capable of being tested by empirical and historical evidence, and of being used to illuminate important practical issues of conduct and policy" (Friedman and Friedman, *Two Lucky People* 192).

10. To be clear, rational-choice theory, also called the maximum-utility theory, never suggests that individuals make conscious rational choices, but only that individual behavior works out, on average, to calculate as if they did so ("The Expected-Utility Hypothesis" 206). This theory mathematically validates Hayek's cognitive psychological approach to the tacitly understood behaviors of the marketplace without ever mentioning Hayek's theory. Jim Aune suggests that such rational-choice theory garners its rhetorical power from the realist style of its scientific and empirical presentation even though Friedman explicitly denies the "realism" of its assumptions. See "Economic Rhetoric and the Realist Style" in Aune's *Selling the Free Market*.

11. For Friedman, positive economic analyses "reveal superficially disconnected and diverse phenomena to be manifestations of a more fundamental and relatively simple structure" ("Methodology of Positive Economics" 33). This tendency to absorb more and more phenomena within limited economic principles also undergirds Chicago School behavioral economics popularized by Friedman's student and fellow Nobel laureate Gary Becker, as well as the more recent freakonomics of Steven Levitt. See, for instance, Becker's early account in *The Economic Approach to Human Behavior* and Levitt and Dubner's *Think Like a Freak*. This all-encompassing approach, however, has been criticized as "economics imperialism" (Boulding; Ben Fine). For a critique of Freakonomics as part of this project, see Chaput's "How to Read Popular Economics" and Chaput and Hanan's "Rhetoric as *Taxis*."

12. From Friedman's perspectives, critics of the classical market model argue that it does not adequately reflect real-world deliberative processes, and so economic theory should be reformulated to align better with lived behavior. He offers Veblen and Keynes as examples, stating that they both believed that economics "rests on outmoded psychology and must be reconstructed in line with each new development in psychology" ("Methodology of Positive Economics" 30). Such criticism, he says, is "beside the point" because it mistakenly aligns economic assumptions with real-world observations (31). For

Friedman, economic science and real-life observations represent two unrelated spheres. When they collide, they promote the dangerous practice of accommodating economics to fit theories of behavior. Economic science should be used to promote proper political policies, but it should have no role in valuations of individual behavior.

13. One of the distinguishing features of Galbraith's description of the free market is its pragmatic explanation of the invisible hand. Galbraith offers a theory of markets in which real-world relations do not rely on affect for the supply-and-demand equilibrium but on competition—a situation in which everyone acts autonomously and no one has disproportional power. Galbraith explains that "in the purely competitive market, individual buyers and sellers are anonymous; no seller can have a group of buyers who are identified as *his* customers" (*Theory of Price Control* 11). A seller in this scenario maximizes profits, which are nonetheless kept low by competition. This version of the classical marketplace allows Galbraith to focus on the uncompetitive nature of corporate power. The modern corporation, he says, does not maximize profit but sets "pricing by custom" (18). In its alignment with other corporations, "the seller is opting for a habitual rather than a profitable pattern of behavior" and uses a "rule-of-thumb" (18). Strikingly, this emphasis on custom and habit represents the implicit affective theory of classical markets as characterized by Smith, Keynes, and Hayek; Galbraith, however, discusses these practices as departures from the competitive tradition.

14. Later in his career, Galbraith offered a softened perspective on the modern corporation. In a 1992 interview with Thomas Karier, he acknowledged that "sometime in the last 10 years I stopped worrying about corporate power and started worrying about corporate inadequacy" (164).

15. The discussion of identification and its repetition intersects significantly with Althusser's formulation of ideological apparatuses. Although Galbraith does not work with theories of ideology here or elsewhere, his *The Economics of Innocent Fraud* comes close to a theory of ideology. For Galbraith, innocent fraud is the belief and perpetuation of a false reality. Among the most pervasive forms of this fraud is the "belief in a market economy in which the consumer is sovereign" (15). His answer to this falsehood is simply a good dose of reality (50). This as well as his lack of engagement with critical social theories signal Galbraith's work as isolated from an ongoing critique of capitalism, a discussion from which his work might have benefited. For instance, Galbraith does not engage with other scholars in his conception of power. The most glaring omission in *The Anatomy of Power* is, of course, Michel Foucault whose power-knowledge dialectic was widely available in English translation as early as the late 1960s. For a treatise on power written in 1983, this book demonstrates an astonishing disregard for the academic practice of peer engagement.

16. Additionally, Friedman was featured in *Fortune* (a magazine that Galbraith once edited) and appeared on the cover of *Time* in December 1969 as well as on the cover of the *New York Times Magazine* in January 1970. During that same period, Galbraith appeared on the cover of *Paris Match,* a popular French magazine, and enjoyed widespread international recognition even as his popularity in the United States was beginning to wane. See Wayne Parson's *The Power of the Financial Press* for further details about their differing receptions in popular media.

17. Friedman was vocal about how important both Hayek and the Mont Pèlerin Society were for his own intellectual growth, noting that "the Mont Pèlerin Society has veritably been a spiritual fount of youth, to which we could all repair once a year or so to

renew our spirits and faith among a growing company of fellow believers" (foreword to *Essays on Hayek* xxi). Additionally, Friedman frequented Hayek's lectures at the University of Chicago and collaborated with him on the production of *New Individualist Review,* a libertarian journal, as well as the Intercollegiate Society of Individualists, a libertarian organization (Lanny Ebenstein 136). However, Ebenstein also notes, "Friedman is more plentiful in his praise of Hayek than the latter was of him" (216). Hayek strongly disagreed with the characterization of economics as a positive science *(Counter-Revolution of Science).* Friedman, in turn, asserts that Hayek and other Austrian economists who dismissed empirical evidence produced "an attitude of human intolerance" (Hammond 101). Interestingly, Galbraith met Hayek a full decade before Friedman did. During his year at Cambridge University, Galbraith commuted to the London School of Economics to hear Hayek's well-attended lectures and, contrary to Friedman's accusation of intolerance, Galbraith characterizes their relationship as both ongoing and friendly (Dunn 222; *Life in Our Times* 78).

18. Friedman discusses the think tank, a relative new political entity at the time, as a key apparatus for mediating between politics and economic theory. Early in his career, Friedman became involved with two such organizations—the American Enterprise Association (founded in 1943) and the Foundation for Economic Education (founded in 1946). He used his membership in the American Enterprise Institute (as it was renamed in 1962) to enter the political playing field, from which he advised presidential candidate Barry Goldwater and later Presidents Richard Nixon and Ronald Reagan (Friedman and Friedman, *Two Lucky People* 340). In this way, he was able to advocate for specific policies such as abandoning the Bretton Woods agreement to allow free-floating currency markets, indexing tax brackets for inflation, and creating school vouchers—all of which he achieved. Further objectives, such as constitutional amendments to balance the federal budget and codified monetary policies, were widely discussed but not achieved. For an exploration of the rhetorical importance of think tanks in the public sphere, see Rob Asen's *Invoking the Invisible Hand.*

19. This essay, published in a Norwegian business magazine, represents one of the few times that Friedman explicitly advocates for neoliberalism. The magazine was edited by his fellow Mont Pèlerin Society member Trygve Hoff, suggesting that its neoliberal tenets were discussed within the organization. Nevertheless, Friedman attributes his version of neoliberalism to the Chicago School generally and to Henry Simons in particular.

20. This differs from Naomi Klein's thesis in *The Shock Doctrine,* which argues that neoliberalism either orchestrates market disaster or takes advantage of natural disaster to introduce an extreme neoliberal agenda that would otherwise be unacceptable. Friedman's approach attempts to change public opinion in advance of those events so that the new policies do not shock their constituencies.

21. For a discussion of how affect contributed to the different receptions of Galbraith's BBC-produced *Age of Innocence* and Friedman's PBS-produced *Free to Choose,* see Chaput's "The Rhetorical Situation and the Battle for Public Sentiment."

22. William Volker, whose fund paid for Hayek's professorship at the University of Chicago as well as Ludwig Mises's position at New York University and also financed the Mont Pèlerin Society (including Friedman's participation in it), believed these financial efforts—dubbed the Free Market Project—would eventually produce a successful book on political and economic freedom (Van Horn and Mirowski 152). According to Van Horn and Mirowski, Friedman's *Free to Choose* (coauthored with Rose Friedman) "made good

on the Free Market Project" by offering "a corporate neoliberal version of *The Road to Serfdom*" (Van Horn and Mirowski 166).

23. Friedman spread the neoliberal doctrine with a style that attracted both experts and the general public. Shortly after his death, Paul Krugman asserted that he was "the best spokesman for the virtues of free markets since Adam Smith" ("Who Was Milton Friedman?" 16). He went even further, saying that he was "possibly the most brilliant communicator of economic ideas to the general public that ever lived" (17). From all accounts, Friedman was highly sensitive to other environments as well. His memoirs, for instance, recall events during which he and his wife, Rose, were in communist Germany. He says that their "feeling of revulsion and fear was so great that we could not bring ourselves to stop for lunch" (Friedman and Freidman, *Two Lucky People* 179). Similarly, he says that "it is difficult to put into words the oppressive feeling that we had while in the Soviet Union. There was nothing concrete to which we could attribute our fear. The atmosphere alone made one feel as though one were being watched constantly" (285). As opposed to these environments from which he felt physically alienated, Friedman's own presence seemed to attract a range of individuals. As Craig Freedman recalls, "he had one of the largest personalities I had ever run across. His ebullience and personality filled the room" (201). An infectious optimist, Friedman was at the center of the economic scene because "people who met Friedman found him impossible to dislike" (Butler, *Milton Friedman: A Concise Guide* 4). In contrast, Galbraith says in his memoirs that "man, at least when educated, is a pessimist" and that he thinks such "pessimism is good" (*Life in Our Times* 324).

24. From Galbraith's perspective, Keynes did not do this. He highlighted a problem—capitalism may be vulnerable to bouts of underinvestment and thus high unemployment, the combination of which brings the circulation of capital to a halt—and also suggested a solution—government spending. But Keynes never adequately explained the source of the problem or the means of its solution. Indeed, Galbraith notes in a number of locations the ambiguity that plagues Keynes's *General Theory*, equating it to the Bible in that it can be interpreted in myriad ways. Ultimately, he concludes that "*The General Theory* was published long before it was finished. Like the Bible and *Das Kapital*, it is deeply ambiguous" and this "helped greatly to win converts" (*Life in Our Times* 216).

25. Galbraith's writing routine in Gstaad, Switzerland, conformed to this practice. He "work[ed] until [he was] tired and then, either in euphoria or frustration, [went] skiing or walking," during which he "continue[d] to ponder." Then, "by next day you often have something more to say" ("Why Do You Go to Gstaad?" 341). This embodied practice correlates well with the rhetorical theory forwarded by Debra Hawhee in *Bodily Arts* as well as her explication of Kenneth Burke's writing process in *Moving Bodies*.

26. Like Galbraith and unlike Friedman, Joseph Schumpeter argues that "scientific performance does not require us to divest ourselves of our value judgments" (346). For Schumpeter, an economist has a "mixture of perceptions and prescientific analysis" that shapes one's research (350). This is not problematic because, in his view, research in turn confirms or denies this initial vision.

27. Friedman endorses an automated Federal Reserve policy as a way to eliminate the discretionary behavior of individuals whose behavior, no matter how competent, interferes with "true" price signals. In his view, supply and demand never adjust instantaneously because individuals and institutions require time to change prices and production. This lag time in adjustment is exacerbated by allowing monetary supply to be in the

hands of imperfect individuals. The contemporary economy has three lags, according to Friedman: (1) "between the need for action and the recognition of this need," (2) "between recognition of the need for action and the taking of action," and (3) "between the action and its effects" ("Monetary and Fiscal Framework" 145–46). Automation eliminates the first two human-created lags, leaving only the one lag between action and effects.

28. Although seemingly unorthodox, I am not the first to call Friedman a Keynesian. Don Patinkin asserts plainly that Friedman's quantity theory relies on an "analytical framework [that] is Keynesian" (886). In fact, many Keynesians note this aspect of Friedman's work, claiming that monetarism allowed him to be both a free-market economist and a Keynesian. Others, such as Lanny Ebenstein, suggest that he "used Keynesian language" as a strategy to dismantle Keynesianism (108).

29. As Friedman says elsewhere, "Fischer's equation plays the same foundation-stone role in monetary theory that Einstein's $E=mc^2$ does in physics" (*Money Mischief* 39).

30. Friedman defines real value as "the volume of goods and services that the money will purchase" and calculates it by dividing total dollars by a price index to create a "standard basket of goods" (*A Theoretical Framework for Monetary Analysis* 2). In this way, such values are both abstract—they represent how much of some hypothetical combination of goods one can purchase with a given dollar amount—and mathematically concrete as the products of precise equations. As ever, Friedman emphasizes the empirical nature of this monetary theory by likening it to "the uniformities that form the basis of the physical sciences" ("Quantity Theory of Money" 21).

31. One of the problems with this consumption function is that because "permanent income cannot be observed directly, it must be inferred from the behavior of consumer units" (*Theory of the Consumption Function* 221). In such inference, one supposes that those who consume heavily are doing so through a rational calculation of future earnings and not because of manufactured desires, as Galbraith would contend. As one might imagine, this assumption has received its fair share of criticism. See, for instance, Rayack's *Not So Free to Choose*.

32. Friedman argues that the Keynesian revolution resulted from the depression of the early 1930s: "I believe the basic source of the revolution and of the reaction against the quantity theory of money was a historical event, namely the great contraction or depression" ("Counter-Revolution in Monetary Theory" 69). He renames this Great Depression the Great Contraction to emphasize that it resulted from government mismanagement of the quantity of money and not from an internal failure in the business cycle. In absolutely unequivocal terms, he argues that "the reduction in the quantity of money was not a consequence of the unwillingness of horses to drink. It was not a consequence of being unable to push a string. It was a direct consequence of the policies followed by the Federal Reserve system" (75).

33. Thus, the wage-price spiral is, he says, "an effect of inflation, not a cause" (*Money Mischief* 220). This runs contrary to Galbraith, who argues that inflation results from the struggle between union power and corporate power. As unions lobby for increased wages, corporations increase consumer prices, and this propels unions to negotiate further wage increases. Belief in this wage-price spiral is one reason he argues for wage and price controls (*American Capitalism* 198–205).

34. Friedman explains price theory in much the same way as Hayek: prices efficiently communicate supply and demand. In other words, "prices serve as guideposts to where resources are wanted most, and, in addition, prices provide the incentive for people to

follow these guideposts" (*Price Theory* 9). In his view, "the problem solved by a price system is an extremely complicated one, involving the coordination of the activities of tens and hundreds of millions of people all over the global and their prompt adjustment to ever-changing conditions" (10). Government interference unravels the entire process.

35. Although he acknowledges a critical tradition for such exploration, he assesses that work as no less outmoded than the conventional wisdom. Thus, Galbraith eliminates both Marx and Veblen as viable theorists for this stage of capitalism. Marx, he says, served the needs of a particular historical moment during which workers were on the brink of starvation. Contemporary capitalism, however, has initiated a "great material increase in the well-being of the average man," creating different problems from those of Marx's era (*Affluent Society* 80). In specific opposition to those who endorse Marxism, Galbraith argues that they simply substitute "one insufficient view of economic society for another" (*Economics and the Public Purpose* 28). More appropriate to the contemporary moment, Veblen addressed the problem that Galbraith does: the competitive market model does not reflect the political economic reality of twentieth century capitalism. Through this insight, says Galbraith, Veblen taught the next generation to engage conventional wisdom with "doubts and pessimism" but provided no tools with which to dismantle that tradition (*Affluent Society* 47). In a relatively swift one-two punch, he eliminates the two most prominent critics of capitalism as simply not helpful for assessing the power of modern corporations.

36. The concept that consumers "vote with their dollars," linking free-market practices with democratic processes, emerges from Paul Samuelson's *Economics*. First published in 1948 and still in print, Samuelson's book was the leading economic textbook throughout the 1950s and 1960s. Friedman popularized this "vote with your dollars" phrase through his many public books and talks.

37. Galbraith calls this the "dependence effect," or the fact that increasing production requires increasing the demand for that production. Not surprisingly, Friedrich Hayek takes issue with Galbraith's dependency effect. In particular, he opposes Galbraith's equivalency between that which is created and that which is unimportant ("Non Sequitur of the 'Dependence Effect'" 313) For Hayek, "to say that a desire is not important because it is not innate is to say that the whole cultural achievement of man is not important" (314). His opposition to Galbraith stems from a belief in cognitive psychology and tacit mimicry as the driving forces for ordering the social world, an organization that aligns with the free market and not rational intervention.

38. In later editions of his book, Galbraith adds a footnote to this discussion that draws attention to Daniel Bell's *The Coming of the Post-Industrial Society*, which tackles the knowledge economy from a sociological rather than economic perspective. Indeed, there is significant overlap in these two works; see especially chapter 2, on the economy, and chapter 6, on governance.

39. This argument, in many ways, presages the Italian autonomous tradition, which contends that the unpaid labor of social reproduction—child care, elder care, and general support for wage workers—is both foundational to capitalism and discounted in Marx's dichotomy between productive and unproductive labor. For different pathways into this argument, see Mariarosa Dalla Costa, Silvia Federici, and Tiziana Terranova.

40. Keynes, the first economist to simultaneously assume a prominent role in policy making and garner popular support for it, worked tirelessly to establish national economic initiatives and craft an international balance of power through the 1944 Bretton

Woods Agreement; however, he was never in the spotlight in the way Friedman and Galbraith were. And Veblen, who addressed the public on a range of issues from university corporatization to consumer culture, refrained from proposing palliative economic policies. These earlier signs of public engagement notwithstanding, Friedman and Galbraith consolidate public support for a host of policy proposals as none before.

41. See, for instance, Joel Spring's *Education and the Rise of the Corporate State* and Raymond Callahan's *Education and the Cult of Efficiency.*

42. Revelatory of its hegemonic status, one that has been strengthened by the failure of Eastern European communism, capitalism is, in the view of J. K. Gibson-Graham (Katherine Gibson and Julie Graham), the last category of our worldview to avoid deconstruction. They offer a corrective to this by outlining a variety of alternative economic practices that emphasize community over individuality. See their *The End of Capitalism (As We Knew It).*

43. This is the position of those who endorse the framing theory of George Lakoff. In his view, words and their metaphoric structure are hardwired into human brains socially and physically. To shift conversations, people must discuss their objectives within an alternative but equally well-established framework. See, for instance, Lakoff's *The Political Mind.*

44. Benjamin famously asserted in "Theses on the Philosophy of History" that "there is no document of civilization that is not at the same time a document of barbarism" (256).

Conclusion

1. This possibility for such a break similarly underscores what Barbara Biesecker calls evental rhetoric. For a theorization of evental rhetoric as a form of radical agency, see "Whither Ideology" and, with William Trapani, "Escaping the Voice of the Mass/ter"; for an example of evental rhetoric, see her "Prospects of Rhetoric for the Twenty-First Century."

2. Antonio Negri characterizes the difference between self-cultivated individuals and those who are externally cultivated as the difference between constituent power *(potentia)* and constituted power *(potestas).* He develops a history of these two power forms in his *Insurgencies.*

3. Although some readers understand Foucault as advocating the form of biopolitics he identifies in American neoliberalism, Esposito disagrees. In his reading of Foucault, "something like definable human nature doesn't exist as such, independent from the meanings that culture and therefore history have, over the course of time, imprinted on it" (29). According to Esposito, this distinction clearly separates Foucault from Chicago School neoliberalism. For a Chicago School endorsement of Foucault, see the discussion of Gary Becker, François Ewald, and Bernard Hartcourt in "Becker on Ewald on Foucault on Becker." For a careful survey of the different schools of thought on biopolitics and the dialogue that connects the Chicago School with Foucault, see Thomas Lemke's *Biopolitics.*

4. For an explanation of Foucault's concept of governmentality, see Thomas Lemke's "'The Birth of Bio-politics.'"

5. For those accustomed to reading Foucault as the advocate, sine qua non, for local analysis of power relations, the more global framework that he employs at the end of his life can be disappointing. Foucault, however, does not dichotomize these two approaches, asserting, at the end of his April 5, 1978, lecture that "there is not a sort of break between the level of micro-power and the level of macro-power" (*Security, Territory, Population*

358). In fact, he says, analyses of micro-power often lead back to concerns of state governance.

6. In Esposito's view, Foucault conflates biopolitics (governing agency) with biopower (individual agency). To distinguish between these governmentalities, he separates biopolitics from biopower: "by the first is meant a politics in the name of life and by the second a life subjected to the command of politics" (15). Michael Hardt similarly argues for a distinction between these terms that, he says, Foucault does not make clear. However, he asserts a different use of these terms. For Hardt, biopower designates "a form of power in which the life of populations becomes the central object of rule" and "biopolitics is the realm in which we have the freedom to make another life for ourselves" ("Militant Life" 159).

7. Several theorists join Brown in her suspicion that Foucault's analysis of political economy in the *Birth of Biopolitics* undermines state power and consequently abdicates critical resistance to the economic stronghold of capitalism. From this perspective, his theory of governmentality and his reading of Smith's invisible hand disarm leftist discourse by eliminating its privileged vantage point. Ute Tellmann, for instance, argues that Foucault "articulates the impossibility of seeing the whole of society from a single vantage point" (16). This reading of the invisible hand, she says, positions the capitalist market as *"the sole site legitimately producing this knowledge of the whole"* because it operates through the seamless guidance of this external agent (22). She expects a leftist critique—one she criticizes Foucault for not performing—to rescue an anticapitalist vision from this construction.

8. This is, in many ways, the same argument put forward by Martha Nussbaum's *Not for Profit.* A humanist education, they both maintain, cultivates the kind of subjects who make democracy possible.

9. It is this notion of ideology as conscious choice that Slavoj Žižek takes to task in his classic *The Sublime Object of Ideology.*

10. She understands this affective intensity as Lacanian *jouissance,* a point picked up by Christian Lundberg. For Lundberg, the struggle against opposition functions as a form of enjoyment for subjects as diverse as those on the Christian right and those on the political left. See "Trope, Affect, and Public Subjectivity" in his *Lacan in Public.*

11. An amplification of communicative memes, according to Dean, draws individuals into the black hole of technology: "the more strident the voices, the more intense the feelings, the stronger is the pull of communication media" (*Democracy and Other Neoliberal Fantasies* 32).

12. Advocating within technological silos, these activities tend to perform and deepen group identification rather than deliberate policy with diverse stakeholders. See Laura Collins's "The Second Amendment as Demanding Subject" for an excellent analysis of this process.

13. Jameson's *Representing Capital* treats the concept of value in ways that intersect with this notion of bodily desire. He argues that because capitalism is not visible in its totality, "one must redouble one's efforts to express the inexpressible" (7). For him, "capitalism constitutes a social formation" united by the market as a surrogate for the invisible totality of the capitalist community; Marx counters with his concept of value or abstract labor as congealed social power (25). Value tracks "extra-economic levels" that are glimpsed in economic analysis that is not political but ethical (35). For Jameson, however,

this remains a representation of reality. For an abbreviated version of this argument, see his "A New Reading of *Capital*."

14. Foucault explicitly states that there is "no governmental rationality of socialism" (*Birth of Biopolitics* 92).

15. In *The Power at the End of the Economy*, Brian Massumi argues that Foucault's *Birth of Biopower* requires us to rethink "the rational in relation to affect" (2). As he sees it, Foucault challenges us to assert our affective potential as what he calls ontopower or the creative "power of becoming" (15). By properly cultivating subjects, "choice spills from the readiness potential of the subject's affective blind spot, nonconsciously" (19). Effective counterpolitics, he says, must practice "operating, like neoliberalism, as an ontopower" (43). For a shorter version of this argument, see "National Enterprise Emergency." A further call to attend to the affective constitution of embodied subjectivities can be found in Martijn Konings's *The Emotional Logic of Capitalism*. Neither text, however, provides the resources for such reconstruction of subjectivities.

16. Barbara Biesecker has long advocated this interpretation of Foucault. "Michel Foucault and the Question of Rhetoric," for instance, argues that "aesthetics of existence" cannot operate from a position of simply reacting against imposed power, but must invest itself as a new subjectivity.

17. He also refers to biopower in the conclusion to *The History of Sexuality*, published that same year.

18. Foucault argues that discipline takes place through various institutions (education, prison, medicine) whereas biopower takes place through the state. Of course, he admits, this is not a complete dichotomy as institutions often take on "a statist dimension in apparatuses" (*Society Must Be Defended* 250). Consequently, disciplinary power and biopower "are not mutually exclusive and can be articulated with each other" (250).

19. Foucault distinguishes between normalization and normation—the normal and the norm—as techniques representative of disciplinary and biopower, respectively. Disciplinary power identifies the normal and positions individuals in or out of that location; biopower monitors individuals and, through a "calculus of probabilities," intervenes on populations so as to maintain an overall statistical norm (*Security, Territory, Population* 57–59).

20. In an undeveloped interjection, Foucault identifies the people as opposed to both the public and the population: "the people are generally speaking those who resist the regulation of the population, who try to elude the apparatus" (*Security, Territory, Population* 44).

21. Foucault indicates this distinction through the analogy that desire "is to the government of populations a bit what ideology was to the disciplines" (*Security, Territory, Population* 74).

22. This is different from the political subject of Greek democracy that prized intellectual discernment so much that its philosophers pursued "*apatheia*: the absence of *pathé*, or the absence of passions" (*Security, Territory, Population* 178). As Foucault explains, *apatheia* attempts to eliminate all those impulses, forces, and emotional triggers that undermine intellectual agency. The possession of such passions transforms the agentive subject into a "slave of what takes place in you, or in your body, or possibly what happens in the world" (178). According to this conception, one avoids enslavement by eliminating bodily passions.

23. As A. Kiarina Kordela explains, ontology "is both transhistorical and historical, insofar as the historical is always a concrete manifestation of transhistorical relations" (xi).

24. Foucault cites exceptions to the rule of modernity. For instance, he acknowledges that Spinoza makes truth dependent on "a series of requirements concerning the subject's very being" (*Hermeneutics of the Subject* 27). This exemption is important, from my perspective, because so many theorists use Spinoza's notion of the ability to affect and be affected as an anchoring moment in affect studies.

25. The ancient Greco-Roman period does not, he admits, have a monopoly on the idea that social change stems from changes within subjects themselves. For instance, he says that both Marxism and psychoanalysis prominently position the transformed subject "at the very heart of, or anyway, at the source and outcome of both of the knowledges" (*Hermeneutics of the Subject* 29). Revolutionary theories based on either the Marxist or psychoanalytical tradition, however, confuse the importance of a transformed individual subjectivity within collective membership—class or party affiliations, for instance. In this way, these theories make "access to the truth" dependent on social or organizational status rather than on the transformation of an embodied subjectivity (29). In other words, they privilege collective thinking over bodily thinking and obedience over freedom.

26. Foucault cites the Cynic Demetrius as saying that this model for education relies on "the image of the athlete" (*Hermeneutics of the Subject* 231). Thus, such training resonates with an ancient Greek tradition, outlined by Debra Hawhee, in which both philosophical or rhetorical knowledge and athletic knowledge dwell in the body and are produced through habituation. See her *Bodily Arts.*

27. Throughout his reading of this self-subjectivation and truth-telling, Foucault positions *parrhesia* outside rhetoric. For instance, he says, *parrhesia* "must free itself from rhetoric, but not only or solely to expel or exclude it, but rather, by being free from its rules, to be able to use it within strict, always tactically delimited limits, where it is really necessary" so that "with regard to rhetoric there is a freedom, a setting free" (*Hermeneutics of the Subject* 373). He insists that *parrhesia* makes "tactical use of rhetoric, but [has] no fundamental, overall, or total obedience to the rules of rhetoric" (403). Consequently, he clearly asserts that "philosophical discourse is not in fact whole and entirely opposed to rhetorical discourse" (348). Needless to say, this has raised red flags among many rhetoricians. Arthur Walzer impressively outlines the history of *parrhesia* as a rhetorical strategy that, he says, is difficult to distinguish from Foucault's supposedly arhetorical version of *parrhesia*. For a discussion on the relationship between rhetoric and these lectures, see Walzer as well as the forum responding to his work by Pat Gehrke, Susan Jarratt, and Bradford Vivian.

28. Further complicating its relationship to rhetoric, *parrhesia* requires speaking truth "only inasmuch as he is capable of receiving it, and receiving it best, at this moment in time . . . what essentially defines the rules of parrhesia is *kairos*" (*Hermeneutics of the Subject* 384). It is, in this way, a contingent practice oriented to concrete change.

29. From Michael Hardt's perspective, Foucault's last two annual lectures on *parrhesia* make up for that fact that his critique of biopolitics "provided no positive propositions regarding the appropriate modes of struggle against neoliberalism" ("Militant Life" 154). According to Hardt, these final lectures theorize individual biopower, his nomenclature for what Foucault calls self-subjectivation, as the strategic alternative to neoliberalism's biopolitics. Indeed, he asserts in the form of a question: "does Foucault's enthusiasm for

the Cynics indicate that he views their biopolitical militancy as a model for effective contemporary political action against neoliberalism and today's forms of biopower?" (160). For an example of rhetorical criticism that uses *parrhesia* and biopolitics from this perspective, see Kelly Happe's "*Parrhēsia*, Biopolitics, and Occupy."

30. The first lecture of this academic year begins with a discussion of Kant's "What Is Enlightenment?" This query into enlightenment also ends his *Hermeneutics of the Subject*. He asserts, in a footnote toward the end of the text, that enlightenment requires us not only to ask "on what our system of objective knowledge rests, it is also to ask on what the modality of the experience of the self rests" (487). He further develops this line of thinking in an separate manuscript titled "What Is Enlightenment?" and anthologized in *The Foucault Reader*. The point he continually comes back to in these discussions is the need to interrogate the instinctual nature of experience—the ways that decisions appear to be made by our bodies rather than our minds.

31. Foucault distinguishes *parrhesia* from rhetoric on the basis of its institutionalized structures and not because *parrhesia* has no suasive force. He clearly notes that *parrhesia* derives its persuasive force through rhetoric (*Government of Self* 53). The point he makes is that *parrhesia* "will triumph only through the weight of its truth and the effectiveness of its persuasion" and not through institutional power (103).

32. In many ways this form of identification functions as mutual recognition, suggesting that we need a fundamentally different understanding of the political relationship among human beings. For an excellent theorization of Hegelian recognition within the biopolitical frame, see Stuart Murray's "Hegel's Pathology of Recognition."

33. See his 1970 lecture "The Discourse on Language" for a further explanation.

34. In addition to revolutionary movements, *parrhesia,* says Foucault, emerges in modern art that "establishes a polemical relationship of reduction, refusal, and aggression to culture, social norms, values, and aesthetic canons" (*Courage of Truth* 188).

35. Foucault characterizes the daily *parrhesiastic* requirement of self-assessment as an administrative duty rather than a judiciary one. The subject, he says elsewhere, "engages in a kind of administrative scrutiny which enables him to reactivate various rules and maxims in order to make them more vivid, permanent, and effective for future behavior" (*Fearless Speech* 149–50). Through a repetition that invigorates and deepens particular capacities, this self-accounting is not performed for the purposes of punishment and reward but for the purposes of calibrating one's instinctive actions with one's willed knowledge.

36. It is important to note that the *bios* Foucault has in mind is neither the *bios politicos* that defines state politics nor is it the natural life *(zoe)* prior to enculturation. Neither, however, is it the bare life theorized by Giorgio Agamben in *Homo Sacer*. Foucault's *bios* exists outside of formal institutions, but it is not bereft of power. On the contrary, it has the power to manufacture its own nature. In this way, his *bios* aligns better with Massumi's theorization of ontopower as preconscious bodily decision making.

37. As conceived by Foucault, the critical potential of *parrhesia* in the ancient world lies in subjectivity and not in truth. In other words, *parrhesia* is an ontological and not an epistemological concern. Foucault, in fact, argues that the question of truth is a modern one that is completely foreign to those thinkers he investigates (*Fearless Speech* 15).

38. In *Fearless Speech* Foucault discusses this "aesthetics of the self" quite lucidly. It demands, he says, an orientation "towards oneself in the role of a technician, of a craftsman, of an artist, who from time to time stops working, examines what he is doing, reminds

himself of the rules of his art, and compares these rules with what he has achieved thus far" (166).

39. In this way, the Cynics enact Foucauldian parody. In "Nietzsche, Genealogy, History," Foucault presents genealogy as a practice dedicated to producing counter-memory through parody, dissociation, and heterogeneity, as well as the replacement of metanarrative with critique (160–64). For an alternative reading of the relationship between these two texts, see Susan Jarratt's "Untimely Historiography."

40. Foucault illustrates this in his reading of Plato's *Alcibiades*. As he explains it, Socrates takes on the role of instructing this privileged youth in the care of his soul so that he might lead others properly within democratic spaces prescribed for such leadership. See the January 13 and January 20 lectures in *Hermeneutics of the Self*. In some ways, this Socratic/Platonic *parrhesia* mirrors the position that Wendy Brown takes in her advocacy of humanistic study as a means to oppose the neoliberal economization of life. For her, if we simply train students properly, they will assert themselves as proper citizen-subjects.

41. An exception to this rule is the recent work of Celeste Condit who argues for the need to reserve a position for the passions separate from emotions and values. For her, the passions are embodied and distinct from the emotions, which operate under the logic of reason. See, for instance, "Chaïm Perelman's Prolegomenon" and "Pathos in Criticism."

42. Daniel Kahneman, psychologist and recipient of the Nobel Prize in Economics, provides a good introduction to how bodies can be primed through external stimuli. According to his research, individual thinking often relies on shortcuts based on past experience. He calls these instinctual responses fast thinking and argues that they take precedence because slow thinking involves both more time and more physical effort. Individuals can be prompted for specific responses by provoking them with external stimuli that unconsciously elicit the desired outcome through such bodily shortcuts. See his *Thinking, Fast and Slow*.

Works Cited

Aaron, Daniel. "Thorstein Veblen: Moralist and Rhetorician." *Antioch Review* 7.3 (1947): 381–90.

Adorno, Theodor. "The Actuality of Philosophy." *TELOS* 31 (1977): 120–33.

———. "Commodity Music Analyzed." *Quasi Una Fantasia: Essays on Modern Music*. Trans. Rodney Livingstone. London: Verso, 1992. 37–52.

———. *Critical Models: Interventions and Catchwords*. Trans. Henry W. Pickford. New York: Columbia UP, 1998.

———. "Crowds and Power: Conversation with Elias Canetti." *Can One Live After Auschwitz? A Philosophical Reader*. Ed. Rolf Tiedemann. Trans. Rodney Livingstone et al. Stanford, CA: Stanford UP, 2003. 182–201.

———. *Culture Industry: Selected Essays on Mass Culture*. Ed. J. M. Bernstein. London: Routledge, 1991.

———. *Current of Music: Elements of a Radio Theory*. Ed. Robert Hullot-Kentor. Cambridge: Polity, 2009.

———. *Essays on Music*. Ed. Richard Leppert. Trans. Susan H. Gillespie. Berkeley: U of California P, 2002.

———. *History and Freedom: Lectures 1964–1965*. Ed. Rolf Tiedemann. Trans. Rodney Livingstone. Cambridge, UK: Polity, 2007.

———. "Is Marx Obsolete?" *Diogenes* 16.1 (1968): 116.

———. "Late Capitalism or Industrial Society? The Fundamental Question of the Present Structure of Society." *Can One Live After Auschwitz? A Philosophical Reader*. Ed. Rolf Tiedemann. Trans. Rodney Livingstone et al. Stanford, CA: Stanford UP, 2003. 111–25.

———. *Metaphysics: Concept and Problems*. Ed. Rolf Tiedemann. Trans. Edmund Jephcott. Stanford, CA: Stanford UP, 2000.

———. *Minimum Moralia: Reflections from Damaged Life*. Trans. E. F. N. Jephcott. London: Verso, 2000.

———. "Music, Language, and Composition." *Essays on Music*. Ed. Richard Leppert. Trans. Susan Gillespie. Berkeley: U of California P, 2002. 113–26.

———. "Music and Language: A Fragment." *Quasi una Fantasia: Essays on Modern Music*. Trans. Rodney Livingstone. London: Verso, 1992. 1–6.

———. "Music and New Music." *Quasi una Fantasia: Essays on Modern Music*. Trans. Rodney Livingstone. London: Verso, 1992. 249–68.

———. *Negative Dialectics*. Trans. E. B. Ashton. New York: Continuum, 1994.

———. *Notes to Literature*. Vol. 1. Trans. Shierry Weber Nicholsen. New York: Columbia UP, 1991.

———. "Opinion Delusion Society." *Critical Models: Interventions and Catchwords.* Trans. Henry W. Pickford. New York: Columbia UP, 1998. 105–22.

———. *Prisms.* Trans. Samuel and Shierry Weber. London: Neville Spearman, 1967.

———. *Problems of Moral Philosophy.* Ed. Thomas Schröder. Trans. Rodney Livingstone. Stanford, CA: Stanford UP, 2001.

———. "Reflections on Class Theory." *Can One Live After Auschwitz? A Philosophical Reader.* Ed. Rolf Tiedemann. Trans. Rodney Livingstone et al. Stanford, CA: Stanford UP, 2003. 93–110.

———. "Veblen's Attack on Culture." *Prisms.* Trans. Samuel and Shierry Weber. London: Neville Spearman, 1967. 73–94.

Adorno, Theodor, Walter Benjamin, Ernst Bloch, Bertolt Brecht, and Georg Lukács. *Aesthetics and Politics.* Afterword by Fredric Jameson. London: Verso, 1994.

Adorno, Theodor, Else Frenkel-Brunswik, Daniel J, Levinson, and R. Nevitt Sanford. *The Authoritarian Personality.* New York: Harper and Brothers, 1950.

Adorno, Theodor, and Max Horkheimer. *Towards a New Manifesto.* Trans. Rodney Livingstone. London: Verso, 2011.

Agamben, Giorgio. *Homo Sacer: Sovereign Power and Bare Life.* Trans. Daniel Heller-Roazen. Stanford, CA: Stanford UP, 1998.

———. "The Mystery of the Economy." *The Kingdom and the Glory: For a Theological Genealogy of Economy and Government.* Trans. Lorenzo Chiesa. Stanford, CA: Stanford UP, 2011. 17–52.

Agrippa, Heinrich Cornelius. "On the Uncertainty and Vanity of the Arts and Sciences." *Renaissance Debates on Rhetoric.* Ed. and trans. Wayne A. Rebhorn. Ithaca, NY: Cornell UP, 2000. 77–81.

Ahmed, Sara. "Affective Economies." *Social Text* 22.2 (2004): 117–39.

———. *The Cultural Politics of Emotion.* New York: Routledge, 2004.

———. "Orientations: Toward a Queer Phenomenology." *GLQ: A Journal of Lesbian and Gay Studies* 12.4 (2006): 543–74.

Akerlof, George A., and Robert J. Schiller. *Animal Spirits: How Human Psychology Drives the Economy, and Why It Matters for Global Capitalism.* Princeton, NJ: Princeton UP, 2009.

Althusser, Louis. "The '1844 Manuscripts' of Karl Marx." *For Marx.* Trans. Ben Brewster. London: Verso, 1990. 153–60

———. "From *Capital* to Marx's Philosophy." *Reading Capital.* London: Verso, 1997. 11–69.

———. "Contradiction and Overdetermination." *For Marx.* Trans. Ben Brewster. New York: Verso, 1993. 87–116.

———. "Ideology and Ideological State Apparatuses." *Lenin and Philosophy and Other Essays.* Trans. Ben Brewster. New York: Monthly Review, 1971. 127–86.

———. "On the Young Marx." *For Marx.* Trans. Ben Brewster. New York: Verso, 1993. 51–86.

———. "Preface to *Capital* Volume One." *Lenin and Philosophy and Other Essays.* New York: Monthly Review, 1971. 71–101.

———. *Reading Capital.* Trans. Ben Brewster. New York: Verso, 1997.

Aristotle. *On Rhetoric: A Theory of Civil Discourse.* Ed. and trans. George Kennedy. New York: Oxford UP, 1991.

Arrighi, Giovanni. *The Long Twentieth Century.* London: Verso, 2000.

Asen, Rob. *Invoking the Invisible Hand: Social Security and the Privatization Debates.* East Lansing: Michigan State UP, 2009.

Aune, James Arnt. "Cultures of Discourse: Marxism and Rhetorical Theory." *Contemporary Rhetorical Theory: A Reader*. Ed. John Lucaites, Celeste Condit, and Sally Caudill. New York: Guilford, 1999. 539–51.

———. "Democratic Style and Ideological Containment." *Rhetoric and Public Affairs* 11.3 (2008): 482–90.

———. "An Historical Materialist Theory of Rhetoric." *American Communication Journal* 6.4 (2003): 1–20.

———. *Rhetoric and Marxism*. Boulder, CO: Westview, 1994.

———. *Selling the Free Market: The Rhetoric of Economic Correctness*. New York: Guildford, 2001.

Axelos, Kōstas. *Alienation, Praxis, and Technē in the Thought of Karl Marx*. Austin: U of Texas P, 1976.

Ayers, C. E. "Veblen's Theory of Instincts Reconsidered." *Thorstein Veblen: A Critical Reappraisal*. Ed. Douglas Dowd. Ithaca, NY: Cornell UP, 1958. 25–37.

Barad, Karen. *Meeting the Universe Halfway: Quantum Physics and the Entanglement of Matter and Meaning*. Durham, NC: Duke UP, 2007.

Baran, Paul, and Paul Sweezy. *Monopoly Capital: An Essay on the American Economic and Social Order*. New York: Monthly Review, 1966.

Bateman, Brad. "Das Maynard Keynes Problem." *Cambridge Journal of Economics* 15 (1991): 101–11.

———. *Keynes's Uncertain Revolution*. Ann Arbor: U of Michigan P, 1996.

Bazerman, Charles. "Money Talks: Adam Smith's Rhetorical Project." *Constructing Experience*. Carbondale: South Illinois UP, 1994.

Beam, Elizabeth, et al. "Mapping the Semantic Structure of Cognitive Neuroscience." *Journal of Cognitive Neuroscience* 26.9 (2014): 1928–48.

Becker, Gary. *The Economic Approach to Human Behavior*. Chicago: U of Chicago P, 1976.

Becker, Gary, François Ewald, and Bernard Hartcourt. "Becker on Ewald on Foucault on Becker." U of Chicago. October 2012. Web: http://ssrn.com/abstract=2142163. Accessed February 2, 2013.

Behrent, Michael. "Liberalism without Humanism: Michel Foucault and the Free-Market Creed, 1976–79." *Modern Intellectual History* 6.3 (2009): 539–68.

Bell, Daniel. *The Coming of Post-Industrial Society*. New York: Basic Books, 1973.

Bender, John, and David Wellbery. "Rhetoricality: On the Modernist Return of Rhetoric." *The Ends of Rhetoric: History, Theory, Practice*. Ed. John Bender and David Wellbery. Stanford, CA: Stanford UP, 1990. 3–39.

Benjamin, Walter. "Theses on the Philosophy of History." *Illuminations*. Trans. Harry Zohn. New York: Schocken, 1969. 253–64.

———. "The Work of Art in the Age of Mechanical Reproduction." *Illuminations*. Trans. Harry Zohn. New York: Schocken, 1969. 217–51.

Bennett, Jane. "The Force of Things: Steps toward an Ecology of Matter." *Political Theory* 32.3 (2004): 347–72.

———. *Vibrant Matter: A Political Ecology of Things*. Durham: Duke UP, 2010.

Berlant, Lauren. *Cruel Optimism*. Durham, NC: Duke UP, 2011.

Bernays, Edward. *Propaganda*. 1928. Brooklyn, NY: Ig Publishing, 2005.

Biesecker, Barbara. "Michel Foucault and the Question of Rhetoric." *Philosophy and Rhetoric* 25.4 (1992): 351–64.

———. "Prospects of Rhetoric for the Twenty-First Century: Speculations on Evental Rhetoric Ending with a Note on Barack Obama." *Reengaging the Prospects of Rhetoric.* Ed. Mark J. Porrovecchio. New York: Routledge, 2010. 16–36.

———. "Whither Ideology? Toward a Different Take on Enjoyment as a Political Factor." *Western Journal of Communication* 75.4 (2011): 445–50.

Biesecker, Barbara, and William Trapani. "Escaping the Voice of the Mass/ter: Late Neoliberalism, Object-Voice, and the Prospects for a Radical Democratic Future." *Advances in the History of Rhetoric* 17.1 (2014): 2–33.

Blundell, John. "Introduction: Hayek, Fisher and *The Road to Serfdom.*" *The Road to Serfdom, with The Intellectuals and Socialism.* London: Institute of Economic Affairs, 2005. 22–33.

———. "Introduction: Hayek and the Second-Hand Dealers in Ideas." *The Road to Serfdom, with The Intellectuals and Socialism.* London: Institute of Economic Affairs, 2005. 96–104.

Boulding, Kenneth. "Economics as a Moral Science." *American Economic Review* 59.1 (1969): 1–12.

Brennan, Teresa. *The Transmission of Affect.* Ithaca, NY: Cornell UP, 2004.

Brown, Bill. "Thing Theory." *Critical Inquiry* 28.1 (2001): 1–21.

Brown, Wendy. *Edgework: Critical Essays.* Princeton, NJ: Princeton UP, 2005.

———. *Regulating Aversion: Tolerance in the Age of Identity and Empire.* Princeton, NJ: Princeton UP, 2006.

———. *Undoing the Demos: Neoliberalism's Stealth Revolution.* New York: Zone Books, 2015.

Buck-Morss, Susan. *The Origin of Negative Dialectics: Theodor W. Adorno, Walter Benjamin, and the Frankfurt Institute.* New York: Free Press, 1977.

Burke, Kenneth. *Counter-Statement.* 1931. Los Altos, CA: Hermes, 1953.

———. "Methodological Repression and/or Strategies of Containment." *Critical Inquiry* 5.2 (1978): 401–16.

———. *A Rhetoric of Motives.* 1950. Berkeley: U of California P, 1969.

Burke, Peter. "The Spread of Italian Humanism." *The Impact of Humanism on Western Europe.* Ed. Anthony Goodman and Angus MacKay. New York: Longman, 1990. 1–22.

Butler, Eamonn. *Milton Friedman: A Concise Guide to the Ideas and Influence of the Free-Market Economist.* Hampshire, UK: Harriman House, 2011.

———. *Milton Friedman: A Guide to His Economic Thought.* New York: Universe, 1985.

Butos, William, ed. *The Social Science of Hayek's 'The Sensory Order.'* Bingley, UK: Emerald, 2010.

Cadwell, Bruce. *Hayek's Challenge: An Intellectual Biography of F. A. Hayek.* Chicago: U of Chicago P, 2005.

———. "Some Reflections on F. A. Hayek's *The Sensory Order.*" *Journal of Bioeconomics* 6 (2004): 239–54.

Calhoun, Craig. *Habermas and the Public Sphere.* Cambridge, MA: MIT Press, 1993.

Callahan, Raymond. *Education and the Cult of Efficiency.* Chicago: U of Chicago, P, 1964.

Campbell, George. "The Nature and Foundation of Eloquence." *The Rhetoric of Blair, Campbell, and Whately.* Ed. James L Golden and Edward P. J. Corbett. Carbondale: Southern Illinois UP, 1990. 145–271.

Cetina, Karin Knorr, and Urs Bruegger. "Traders' Engagement with Markets: A Postsocial Relationship." *Theory, Culture and Society* 19.5/6: 161–85.

Chaput, Catherine. "Affect and Belonging in Late Capitalism: A Speculative Narrative on the Unexamined Rhetoricity of Reality TV." *International Journal of Communication* 5.1 (2011): 1–20.

———. "How to Read Popular Economics: An Exploration into Neoliberal Propaganda and Its Affectivity." *Managing American Democracy: Propaganda and the Production of Political Rhetorics and Realities.* Ed. M. J. Braun and Gae Lyn Henderson. Carbondale: Southern Illinois UP, 2016. 157–80.

———. "Rhetorical Circulation in Late Capitalism: Neoliberalism and the Overdetermination of Affective Energy." *Philosophy and Rhetoric* 43.1 (2010): 1–25.

———. "The Rhetorical Situation and the Battle for Public Sentiment: How Friedman Surpassed Galbraith at the Dawn of Neoliberalism." *Communication and the Economy: History, Value, and Agency.* Ed. Josh Hanan and Mark Hayward. New York: Peter Lang, 2013. 187–208.

Chaput, Catherine, and Joshua S. Hanan. "Economic Rhetoric as *Taxis*: Neoliberal Governmentality and the Dispositif of Freakonomics." *Journal of Cultural Economy* 8.1 (2014): 1–20.

Cherrier, Béatrice. "The Lucky Consistency of Milton Friedman's Science and Politics, 1933–1963." *Building Chicago Economics: New Perspectives on the History of America's Most Powerful Economics Program.* Ed. Robert Van Horn, Philip Mirowski, and Thomas A. Stapleford. Cambridge: Cambridge UP, 2011. 335–67.

Cloud, Dana. *Control and Consolation in American Culture and Politics.* Thousand Oaks, CA: Sage, 1998.

———. "The Materialist Dialectic as a Site of *Kairos*: Theorizing Rhetorical Intervention in Material Social Relations." *Rhetoric, Materiality, and Politics.* Ed. Barbara A. Biesecker and John Lucaites. New York: Peter Lang, 2009. 293–320.

———. "Therapy, Silence, and War: Consolation and the End of Deliberation in the 'Affected' Public." *Poroi* 2.1 (2003): 125–42.

Cloud, Dana L., and Kathleen Eaton Feyh. "Reason in Revolt: Emotional Fidelity and Working Class Standpoint in the 'Internationale.'" *Rhetoric Society Quarterly* 45.4 (2015): 300–318.

Clough, Patricia. *Autoaffection: Unconscious Thought in the Age of Technology.* Minneapolis: U of Minnesota P, 2000.

Clough, Patricia, Greg Goldberg, Rachel Schiff, Adam Weeks, and Craig Willse. "Notes Towards a Theory of Affect-Itself." *Ephemera* 7 (2007): 60–77.

Cole, Thomas. *The Origins of Rhetoric in Ancient Greece.* Baltimore: Johns Hopkins UP, 1991.

Collins, Laura. "The Second Amendment as Demanding Subject: Figuring the Marginalized Subject in Demands for an Unbridled Second Amendment. *Rhetoric & Public Affairs* 17.4 (2014): 737–56.

Cook, Deborah. "The Sundered Totality: Adorno's Freudo-Marxism." *Journal for the Theory of Social Behavior* 25.2 (1995): 191–215.

Cook, Harold. "Body and Passions: Materialism and the Early Modern State." *OSIRIS* 17 (2002): 25–48.

Coole, Diana, and Samantha Frost, eds. *New Materialisms: Ontology, Agency, and Politics.* Durham, NC: Duke UP, 2010.

Condit, Celeste. "Chaïm Perelman's Prolegomenon to a New Rhetoric: How Should We Feel?" *Reengaging the Prospects of Rhetoric.* Ed. Mark J. Porrovecchio. New York: Routledge, 2010. 96–111.

———. "Pathos in Criticism: Edwin Black's Communism-As-Cancer Metaphor." *Quarterly Journal of Speech* 99.1 (2013): 1–26.

Dalla Costa, Mariarosa. *Women, Development, and Labor of Reproduction: Struggles and Movements*. Ed. Giovanna Dalla Costa. Trenton, NJ: African World Press, 1999.

Davies, William, and Linsey McGoey. "Rationalities of Ignorance: On Financial Crisis and the Ambivalence of Neo-liberal Epistemology." *Economy and Society* 41.1 (2012): 64–83.

Davis, Diane. *Inessential Solidarity: Rhetoric and Foreigner Relations*. Pittsburgh: U of Pittsburgh P, 2010.

———. "Identification: Burke and Freud on Who You Are." *Rhetoric Society Quarterly* 38.2 (2008): 123–47.

Dean, Jodi. *The Communist Horizon*. London: Verso, 2012.

———. *Democracy and Other Neoliberal Fantasies: Communicative Capitalism and Left Politics*. Durham, NC: Duke UP, 2009.

———. "Enjoying Neoliberalism." *Cultural Politics* 4 (2008): 47–72.

Deleuze, Gilles. "Postscript on Control Societies." *Negotiations*. New York: Columbia UP, 1995. 177–82.

Deleuze, Gilles, and Félix Guattari. *Anti-Oedipus: Capitalism and Schizophrenia*. Trans. Robert Hurley, Mark Seem, and Helen R. Lane. London: Continuum, 2004.

———. *A Thousand Plateaus: Capitalism and Schizophrenia*. Trans. Brian Massumi. Minneapolis: U of Minnesota P, 1987.

———. "Percept Affect and Concept." *What Is Philosophy?* Trans. Hugh Tomlinson and Graham Burchill. London: Verso, 1994. 163–200.

Derrida, Jacques. *Specters of Marx: The State of the Debt, the Work of Mourning, and the New International*. Trans. Peggy Kamuf. New York: Routledge, 1994.

Diggins, John P. *The Bard of Savagery: Thorstein Veblen and Modern Social Theory*. New York: Seabury, 1978.

Dowd, Douglas. "Depths below Depths: The Intensification, Multiplication, and Spread of Capitalism's Destructive Force from Marx's Time To Ours." *Radical Political Economics* 34 (2002): 247–66.

———. *Thorstein Veblen*. New York: Washington Square, 1966.

———. "The Theory of Business Enterprise." *Veblen's Century: A Collective Portrait*. Ed. Irving Louis Horowitz. New Brunswick, NJ: Transaction, 2002: 195–202.

Dorfman, Joseph. *Thorstein Veblen and His America*. New York: Viking, 1934.

Drosos, Dionysios. "Adam Smith and Karl Marx: Alienation in Market Society." *History of Economic Ideas* 4.1–2 (1996): 325–51.

Dunn, Stephen P. "The Origins of the Galbraithian System: Stephen P. Dunn in Conversation with J. K. Galbraith." *Interviews with John Kenneth Galbraith*. Ed. James Ronald Stanfield and Jacqueline Bloom Stanfield. Jackson: UP of Mississippi, 2004. 217–37.

Ebenstein, Alan. *Hayek's Journey: The Mind of Friedrich Hayek*. New York: Palgrave, 2003.

Ebenstein, Lanny. *Milton Friedman: A Biography*. New York: Palgrave, 2007.

Engels, Friedrich. *Anti-Dühring: Herr Eugen Dühring's Revolution in Science*. New York: International Publishers, 1966.

Erikson, Kai. "On Work and Alienation." *American Sociological Review* 51.1 (1986): 1–8.

Esposito, Roberto. *Bios: Biopolitics and Philosophy*. Trans. Timothy Campbell. Minneapolis: U of Minnesota P, 2008.

"Extrahuman Rhetoric: Addressing the Animal, the Object, the Dead, and the Divine." Special issue, *Philosophy and Rhetoric* 47.4 (2014).

Fanon, Frantz. *Black Skin, White Masks*. Trans. Charles Lam Markmann. New York: Grove, 1968.

Federici, Silvia. *Revolution at Point Zero: Housework, Reproduction, and Feminist Struggle*. Oakland, CA: PM, 2012.

Ferguson, Adam. *An Essay on the History of Civil Society*. London: Cadell, 1767.

Feuerbach, Ludwig. *The Essence of Christianity*. Trans. M. Evans. New York: Harper and Row, 1967.

Feulner, Edwin. "Foreword: The Intellectuals and Socialism." *The Road to Serfdom, with The Intellectuals and Socialism*. London: Institute of Economic Affairs, 2005. 93–95.

Fine, Ben. "Economics Imperialism and Intellectual Progress: The Present as History of Economic Thought?" *History of Economics Review* 32 (2000): 10–36.

Fine, Gary Alan. "The Social Construction of Style: Thorstein Veblen's *The Theory of the Leisure Class* as Contested Text." *Sociology Quarterly* 35.3 (1994): 457–72.

Fleming, David. "Rhetoric as a Course of Study." *College English* 61.2 (1998): 169–91.

Flew, Terry. "Michel Foucault's *The Birth of Biopolitics* and Contemporary Neo-Liberalism Debates." *Thesis Eleven* 108.1 (2012): 2–40.

Forman-Barzilai, Fonna. "Sympathy in Space(s): Adam Smith on Proximity." *Political Theory* 33.2 (2005): 189–217.

Foucault, Michel. "Adorno, Horkheimer, and Marcuse: Who is a 'Negator of History'? *Remarks on Marx: Conversations with Duccio Trombadori*. Trans. R. James Goldstein and James Cascaito. New York: Semiotext(e), 1991. 115–29.

———. *The Birth of Biopolitics*. Trans. Graham Burchell. New York: Picador, 2008.

———. *The Care of the Self*. Trans. Robert Hurley. New York: Vintage, 1988.

———. *The Courage of Truth*. Trans. Graham Burchell. New York: Picador, 2012.

———. "The Discourse on Language." *The Archeology of Knowledge*. Trans. A. M. Sheridan Smith. New York: Pantheon, 1972. 215–37.

———. *Fearless Speech*. Los Angeles: Semiotext(e): 2001.

———. *The Government of Self and Others*. Trans. Graham Burchell. New York: Picador, 2011.

———. *The Hermeneutics of the Subject*. Trans. Graham Burchell. New York: Picador, 2005.

———. *The History of Sexuality: An Introduction*. Trans. Robert Hurley. New York: Vintage, 1990.

———. "Nietzsche, Genealogy, History." *Language, Counter-Memory, Practice: Selected Essays and Interviews*. Ithaca, NY: Cornell UP, 1977. 139–64.

———. *Security, Territory, Population*. Trans. Graham Burchell. Ed. Michel Senellart. New York: Palgrave, 2007.

———. *Society Must Be Defended*. Trans. Graham Burchell. New York: Picador, 1997.

———. "What Is Enlightenment?" *The Foucault Reader*. Ed. Paul Rabinow. New York: Pantheon, 1984. 32–50.

Frank, Robert H. "Right for the Wrong Reasons: Why Galbraith Never Got the Prize." *New York Times*, May 11, 2006. Web: https://www.nytimes.com/2006/05/11/business/11scene.html. Accessed January 22, 2015.

Frantz, Roger. "Intuitive Elements of Adam Smith." *Journal of Socio-Economics* 29 (2000): 1–19.

Freedman, Carl, and Neil Lazarus. "The Mandarin Marxism of Theodor Adorno." *Rethinking Marxism* 1.4 (1988): 85–111.

Freedman, Craig. *Chicago Fundamentalism: Ideology and Methodology in Economics*. Hackensack, NJ: World Scientific, 2008.

Freud, Sigmund. *Civilization and its Discontents.* Trans. James Strachey. New York: Norton, 1962.

———. *The Future of an Illusion.* Trans. James Strachey. New York: Norton, 1989.

———. *Group Psychology and the Analysis of the Ego.* Trans. James Strachey. New York: Liveright, 1951.

———. *Totem and Taboo.* Trans. A. A. Brill. New York: Vintage, 1946.

Friedman, Milton. "The Counter-Revolution in Monetary Theory." *Money, Inflation and the Constitutional Position of the Central Bank.* London: Institute of Economic Affairs, 2003. 64–90.

———. *Dollars and Deficits: Living with America's Economic Problems.* Englewood Cliffs, NJ: Prentice-Hall, 1968.

———. "The Expected-Utility Hypothesis and the Measurability of Utility." *The Essence of Friedman.* Ed. Kurt R. Leube. Stanford, CA: Hoover Institution P, 1987. 206–21.

———. "Foreword." *Essays on Hayek.* Ed. Fritz Machlup. New York: Routledge, 1977. xxi–xxiv.

———. "The Methodology of Positive Economics." *Essays in Positive Economics.* Chicago: U of Chicago P, 1953. 3–43.

———. *Money Mischief: Episodes in Monetary History.* New York: Harcourt, 1992.

———. "Monetary and Fiscal Framework for Economic Stability." *Essays in Positive Economics.* Chicago: U of Chicago P, 1953. 133–56.

———. "The Monetary Theory and Policy of Henry Simons." *Journal of Law and Economics* 10 (1967): 1–13.

———. "Neo-Liberalism and its Prospects." *Farmand,* February 17, 1951, 89–93.

———. "Nobel Lecture: Inflation and Unemployment." *Milton Friedman on Economics: Selected Papers.* Chicago: U of Chicago P, 2007. 1–22.

———. *Price Theory.* Chicago: Aldine, 1976.

———. "The Quantity Theory of Money—A Restatement." *Studies in the Quantity Theory of Money.* Ed. Milton Friedman. Chicago: U of Chicago P, 1956.

———. "The Role of Monetary Policy." *American Economic Review* 58.1 (1968): 1–17.

———. *A Theoretical Framework for Monetary Analysis.* New York: National Bureau of Economic Research, 1971.

———. *A Theory of the Consumption Function.* Princeton, NJ: Princeton UP, 1957.

———. "Value Judgments in Economics." *Human Values and Economic Policy.* Ed. Sidney Hook. New York: New York UP, 1967. 85–93.

Friedman, Milton, and Rose Friedman. *Capitalism and Freedom.* Chicago: U of Chicago P, 2002.

———. *Free to Choose: A Personal Statement.* New York: Harcourt, 1990.

———. *Two Lucky People: Memoirs.* Chicago: U of Chicago P, 1998.

Friedman, Milton, and Anna Jacobson Schwartz. *A Monetary History of the United States, 1867–1960.* Princeton: Princeton UP, 1963.

———. *The Great Contraction, 1929–1933.* Princeton, NJ: Princeton UP, 1965.

Frijters, Paul, and Andrew Leigh. "Materialism on the March: From Conspicuous Leisure to Conspicuous Consumption?" *Journal of Socio-Economics* 37 (2008): 1937–45.

Gabriel, Mary. *Love and Capital: Karl and Jenny Marx and the Birth of a Revolution.* New York: Little, Brown, 2011.

Galbraith, John Kenneth. *The Affluent Society.* Boston: Houghton Mifflin, 1976.

———. *American Capitalism: The Concept of Countervailing Power.* Boston: Houghton Mifflin, 1952.

———. *The Anatomy of Power.* Boston: Houghton Mifflin, 1983.

———. *Economics and the Art of Controversy.* New Brunswick, NJ: Rutgers UP, 1955.

———. *Economics and the Public Purpose.* Boston: Houghton Mifflin, 1973.

———. *The Economics of Innocent Fraud.* New York: Penguin, 2005.

———. "The Founding Faith: Adam Smith's *Wealth of Nations.*" *The Essential Galbraith.* Ed. Andrea D. Williams. Boston: Houghton Mifflin, 2001. 153–68.

———. *The Galbraith Reader.* Ipswich, MA: Gambit, 1977.

———. *The Great Crash, 1929.* Boston: Houghton Mifflin, 1972.

———. "How Keynes Came to America." *Economics Peace and Laughter.* Ed. Andrea Williams. Boston: Houghton Mifflin, 1971. 43–59.

———. "The Language of Economics." *Economics, Peace and Laughter.* Ed. Andrea Williams. Boston: Houghton Mifflin, 1971. 26–42.

———. *A Life in Our Times: Memoirs.* Boston: Houghton Mifflin, 1981.

———. *The New Industrial State.* Boston: Houghton Mifflin, 1985.

———. *A Short History of Financial Euphoria.* New York: Penguin, 1994.

———. *A Theory of Price Control.* Cambridge: Harvard UP, 1952.

———. "Who Was Thorstein Veblen?" *The Essential Galbraith.* Ed. Andrea D. Williams. Boston: Houghton Mifflin, 2001. 200–223.

———. "Why Do You Go to Gstaad?" *Economics, Peace and Laughter.* Ed. Andrea D. Williams. Boston: Houghton Mifflin, 1971. 337–43

———. "Writing, Typing, and Economics." *Atlantic.* March 1978. Web: https://www.theatlantic.com/magazine/archive/1978/03/writing-typing-and-economics/305165/. Accessed September 25, 2015.

Gaonkar, Dilip Parameshwar. "The Idea of Rhetoric in the Rhetoric of Science." *Rhetorical Hermeneutics: Invention and Interpretation in the Age of Science.* Ed. Alan G. Gross and William M. Keith. Albany: State U of New York P, 1997. 25–85.

Gehrke, Pat J., Susan C. Jarratt, Bradford Vivian, Arthur E. Walzer. "Forum on Art Walzer's 'Parrēsia, Foucault, and the Classical Rhetorical Tradition.'" *Rhetoric Society Quarterly* 43.4 (2013): 355–81.

Gibson, Nigel. "Rethinking an Old Saw: Dialectical Negativity, Utopia, and *Negative Dialectics* in Adorno's Hegelian Marxism." *Adorno: A Critical Reader.* Ed. Nigel Gibson and Andrew Rubin. Oxford, UK: Blackwell, 2002. 257–91.

Gibson-Graham, J. K. *The End of Capitalism (As We Knew It): A Feminist Critique of Political Economy.* Minneapolis: U of Minnesota P, 1996.

Gifford, Adam. "The Knowledge Problem, Determinism, and *The Sensory Order.*" *Review of Austrian Economics* 20 (2007): 269–91.

Godfrey, Richard. "Sucking, Bleeding, Breaking: On the Dialectics of Vampirism, Capital, and Time." *Culture and Organization* 10 (2004): 25–36.

Golden, James L., and Edward P. J. Corbett. *The Rhetoric of Blair, Campbell, and Whately.* Carbondale: Southern Illinois UP, 1990.

Gordon, Wendell. "What of Friedman's *Free to Choose?*" *Journal of Economic Issues* 16.1 (1982): 301–7.

Gorgias. "Encomium of Helen." *The Rhetorical Tradition: Readings from Classical Times to the Present.* Ed. Patricia Bizzell and Bruce Herzberg. Boston: Bedford, 1990. 40–42.

Gramsci, Antonio. *Selections from the Prison Notebooks.* Ed. and trans. Quintin Hoare and Geoffrey Nowell-Smith. New York: International Publishers, 1992.

Greene, Ronald Walter. "Another Materialist Rhetoric." *Critical Studies in Mass Communication* 15 (1998): 21–41.

———. Rhetoric and Capitalism: Rhetorical Agency as Communicative Labor. *Philosophy and Rhetoric* 37 (2004): 188–206.

———. "Rhetorical Capital: Communicative Labor, Money/Speech, and Neo-Liberal Governance." *Communication and Critical/Cultural Studies* 4.3 (2007): 327–33.

———. "Rhetorical Materialism: The Rhetorical Subject and the General Intellect." *Rhetoric, Materiality, and Politics.* Ed. Barbara Biesecker and John Lucaites. New York: Peter Lang, 2009. 44–66.

Gregg, Melissa. *Cultural Studies' Affective Voices.* New York: Palgrave, 2006.

Grossberg, Lawrence. *We Gotta Get Out of This Place: Popular Conservatism and Post-Modern Culture.* New York: Routledge, 1992.

Habermas, Jürgen. "A Generation Apart from Adorno." *Philosophy and Social Criticism* 18.2 (1992): 119–24.

———. *The Structural Transformation of the Public Sphere.* Cambridge, MA: MIT Press, 1991.

Hammond, J. Daniel. "An Interview with Milton Friedman on Methodology." *Research in the History of Economic Thought and Methodology* 10 (1992): 91–118.

Happe, Kelly E. "*Parrhēsia*, Biopolitics, and Occupy." *Philosophy and Rhetoric* 48.2 (2015): 211–23.

Harcourt, Bernard. *The Illusion of Free Markets.* Cambridge, MA: Harvard UP, 2011.

Hardt, Michael. "Affective Labor." *Boundary 2* 26.2 (1999): 89–100.

———. "Militant Life." *New Left Review* 64 (2010): 151–60.

Hardt, Michael, and Antonio Negri. *Commonwealth.* Cambridge, MA: Harvard UP, 2009.

———. *Empire.* Cambridge, MA: Harvard UP, 2000.

———. *Multitude: War and Democracy in the Age of Empire.* New York: Penguin, 2000.

Harman, Graham. *Tool-Being: Heidegger and the Metaphysics of Objects.* Chicago: Open Court, 2002.

Harvey, David. *Justice, Nature, and the Geography of Difference.* Oxford, UK: Blackwell, 1996.

Hawhee, Debra. *Bodily Arts: Rhetoric and Athletics in Ancient Greece.* Austin: U of Texas P, 2005.

———. *Moving Bodies: Kenneth Burke at the Edges of Language.* Columbia: U of South Carolina P, 2012.

Hayek, Friedrich. *The Confusion of Language in Political Thought.* Occasional Paper 20. London: Institute of Economic Affairs, 1968.

———. *The Constitution of Liberty: The Definitive Edition.* Chicago: U of Chicago P, 2011.

———. *The Counter-Revolution of Science: Studies on the Abuse of Reason.* Glencoe, IL: Free Press, 1952.

———. "Dr. Bernard Mandeville." *New Studies in Philosophy, Politics, Economics, and the History of Ideas.* Chicago: U of Chicago P, 1978. 249–66.

———. "Economics and Knowledge." 1948. *Individualism and Economic Order.* Chicago: U of Chicago P, 1980. 33–56.

———. "The Economy, Science, and Politics." *Studies in Philosophy, Politics, and Economics.* Chicago: U of Chicago P, 1967. 251–69.

———. *The Fatal Conceit: Errors of Socialism.* Chicago: U of Chicago P, 1988.

———. "Individualism: True and False." *Individualism and Economic Order.* Chicago: U of Chicago P, 1980.

———. "The Intellectuals and Socialism." 1949. *The Road to Serfdom, with The Intellectuals and Socialism.* London: Institute of Economic Affairs, 2005. 105–29.

———. *The Mirage of Social Justice.* Chicago: U of Chicago P, 1978.

———. "The Non Sequitur of the 'Dependence Effect.'" *Studies in Philosophy, Politics, and Economics.* Chicago: U of Chicago P, 1967. 313–17.

———. "Opening Address to a Conference at Mont Pèlerin." *Studies in Philosophy, Politics, and Economics.* Chicago: U of Chicago P, 1967. 148–59.

———. *The Political Order of a Free People.* Chicago: U of Chicago P, 1979.

———. *Prices and Production.* London: Routledge, 1935.

———. *The Pure Theory of Capital.* Chicago: U of Chicago P, 1989.

———. *The Road to Serfdom.* Chicago: U of Chicago P, 2007.

———. *Rules and Order.* Chicago: U of Chicago P, 1973.

———. "Rules, Perception, and Intelligibility." *Studies in Philosophy, Politics, and Economics.* Chicago: U of Chicago P, 1967. 43–65.

———. *The Sensory Order: An Inquiry into the Foundations of Theoretical Psychology.* Chicago: U of Chicago P, 1963.

———. "The Theory of Complex Phenomena." *Studies in Philosophy, Politics, and Economics.* Chicago: U of Chicago P, 1967. 22–42.

———. "The Transmission of the Ideals of Economic Freedom." 1951. *Econ Journal Watch* 9.2 (2012): 163–69.

Heath, Eugene. "Rules, Function, and the Invisible Hand: An Interpretation of Hayek's Social Theory." *Philosophy of the Social Sciences* 22.1 (1992): 28–45.

Hegel, G. W. F. *The Phenomenology of Mind.* Trans. J. B. Baillie. Mineola, NY: Dover, 2003.

Henriques, Julian. "The Vibrations of Affect and Their Propagation on a Night Out on Kingston's Dancehall Scene." *Bodies and Society* 16.1 (2010): 57–89.

Herring, Rodney, and Mark Garrett Longaker. "Wishful, Rational, and Political Thinking: The Labor Theory of Value as Rhetoric." *Argumentation and Advocacy* 50.4 (2014): 193–209.

Hession, Charles. *John Galbraith and His Critics.* New York: Norton, 1972.

Hill, Forest G. "Veblen and Marx." *Thorstein Veblen: A Critical Reappraisal.* Ed. Douglas Dowd. Ithaca, NY: Cornell UP, 1958.

Hirschman, Albert O. *The Passions and the Interests: Political Arguments for Capitalism before Its Triumph.* Princeton, NJ: Princeton UP, 1997.

———. *The Rhetoric of Reaction: Perversity, Futility, Jeopardy.* Cambridge, MA: Harvard UP, 1991.

Hobbes, Thomas. *Leviathan.* Baltimore: Penguin, 1968.

Hoggart, Richard. *The Uses of Literacy.* London: Transaction, 1957.

Horkheimer, Max. "Authority and the Family." *Critical Theory: Selected Essays.* Trans. Matthew J. O'Connell. New York: Continuum, 1982. 47–128.

Horkheimer, Max, and Theodor Adorno. *Dialectic of Enlightenment.* Trans. John Cumming. New York: Continuum, 1994.

Horwitz, Steven. "From *The Sensory Order* to the Liberal Order: Hayek's Non-Rationalist Liberalism." *Review of Austrian Economics* 13 (2000): 23–40.

Hullot-Kentor, Robert. Translator's Introduction. *Aesthetic Theory.* By Theodor Adorno. Minneapolis: U of Minnesota P, 1997. xi–xxi.

Jack, Jordynn. *Neurorhetorics.* New York: Routledge, 2012.

———. "What Are Neurorhetorics?" *Rhetoric Society Quarterly* 40.5 (2010): 405–10.

Jack, Jordynn, and Paul Appelbaum. "'This is Your Brain on Rhetoric': Research Directions for Neurorhetorics." *Rhetoric Society Quarterly* 40.5 (2010): 411–37.

James, William. *Principles of Psychology.* Vol. 2. New York: Henry Holt, 1896.

———. "What Is an Emotion?" *Mind* 9 (1884): 188–205.

Jameson, Fredric. *Late Marxism: Adorno, or, The Persistence of the Dialectic.* Verso: London, 1990.

———. *Marxism and Form: Twentieth-Century Dialectical Theories of Literature.* Princeton, NJ: Princeton UP, 1974.

———. "A New Reading of *Capital.*" *Mediations* 25 (2010): 5–14.

———. *Representing* Capital: *A Reading of Volume One.* New York: Verso, 2011.

Jarratt, Susan. "Untimely Historiography? Foucault's 'Greco-Latin' Trip." *Rhetoric Society Quarterly* 44.3 (2014): 220–33.

Jaskinski, James. "The Status of Theory and Method in Rhetorical Criticism." *Western Journal of Communication* 65.3 (2001): 249–70.

Jay, Martin. *Adorno.* Cambridge, MA: Harvard UP, 1984.

———. *The Dialectical Imagination: A History of the Frankfurt School and the Institute of Social Research.* Berkeley: U of California P, 1996.

Jennings, Ann, and William Waller. "The Place of Biological Science in Veblen's Economics." *History of Political Economy* 30.2 (1998): 189–217.

Jerome. "Letter XXII. To Eustochium." Christian Classics Ethereal Library. Web: http:www.ccel.org/ccel/schaff/npnf206.v.XXII.html. 1–12. Accessed November 3, 2014.

Kahn, Victoria, Neil Saccamano, and Daniela Coli, eds. *Politics and the Passions, 1500–1850.* Princeton, NJ: Princeton UP, 2006.

Kahneman, Daniel. *Thinking, Fast and Slow.* New York: Farrar, Straus and Giroux, 2011.

Kalyvas, Andreas, and Ira Katznelson. "The Rhetoric of the Market: Adam Smith on Recognition, Speech, and Exchange." *Review of Politics* 63.3 (2001): 549–79.

Kaplan, Michael. "Iconomics: The Rhetoric of Speculation." *Public Culture* 15.3 (2003): 477–93.

Karier, Thomas. "John Kenneth Galbraith Looks Back at the Reagan-Bush Era." *Interviews with John Kenneth Galbraith.* Ed. James Ronald Stanfield and Jacqueline Bloom Stanfield. Jackson: UP of Mississippi, 2004. 161–68.

Kennedy, Gavin. "Adam Smith and the Role of the Invisible Hand Metaphor." *Economic Affairs* 31.1 (2011): 53–57.

Kennedy, George. "A Hoot in the Dark: The Evolution of General Rhetoric." *Philosophy and Rhetoric* 25 (1992): 1–21.

———. *Comparative Rhetoric: An Historical and Cross-Cultural Introduction.* Oxford: Oxford UP, 1998.

Keynes, John Maynard. *The Collected Writings of John Maynard Keynes.* Vol. 13. Ed. Donald Moggridge. London: Macmillan, 1973.

———. "The Economic Consequences of the Peace." 1919. *The End of Laissez-Faire/The Economic Consequences of Peace.* Amherst, NY: Prometheus, 2004. 47–298.

———. *The End of Laissez-Faire.* London: Hogarth Press, 1927.

———. *Essays in Persuasion.* New York: Norton, 1963.

———. *The General Theory of Employment, Interest, and Money.* Lexington, KY: CreateSpace Independent Publishing, 2011.

———. "The General Theory of Employment Summary." *Quarterly Journal of Economics* 51.2 (1937): 209–23.

———. "A Short View of Russia." *Laissez-Faire and Communism.* New York: New Republic, 1926. 83–144.

———. *A Tract on Monetary Reform.* London: Macmillan, 1923.

———. *A Treatise on Money.* London: Macmillan, 1930.

———. *A Treatise on Probability.* London: Macmillan, 1921.

King, J. E. "Keynes and 'Psychology.'" *Economic Papers* 29.1 (2010): 1–12.

Klein, Naomi. *The Shock Doctrine: The Rise of Disaster Capitalism.* New York: Metropolitan, 2007.

Kohler, Evelyne, Christine Keysers, M. Allesandra Umiltà, Leonardo Fogassi, Vittorio Gallese, and Giacomo Rizzollotti. "Hearing Sounds, Understanding Actions: Action Representation in Mirror Neurons." *Science* 29 (2002): 846–48.

Konings, Martijn. *The Emotional Logic of Capitalism: What Progressives Have Missed.* Stanford, CA: Stanford UP, 2015.

Kordela, A. Kiarina. *Being, Time, Bios: Capitalism and Ontology.* Albany: State U of New York P, 2013.

Kresge, Stephen, and Leif Wenar, eds. *Hayek on Hayek: An Autobiographical Dialogue.* U of Chicago P, 1994.

Krugman, Paul. *Peddling Prosperity: Economic Sense and Nonsense in the Age of Diminished Expectations.* New York: Norton, 1995.

———. "Who Was Milton Friedman?" *New York Review of Books,* February 15, 2005. Web: https://www.nybooks.com/articles/2007/02/15/who-was-milton-friedman/. Accessed June 14, 2016.

Kuttner, Robert. *Everything for Sale: The Virtues and Limits of Markets.* New York: Knopf, 1997.

Lakoff, George. "Neural Social Science." *Handbook of Neurosociology.* Ed. David D. Franks and Jonathon H. Turner. Amsterdam: Springer, 2003. 9–25.

———. *The Political Mind: A Cognitive Scientist's Guide to Your Brain and Its Politics.* New York: Penguin, 2009.

Lakoff, George, and Mark Johnson. *Philosophy in the Flesh: The Embodied Mind and Its Challenge to Western Thought.* New York: Basic, 1999.

Latour, Bruno. *Reassembling the Social: An Introduction to Actor-Network-Theory.* Oxford: Oxford UP, 2005.

———. "Why Has Critique Run Out of Steam? From Matters of Fact to Matters of Concern." *Critical Inquiry* 30 (2004): 225–47.

Lazzarato, Maurizio. "Biopolitics and Bioeconomics: A Politics of Multiplicity." Trans. Arianna Bove and Erik Empson. *Multitudes* 22 (2005). Web: http://www.multitudes.net/biopolitics-bioeconomics-a/. Accessed August 22, 2016.

Leathers, Charles. "Veblen and Hayek on Instincts and Evolution." *Journal of the History of Economic Thought* 12 (1990): 162–78.

Le Bon, Gustave. *The Crowd: A Study of the Popular Mind.* 1895. London: Ernest Benn, 1952.

Lekachman, Robert. Introduction. *The Theory of the Leisure Class.* By Thorstein Veblen. New York: Penguin, 1994. v–xi.

Lemke, Thomas. *Biopolitics: An Advanced Introduction.* Trans. Eric Frederick Trump. New York: New York UP, 2011.

———. "'The Birth of Bio-politics': Michel Foucault's Lecture at the Collège de France on Neo-Liberal Governmentality." *Economy and Society* 30.2 (2001): 190–207.

Levitt, Steven, and Stephen Dubner. *Think Like a Freak.* New York: Morrow, 2014.

Lewis, Anthony. "The World through Galbraith's Eyes." *Interviews with John Kenneth Galbraith.* Ed. James Ronald Stanfield and Jacqueline Bloom Stanfield. Jackson: UP of Mississippi, 2004. 3–15.

Lewis, Paul. "Emergent Properties in the Work of Friedrich Hayek." *Journal of Economic Behavior and Organization* 82 (2012): 368–78.

Lippmann, Walter. *Public Opinion.* 1922. New York: Free Press, 1997.

Locke, John. *Of Civil Government.* Ann Arbor, MI: J. W. Edwards, 1946.

Locke, Carter. *Market Matters: Applied Rhetoric Studies and Free Market Competition.* Cresskill, NJ: Hampton, 2005.

Longaker, Mark Garrett. *Rhetorical Style and Bourgeois Virtue: Capitalism and Civil Society in the British Enlightenment.* University Park: Pennsylvania State UP, 2015.

Longinus. *On the Sublime.* Trans. H. L. Havell. The Project Gutenberg. Web: http://www.gutenberg.org/files/17957/17957-h/17957-h.htm. Accessed August 13, 2014.

Lukács, Georg. "Reification and the Consciousness of the Proletariat." *History and Class Consciousness: Studies in Marxist Dialectics.* Cambridge, MA: MIT Press, 1990. 83–222.

Lundberg, Christian. *Lacan in Public: Psychoanalysis and the Science of Rhetoric.* Tuscaloosa: U of Alabama P, 2012.

Lundberg, Christian, and Joshua Gunn. "'Ouija Board, Are There Any Communications?' Agency, Ontotheology, and the Death of the Humanist Subject, or, Continuing the ARS Conversation." *Rhetoric Society Quarterly* 35.4 (2005): 83–105.

Lynch, Paul, and Nathaniel Rivers. *Thinking with Bruno Latour in Rhetoric and Composition.* Carbondale: Southern Illinois UP, 2015.

Maidan, Michael. "Karl Marx on Technology and Alienation." *Critique* 39.2 (2011): 322–24.

Marsh, Leslie, ed. *Hayek in Mind: Hayek's Philosophical Psychology.* Bingley, UK: Emerald, 2011.

Marx, Karl. *A Contribution to the Critique of Political Economy.* 1859. New York: International Publishers, 1999.

———. *Capital.* Vol. 1. 1867. Trans. Ben Fowkes. New York: Penguin, 1990.

———. "Critique of the Gotha Program." 1891. *The Marx-Engels Reader.* Ed. Robert Tucker. New York: Norton, 1978. 525–41.

———. *Economic and Philosophic Manuscripts of 1844.* 1934. Ed. Dirk J. Struik. Trans. Martin Milligan. New York: International Publishers, 1964.

———. "For a Ruthless Criticism of Everything Existing." 1844. *The Marx-Engels Reader.* Ed. Robert Tucker. New York: Norton, 1978. 12–15.

———. "On the Jewish Question." 1843. *The Marx-Engels Reader.* Ed. Robert C. Tucker. New York: Norton, 1978. 26–52.

Marx, Karl, and Frederick Engels. *The German Ideology.* 1932. Ed. C. J. Arthur. New York: International Publishers, 1995.

Marx Reloaded. Dir. Jason Barker and Alexandra Weltz. Films Noirs, Medea Film, and Zweites Deutsches Fernsehen, 2011.

Marzola, Alessandra. "Rhetoric and Imagination in the Economic and Political Writings of J. M. Keynes." *John Maynard Keynes: Language and Method.* Ed. Alessandra Marzola and Francesco Silva. Aldershot, UK: Edward Elgar, 1994. 192–223.

Massumi, Brian. "Fear (The Spectrum Said)." *positions* 13.2 (2005): 31–48.

———. "National Enterprise Emergency: Steps Toward an Ecology of Powers." *Beyond Biopolitics: Essays on the Governance of Life and Death.* Ed. Patricia Ticineto Clough and Craig Willse. Durham, NC: Duke UP, 2011. 19–45.

———. *Ontopower: War, Power, and the State of Perception.* Durham, NC: Duke UP, 2015.

———. *Parables for the Virtual: Movement, Affect, Sensation.* Durham, NC: Duke UP, 2002.

———. *The Power at the End of the Economy*. Durham, NC: Duke UP, 2015.

Mays, Chris, Nathaniel Rivers, and Kellie Sharp-Hoskins. *Kenneth Burke + The Posthuman*. University Park: Pennsylvania State UP, 2017.

McCloskey, Deirdre N. *Bourgeois Dignity: Why Economics Can't Explain the Modern World*. Chicago: U of Chicago P, 2010.

———. *The Bourgeois Virtues: Ethics for an Age of Commerce*. Chicago: U of Chicago P, 2006.

———. "Other Things Equal: Keynes Was a Sophist, and a Good Thing, Too." *Eastern Economic Journal* 22.2 (1996): 231–34.

McGee, Michael Calvin. "In Search of the 'People': A Rhetorical Alternative." *Contemporary Rhetorical Theory: A Reader*. Ed. John Louis Lucaites, Celeste Michelle Condit, and Sally Caudill. New York: Guilford, 1999. 341–56.

McKenna, Stephen J. *Adam Smith: The Rhetoric of Propriety*. Albany: State U of New York P, 2006.

McKerrow, Raymie. "Corporeality and Cultural Rhetoric: A Site for Rhetoric's Future." *Southern Communication Journal* 63.4 (1998): 315–28.

———. "Critical Rhetoric: Theory and Praxis." *Contemporary Rhetorical Theory: A Reader*. New York: Guilford Press, 1999. 441–63.

McQuade, Thomas, and William Butos. "The Sensory Order and Other Adaptive Classifying Systems." *Journal of Bioeconomics* 7 (2005): 335–58.

Merchant, Jamie. "Immanence, Governmentality, Critique: Toward a Recovery of Totality in Rhetorical Theory." *Philosophy and Rhetoric* 47.3 (2014): 227–50.

Miller, Carolyn. "What Can Automation Tell Us about Agency?" *Rhetoric Society Quarterly* 37.2 (2007): 137–57.

Mirowski, Philip. *More Heat Than Light: Economics as Social Physics, Physics as Nature's Economics*. Cambridge: Cambridge UP, 1989.

Mises, Ludwig. *Human Action: A Treatise on Economics*. Indianapolis: Liberty Fund, 2007.

Morrissette, Jason J. "Marxferatu: The Vampire Metaphor as a Tool for Teaching Marx's Critique of Capitalism." *PS: Political Science and Politics* 46.3 (2013): 637–42.

Mouhammed, Adil H. "Veblen and Keynes." *International Journal of Politics, Culture, and Society* 13.2 (1999): 169–86.

Muller, Jerry. *Adam Smith in His Time and Ours: Designing the Decent Society*. New York: Free Press, 1993.

Murphey, Murray G. "The Instinct of Workmanship and the State of Industrial Arts." *Veblen's Century: A Collective Portrait*. Ed. Irving Louis Horowitz. New Brunswick, NJ: Transaction, 2002. 229–53.

Murray, Stuart. "Hegel's Pathology of Recognition: A Biopolitical Fable." *Philosophy and Rhetoric* 48.4 (2015): 443–72.

Negri, Antonio. "Art and Culture in the Age of Empire and the Time of the Multitudes." Trans. Max Henninger. *SubStance* 36.1 (2007): 48–55.

———. *Insurgencies: Constituent Power and the Modern State*. Trans. Maurizia Boscagli. Minneapolis: U of Minnesota P, 2009.

———. "The Political Monster." *Praise of the Common: A Conversation on Philosophy and Politics*. Minneapolis: U of Minnesota P, 2009. 193–218.

———. "Value and Affect." *Boundary* 2 26.2 (1999): 77–88.

Nussbaum, Martha. *Not For Profit: Why Democracy Needs the Humanities*. Princeton, NJ: Princeton UP, 2010.

O'Donnell, Roderick. "Keynes as a Writer: Three Case Studies." *The History of Political Economy.* Ed. Peter D. Groenewegen, Tony Aspromourgos, and John Kees Lodewijks. London: Routledge, 2004. 197–216.

———. *Keynes: Philosophy, Economics, and Politics.* New York: St. Martin's, 1989.

———. "Keynes's Principles of Writing (Innovative) Economics." *Economic Record* 82.259 (2006): 396–407.

———. "The Thick and Thin of Controversy." *The Philosophy of Keynes's Economics: Probability, Uncertainty, and Convention.* Ed. Jochen Runde and Sohei Mizuhara. London: Routledge, 2003. 85–99.

Ollman, Bertell. *Alienation: Marx's Conception of Man in a Capitalist Society.* Cambridge: Cambridge UP, 1977.

———. *Dance of the Dialectics: Steps in Marx's Method.* Chicago: University of Illinois Press, 2003.

Olson, Mancur. "Esthetics, Economics, and Wit." *Unconventional Wisdom: Essays on Economics in Honor of J. K. Galbraith.* Ed. Samuel Bowles, Richard Edwards, and William G. Shepherd. Boston: Houghton Mifflin, 1989. 81–87.

Parker, Richard. *John Kenneth Galbraith: His Life, His Politics, His Economics.* Chicago: U of Chicago P, 2005.

Parsons, Wayne. *The Power of the Financial Press: Journalism and Economic Opinion in Britain and America.* New Brunswick, NJ: Rutgers UP, 1990.

Paster, Gail Kern, Katherine Rowe, and Mary Floyd-Wilson, eds. *Reading the Early Modern Passions: Essays in the Cultural History of Emotion.* Philadelphia: University of Pennsylvania Press, 2004.

Patinkin, Don. "Friedman on the Quantity Theory and Keynesian Economics." *Milton Friedman's Monetary Framework: A Debate with His Critics.* Chicago: U of Chicago P, 1974. 111–31.

Patrizi, Francesco. "Ten Dialogues on Rhetoric." *Renaissance Debates on Rhetoric.* Ed. and trans. Wayne A. Rebhorn. Ithaca, NY: Cornell UP, 2000. 184–202.

Penner, Devin. "The Limits of Radical Institutionalism: A Marxian Critique of Thorstein Veblen's Political Economy." *Review of Radical Political Economics* 43.2 (2011): 154–71.

Perelman, Chaïm, and Lucie Olbrechts-Tyteca. *The New Rhetoric: A Treatise on Argumentation.* South Bend: U of Notre Dame P, 1991.

Petrarch, Francis. "Letter to Tommaso da Messina, Concerning the Study of Eloquence." *Renaissance Debates on Rhetoric.* Ed. and trans. Wayne A. Rebhorn. Ithaca: Cornell UP, 2000.15–26.

Plato. "Gorgias." *The Rhetorical Tradition: Readings from Classical Times to the Present.* Ed. Patricia Bizzell and Bruce Herzberg. Boston: Bedford, 1990. 61–112.

———. *Phaedrus. The Rhetorical Tradition: Readings from Classical Times to the Present.* Ed. Patricia Bizzell and Bruce Herzberg. Boston: Bedford, 1990. 113–43.

Poovey, Mary. *A History of the Modern Fact: Problems of Knowledge in the Sciences of Wealth and Society.* Chicago: U of Chicago P, 1998.

Rancière, Jacques. *Disagreement.* Trans. Julie Rose. Minneapolis: U of Minnesota P, 2004.

Rayack, Elton. *Not So Free to Choose: The Political Economy of Milton Friedman and Ronald Reagan.* New York: Praeger, 1987.

Rashid, Salim. *The Myth of Adam Smith.* Northampton, MA: Edward Elgar, 1998.

Rebhorn, Wayne A. *The Emperor of Men's Minds: Literature and the Renaissance Discourse of Rhetoric.* Ithaca, NY: Cornell UP, 1995.

Rice, Jenny Edbauer. "The New 'New': Making a Case for Critical Affect Studies." *Quarterly Journal of Speech* 94.2 (2008): 200–212.

Rickert, Thomas. *Ambient Rhetoric: The Attunements of Rhetorical Being.* Pittsburgh: U of Pittsburgh P, 2013.

Riley, Denise. *Impersonal Passion: Language as Affect.* Durham, NC: Duke UP, 2005.

Robinson, Joan. *Essays in the Theory of Employment.* London: Macmillan, 1937.

Rose, Gillian. *The Melancholy Science: An Introduction to the Thought of Theodor W. Adorno.* New York: Columbia UP, 1979.

Runde, Jochen, and Sohei Mizuhara. *The Philosophy of Keynes's Economics: Probability, Uncertainty, and Convention.* London: Routledge, 2003.

Rutherford, Malcolm. "Thorstein Veblen and the Process of Institutional Change." *History of Political Economy* 16.3 (1984): 331–48.

Sabooglu, Müfit. "Hayek and Spontaneous Orders." *Journal of the History of Economic Thought* 18 (1996): 347–64.

Sacks, Oliver. *An Anthropologist on Mars: Seven Paradoxical Tales.* New York: Vintage, 1995.

———. *The Mind's Eye.* New York: Vintage, 2010.

———. *Seeing Voices: A Journey into the World of the Deaf.* New York: Vintage, 1989.

Samuelson, Paul. *Economics: An Introductory Analysis.* York, PA: McGraw Hill, 1948.

———. "Galbraith as Artist and Scientist." *Unconventional Wisdom: Essays on Economics in Honor of J. K. Galbraith.* Ed. Samuel Bowles, Richard Edwards, and William G. Shepherd. Boston: Houghton Mifflin, 1989. 123–28.

———. "Marxian Economics as Economics." *American Economic Review* 57.2 (1967): 616–23.

Schiappa, Edward. "Second Thoughts on the Critique of Big Rhetoric." *Philosophy and Rhetoric* 34.3 (2001): 260–74.

Schliesser, Eric. "Reading Adam Smith after Darwin: On the Evolution of Propensities, Institutions, and Sentiments." *Journal of Economic Behavior and Organization* 77 (2011): 14–22.

Schumpeter, Joseph A. "Science and Ideology." *American Economic Review* 39.2 (1949): 345–59.

Shannon, Christopher. *Conspicuous Criticism: Tradition, the Individual, and Culture in American Social Thought from Veblen to Mills.* Baltimore: Johns Hopkins UP, 1996.

Simons, Herbert. "Rhetorical Hermeneutics and the Project of Globalization." *Quarterly Journal of Speech* 85 (1999): 86–109.

Skidelsky, Robert. *John Maynard Keynes.* Vol. 1, *Hopes Betrayed, 1883–1920.* London: Macmillan, 1983.

———. *John Maynard Keynes.* Vol. 2, *The Economist as Saviour, 1920–1937.* London: Macmillan, 1992.

———. *John Maynard Keynes.* Vol. 3, *Fighting for Freedom, 1937–1946.* London: Macmillan, 2000.

Smart, Barry. "An Economic Turn: Galbraith and Classical Sociology." *Journal of Classical Sociology* 9.3 (2003): 337–46.

———. "Economics, Politics and Sociology: On the Contribution of Galbraith's Unconventional Wisdom to the Discourse of Classical Sociology." *Journal of Classical Sociology* 3.1 (2009): 47–66.

Smith, Adam. *Lectures on Rhetoric and Belles Lettres.* 1963. Ed. J. C. Bryce. Indianapolis: Liberty Fund, 1985.

———. "The History of Astronomy." *Essays in Philosophical Subjects.* London: Cadell and Davies, 1795. 1–93.

———. *The Theory of Moral Sentiments.* 1759. Ed. Knud Haakonssen. Cambridge: Cambridge UP, 2002.

———. *The Wealth of Nations.* 1776. Amherst, NY: Prometheus Books, 1991.

Smith, Andrew. "Reading Wealth in Nigeria: Occult Capitalism and Marx's Vampires." *Historical Materialism* 9 (2001): 39–59.

Soelle, Dorothee. *To Work and to Love: A Theology of Creation.* Philadelphia: Fortress P, 1984.

Spindler, Michael. *Veblen and Modern America: Revolutionary Iconoclast.* London: Pluto, 2002.

Spring, Joel. *Education and the Rise of the Corporate State.* Mahwah, NJ: Lawrence Erlbaum, 1998.

Stapleford, Thomas. "Positive Economics for Democratic Policy: Milton Friedman, Institutionalism, and the Science of History." *Building Chicago Economics: New Perspectives on the History of America's Most Powerful Economics Program.* Ed. Robert Van Horn, Philip Mirowski, and Thomas A. Stapleford. Cambridge: Cambridge UP, 2011. 3–35.

Stormer, Nathan. "Rhetoric's Diverse Materiality: Polythetic Ontology and Genealogy." *Review of Communication.* 16.4 (2016): 299–316.

Tellmann, Ute. "Foucault and the Invisible Economy." *Foucault Studies* 6 (2009): 5–24.

Terranova, Tiziana. "Another Life: The Nature of Political Economy in Foucault's Genealogy of Biopolitics." *Theory, Culture & Society* 26.6 (2009): 234–62.

———. "Free Labor: Producing Culture for the Digital Economy." *Social Text* 63 18.2 (2000): 33–57.

Tompkins, Silvan. *Affect, Imagery, Consciousness: The Complete Edition.* New York: Springer, 2008.

Törrönen, Jukka. "On the Road to Serfdom? An Analysis of Friedrich Hayek's Socio-Political Manifesto as a Pending Narrative." *Social Semiotics* 13.3 (2003): 305–20.

Tronti, Mario. "The Strategy of Refusal." *Autonomia: Post-Political Politics.* Ed. Sylvere Lotringer and Christian Marazzi. New York: Semiotext(e), 2012. 28–35.

Turpin, Paul. *The Moral Rhetoric of Political Economy: Justice and Modern Economic Thought.* New York: Routledge, 2011.

Van Horn, Robert, and Phillip Mirowski. "The Rise of the Chicago School of Economics and the Birth of Neoliberalism." *The Road From Mont Pèlerin: The Making of the Neoliberal Thought Collective.* Ed. Philip Mirowski and Dieter Plehwe. Cambridge, MA: Harvard UP, 2009. 139–78.

Veblen, Thorstein. *Absentee Ownership and Business Enterprise in Recent Times: The Case of America.* New York: Viking, 1923.

———. "Conspicuous Consumption of Language." *Quarterly Journal of Speech* 39.3 (1953): 306.

———. *The Instinct of Workmanship and the State of the Industrial Arts.* New York: Macmillan, 1914.

———. *The Nature of Peace and the Terms of Its Perpetuation.* New York: Macmillan, 1917.

———. Rev. of *The Economic Consequences of the Peace,* by John Maynard Keynes. *Political Science Quarterly* 35.3 (1920): 467–72.

———. "The Socialist Economics of Karl Marx." *The Place of Science in Modern Civilisation and Other Essays.* New York: Viking, 1919. 409–56.

———. *The Theory of Business Enterprise*. New York: Scribner's, 1910.

———. *The Theory of the Leisure Class*. 1899. New York: Penguin, 1994.

———. *Vested Interests and the Common Man*. New York: B. W. Huebsch, 1919.

Verbeek, Peter-Paul. *What Things Do: Philosophical Reflections on Technology, Agency, and Design*. University Park: Pennsylvania State UP, 2005.

Walker, Donald A. "Thorstein Veblen's Economic System." *Economic Inquiry* 15 (1977): 213–36.

Waller, William. "John Kenneth Galbraith: Cultural Theorist of Consumption and Power." *Journal of Economic Issues* 42.1 (2008): 13–24.

Waller, William, and Linda R. Robertson. "Why Johnny (Ph.D., Economics) Can't Read: A Rhetorical Analysis of Thorstein Veblen and a Response to Donald McCloskey's *Rhetoric of Economics*." *Journal of Economic Issues* 24.4 (1990): 1027–44.

Walters, Shannon. *Rhetorical Touch: Disability, Identification, Haptics*. Columbia: U of South Carolina P, 2014.

Walzer, Arthur. "*Parrēsia*, Foucault, and the Classical Rhetorical Tradition." *Rhetoric Society Quarterly* 43 (2013):1–21.

Wapshott, Nicholas. *Keynes Hayek: The Clash That Defined Modern Economics*. New York: Norton, 2011.

Wasserstein, Bruce. Rev. of *Money: Whence It Came, Where It Went*, by John Kenneth Galbraith. *Columbia Law Review* 76 (1976): 175–86.

Watkins, Evan. *Everyday Exchanges: Market Work and Capitalist Common Sense*. Stanford, CA: Stanford UP, 1998.

West, E. G. "The Political Economy of Alienation: Karl Marx and Adam Smith." *Oxford Economic Papers* 21.1 (1969): 1–23.

Whately, Richard. *Introductory Lectures on Political Economy*. New York: Augustus M. Kelley, 1966.

Wheen, Francis. *Karl Marx: A Life*. New York: Norton, 1999.

Widmaier, Wesley. "Theory as a Factor and the Theorist as an Actor: The 'Pragmatist Constructivist' Lessons of John Dewey and John Kenneth Galbraith." *International Studies Review* 6 (2004): 427–45.

Wiggershaus, Rolf. *The Frankfurt School: Its History, Theories, and Political Significance*. Trans. Michael Robertson. Cambridge, MA: MIT Press, 1998.

Williams, Raymond. *The Long Revolution*. 1961. Peterborough, ON: Broadview, 2001.

———. *Marxism and Literature*. Oxford: Oxford UP, 1977.

Wray, L. Randall. "Veblen's Theory of Business Enterprise and Keynes's Monetary Theory of Production." *Journal of Economic Issues* 41.2 (2007): 617–24.

Zak, Paul. "The Physiology of Moral Sentiments." *Journal of Economic Behavior & Organization* 77 (2011): 53–65.

Žižek, Slavoj. "Class Struggle or Postmodernism? Yes, Please!" *Contingency, Hegemony, Universality: Contemporary Dialogues on the Left*. Ed. Judith Butler, Ernesto Laclau, and Slavoj Žižek. London: Verso, 2000. 90–135.

———. *The Plague of Fantasies*. London: Verso, 1997.

———. *The Sublime Object of Ideology*. New York: Verso, 2009.

Index